THE OAK RIDGES MORAINE BATTLES

Development, Sprawl, and Nature Conservation in the Toronto Region

The Oak Ridges Moraine, a unique landform in southern Ontario, has generated heated battles over the future of nature conservation, urban sprawl, and development in the Toronto region in recent years. This book provides a detailed yet wide-ranging history and policy analysis of planning issues and citizen activism on the Moraine's future in the face of rapid urban expansion.

The Oak Ridges Moraine Battles captures behind-the-scenes aspects of a story that received a great deal of attention in local and national news, and that ultimately led to provincial legislation aimed at protecting the Moraine and Ontario's Greenbelt. By giving voice to a range of stakeholders – residents, activists, civil servants, scientists, developers, and aggregate and other resource users – the book demonstrates how space on the urban periphery was reshaped in the Toronto region. The authors ask hard questions about who is included and excluded in decision-making when the preservation of nature is at odds with the relentless process of urbanization.

L. ANDERS SANDBERG is a professor in the Faculty of Environmental Studies at York University.

GERDA R. WEKERLE is a professor in the Faculty of Environmental Studies at York University.

LIETTE GILBERT is an associate professor in the Faculty of Environmental Studies at York University.

L. ANDERS SANDBERG,
GERDA R. WEKERLE, AND
LIETTE GILBERT

The Oak Ridges
Moraine Battles

Development, Sprawl, and Nature
Conservation in the Toronto Region

UNIVERSITY OF TORONTO PRESS
Toronto Buffalo London

© University of Toronto Press 2013
Toronto Buffalo London
www.utppublishing.com
Printed in Canada

ISBN 978-1-4426-4514-1 (cloth)
ISBN 978-1-4426-1302-7 (paper)

Printed on acid-free, 100% post-consumer recycled paper with vegetable-based inks.

Library and Archives Canada Cataloguing in Publication

Sandberg, L. Anders, 1953–
The Oak Ridges Moraine battles : development, sprawl, and nature conservation in the
Toronto Region / L. Anders Sandberg, Gerda R. Wekerle, and Liette Gilbert.

Includes bibliographical references and index.
ISBN 978-1-4426-4514-1 (bound). – ISBN 978-1-4426-1302-7 (pbk.)

1. Nature conservation – Ontario – Oak Ridges Moraine – Citizen participation.
2. Nature conservation – Ontario – Oak Ridges Moraine – Planning.   3. Nature
conservation – Ontario – Toronto Region.   4. Oak Ridges Moraine (Ont.) – Economic
conditions.   5. Oak Ridges Moraine (Ont.) – Population.   6. Oak Ridges
Moraine (Ont.) – History.   I. Wekerle, Gerda R.   II. Gilbert, Liette   III. Title.

QH77.C3S25 2013   333.7209713′5   C2012-908150-7

This book has been published with the help of a grant from the Canadian Federation
for the Humanities and Social Sciences, through the Aid to Scholarly Publications
Program, using funds provided by the Social Sciences and Humanities Research
Council of Canada.

University of Toronto Press acknowledges the financial assistance to its publishing program of the Canada Council for the Arts and the Ontario Arts Council.

University of Toronto Press acknowledges the financial support for its publishing activities of the Government of Canada through the Canada Book Fund.

Contents

Illustrations

Tables

Preface and Acknowledgments

In 2000, our attention was captured by the headlines of the *Toronto Star*, the *Globe and Mail*, and the *National Post*, the three major Canadian daily newspapers, which featured stories about the fight of local residents on the urban fringe of Toronto against developers who were planning to build extensive housing subdivisions in Richmond Hill, a threat to the natural integrity of the Oak Ridges Moraine. These residents had fled the hustle and bustle of the city for their own rural retreat on the scenic Moraine and were now facing the prospect of urban sprawl. At the time, we thought we saw something very special about the battle, namely the unlikely alliance between ex-urbanites, who were often well off and conservative in political orientation, and the radical environmentalists and liberal downtown residents who were collectively fighting the developers.

These battles triggered the Conservative government of Premier Mike Harris to pass the *Oak Ridges Moraine Conservation Act* and the *Oak Ridges Moraine Conservation Plan* in 2001 and 2002, respectively. The Plan has been celebrated widely as a progressive regulation that conserves the 160 km long Moraine and stops sprawl in its tracks; in addition, it conserves nature and affirms Moraine residents and others as belonging to the Oak Ridges Moraine.

When we first planned this book, our intent was to document and celebrate the battles waged by residents on the Moraine and to discuss their wider implications and promises. The Oak Ridges Moraine is now ten years older. The headlines of the Moraine battles in the newspapers have disappeared. The Greenbelt, a new initiative of the current Liberal government, is the new kid on the block. The time that has passed since the Oak Ridges Moraine battles raged in Richmond Hill in 2000 has given us a wider perspective on the issue of environmental activism. So has the historical research that we have done on the Moraine. Inevitably, there will be many different stories of the shifts in the planning of the Oak Ridges Moraine. This book is our attempt to make sense of the stories that have been told to us, both in the heat of battles and in their aftermath, combined with our own observations and analysis of events and their meanings.

The Oak Ridges Moraine Battles critically engages the questions of what it means to manage growth; the battles over sprawl, conservation, and belonging; and their potential to build a better world. We view the dynamics of policy change on the Oak Ridges Moraine through the multiple and shifting lenses of key participants and decision makers. We do not ask the questions posed by conventional planners of growth and conservation. Instead, we interrogate the very frames through which planners pose questions. We then suggest new ways of conceiving of nature, sprawl, conservation, and belonging.

We were inspired to think about the everyday encounters of various human and non-human actors on the Moraine. By documenting these encounters, we wish to convey the message that the Oak Ridges Moraine is not a categorical absolute that can be understood as an ecological marvel frozen in time and space; it has a history, it evolves, and it is constantly made, unmade, and remade. We owe a huge gratitude to the many people who have taken part in the battles surrounding the Oak Ridges Moraine and who have shared their experiences with us through informal talks and formal interviews, documents, and policy papers. There are far too many of them to mention here, but some of them are referenced in the book.

The Aid to Scholarly Publications Program of the Social Science Federation of Canada approved a grant in support of this book's publication, for which we are most thankful. We are also grateful to the Social Science and Humanities Research Council for providing funding to complete this research through grant no. 410-2002-1483. This funding allowed us to support, work with, and/or be inspired by doctoral and master's degree students in York University's Faculty of Environmental Studies: Teresa Abbruzzese, Christina Addorisio, Hajo Beeckman, Matthew Binstock, Ganjin Davies, Britt Erickson, Elsa Fancello, Marcel Gelein, Vera Hofmann, Lucrezia Iandoli, Paul Jackson, Penny Kaill-Vinish, Susan Lloyd-Swail, Clarine Lee-Macaraig, Don Leffers, Shannon Logan, Colin Lund, Marvin Macaraig, Julianna MacDonald, Claire

Malcolmson, Michael McMahon, Tiffany Onesi, Letizia Orsi, Anna Rita Papa, Andrew Pask, Sandra Patano, Susan Robertson, Stephanie Rutherford, Lindsey Savage, Jocelyn Thorpe, Jelena Vesic, Lisa Wallace, Melanie Walther, and James Young. We were buoyed by their enthusiastic study of the dynamics of natural and political change on and beyond the Oak Ridges Moraine and benefitted from conversations and astute insights. After graduation many of these students became academics, policymakers, planners, and leaders in their communities. We would also like to thank four anonymous reviewers and Jon Johnson and Matthew Binstock for providing insightful and specific comments and suggestions for improvements of the book. Rajiv Rawat drew all the beautiful maps in the book. The Faculty of Environmental Studies, York University, provided us with both unstinting support through matching funds that allowed us to work with more students over several years, and encouragement of our research efforts. Rhoda Reyes, Research Officer in the Faculty of Environmental Studies, provided grants management assistance that was professional and supportive. We are grateful for various opportunities to try out our ideas at workshops through invitations from the Goethe Institute (Toronto); York University's City Institute; the Research Gallery at the Congress of Social Sciences and Humanities held at York University; St Francis Xavier University's Centre for Policy and Governance; and diverse academic conferences.

We would like to thank the staff at the University of Toronto Press who guided the manuscript to its completion, in particular our editors, Virgil Duff and Doug Hildebrand. We are also indebted to our copy editor, Angela Wingfield, for her detailed review of the book.

Anders Sandberg is grateful to his partner, Maria Legerstee, for her support and understanding. She knows the time and effort that it takes to write a book because she has written a few books herself. Gerda Wekerle thanks her spouse, Slade Lander, for his unstinting support and tolerance beyond the call of duty in harbouring rooms full of boxes of Moraine research materials for too many years to count. Liette Gilbert expresses her gratitude to Jorge Alonso and to her family for their unconditional support and love.

Toronto, 23 March 2012

THE OAK RIDGES MORAINE BATTLES

Development, Sprawl, and Nature Conservation
in the Toronto Region

Chapter One

Development, Sprawl, and Conservation on the Oak Ridges Moraine

At the turn of the twenty-first century the Oak Ridges Moraine became known as a conservation object threatened by urban sprawl (figure 1.1). The Jefferson salamander was widely used as an iconic symbol to rally support for the conservation of the Moraine. The picture of the threatened salamander perched on the hand of a prominent environmentalist in front of the Osgoode Hall law courts in downtown Toronto near the financial district offers a stark image of the fragility of nature when confronted with the constraints of the legal system and the financial markets. Appearing on the front page of the *Toronto Star*, the photograph constituted a media coup for the defenders of the Moraine. It mattered little that the salamander, named Melissa, originated in Waterloo and had been transported to Toronto in a moistened plastic container (Swainson, 2002d).

However, the Jefferson salamander was only one of a series of actors in the conservation battles over the Oak Ridges Moraine. Starting in 1999, a cacophony of newspaper headlines in the Greater Toronto Area alerted the public and policymakers to the ongoing battles over urbanization in the region bordering on Toronto and stretching to the north. Resistance to development is part of the ongoing story of urbanization. What was new was the source of resistance: middle-class, predominantly white, homeowners living in suburban and exurban low-density settlements that were a mix of subdivision housing developments, estate homes, horse farms, hamlets, villages, kettle lakes, forests, and some farms. In alliances with local naturalist groups and regional, national, and international environmental organizations these exurban residents challenged sprawl. Reports of opposition to development came from a proliferation of sites across the region: resistance

Figure 1.1: Jefferson salamander at Osgoode Hall

The Jefferson salamander is a central fauna and symbol in the battles for nature conservation in the Greater Toronto Area, including the struggles surrounding the Oak Ridges Moraine. This salamander was a key exhibit in an unsuccessful lawsuit to stop the tree cutting in the Jefferson Forest for a road. Singer and anti-quarry activist Sarah Harmer paid tribute to the small creature in the song "Salamandre." Source: *Toronto Star*, 17 September 2002, A03; Bernard Weil/ GetStock.com

to the extension of a major highway; challenges to multiple develop-ment proposals in suburban and exurban areas; mobilization against a massive sewer pipe; and many more. What was inciting these gen-erally quiescent homeowners to chain themselves to trees, storm pub-lic meetings, lobby municipal, regional, and provincial politicians, and demand change in land use policy? Municipalities across the region seemed to be under siege from these newly environmentally conscious residents. The Conservative provincial government of Premier Mike Harris, a champion of free enterprise and untrammelled growth, was under intense pressure from its suburban supporters to act against sprawl and the despoliation of nature. Conflicts over land use moved beyond contention over changes to specific sites to a more generalized debate about the values of growth, nature, and belonging over a very large region. The political climate of the Toronto region seemed to have dramatically changed.

Reportage of local battles over development scattered across the region identified the site of these contestations as the Oak Ridges Moraine, often described as a land use spanning 160 kilometres north of Toronto; a unique piece of natural habitat; an attractive landform with kettle lakes carved by glaciers, with forests and the headwaters of rivers; and a water resource for the region. Media coverage identified the rival claims to the future of the Moraine: housing development and associated infrastructure, aggregate extraction, and conservation of natural heritage. The *Toronto Star*, in particular, devoted space to continuous coverage of the technical details of the planning hearings on development applications in municipalities and at the Ontario Municipal Board, a quasi-judicial appeal body appointed by the provincial government. Newspaper articles with large colourful graphics introduced a primarily urban readership to a new language of ecological conservation, showing the significance of underground aquifers, watersheds and headwaters, and natural habitats for rare plant and animal species. The battles to conserve the Oak Ridges Moraine made visible what was perceived to be a key challenge – how to reconcile the pressures of growth in a fast-growing region with the demands to conserve an endangered natural feature and ecosystem. With the passing of the *Oak Ridges Moraine Conservation Act* and the *Oak Ridges Moraine Conservation Plan* in 2001 and 2002, respectively, the conservation forces appeared to have won a landmark battle (Ontario Ministry of Municipal Affairs and Housing, 2001a, 2002a).

In this book we challenge the stories about the battles over urban sprawl and conservation on the Oak Ridges Moraine. A critical political ecology approach that addresses the linkages in the condition and the change of social and environmental systems, with explicit considerations of power (Robbins, 2004; Heynen et al., 2006), informs our empirical studies. We draw upon regional studies and studies of politics, ecology, environmental planning, social movement, and actor-network theories to illuminate a particular chapter in Ontario environmental politics that has reshaped the ways in which we think about conservation and development planning on the rural-urban periphery and about citizen engagement in these processes. Political ecology emphasizes the centrality of political, economic, and social power in understanding ecological issues. The case of the Oak Ridges Moraine is a prominent example of the actions of residents and environmentalists playing a key role in placing the conservation of the Moraine on the public agenda. We are inspired by a literature that takes seriously the ability of residents and environmentalists to build place-based coalitions and social movements that consider action both within and outside government structures to promote their vision (Rootes, 2007; Woods, 2005, 2007). Social movements may do so by strategically formulating and timing their actions for maximum impact in the media and on political decision makers. They may also take part and advance their positions as stakeholders and partners in state institutions and government-sanctioned programs. As the title of our book suggests, there were and continue to be political battles, subplots, and power machinations over the Oak Ridges Moraine among human actors, such as developers, aggregate operators, residents, environmentalists, experts, politicians, and civil servants.

This book also addresses the politics associated with the creation of a new regulatory regime and of institutional changes that seek to reconcile the imperatives of growth with the demands for conservation. We delineate the multiple, overlapping, and contingent stories of historically grounded actors and institutions that have constructed various and changing responses to sprawl, to growth management, and to the conservation of nature on the Moraine over time, and especially in the past few decades. In telling the story of the Moraine battles and recent outcomes, we map the shifts in power and influence of the development and aggregate industries, municipal and provincial governments, state agencies, government bureaucrats, politicians, planners, and new governance arrangements. We draw upon recent work on decentred institutional analysis (Bevir and Rhodes, 2003, 2006; Gibbs and Krueger, 2012). Decentred accounts emphasize "how meanings and so actions are created, recreated and changed in ways that can modify and even transform institutions" (Bevir and Rhodes, 2003: 63). They offer a detailed genealogical approach to policy change, draw attention to the role of the ideas and actions of individuals, and construct policy stories that are historically contingent.

Political ecologists also propose that there are other more intangible actors and interactions. We are inspired by the proposition that any phenomenon or process – such as a landform or a nature conservation effort – is influenced by many factors, not only by the stakeholders involved in the heat of immediate battles. We also consider the bio-physical and social contexts – the frames and the daily meetings or encounters through which these stakeholders operate – such as the state of expertise, the techniques involved in making measurements, and the agency of the biophysical processes themselves (Walker, 2005). Encounters include not only the public battles reported in newspapers but also the historical legacies and the often subtle and unchallenged everyday practices that frame people's lives.

Bruno Latour (1987, 2004; Latour, Woogar, and Salk, 1986) argues that any arbitrarily defined object, whether it be a laboratory, an institution, a piece of legislation, or a landform, is a complex, complicated, and unpredictable assemblage of actors in which the role and significance of any actor should be considered undetermined and subject to careful examination and assessment. Latour's concept of actor networks suggests that it is the historical representations, the landforms, the hydrogeologies, the flora, the fauna, and the legislation concerning the Oak Ridges Moraine that can be potent actors rather than passive objects in influencing socio-political outcomes (Latour, 2004; Law and Hassard, 1999; Valverde, 2005, 2008; Robbins, 2004). When we refer to non-human natures as actors, it does not mean that these actors have a consciousness and can "speak" and "listen" (though some cultures do believe this is the case); it means that non-human actors can react in unpredictable and contingent ways that are difficult for humans to comprehend, control, or manipulate. It also means that concepts and technologies that humans admittedly construct and shape can create path dependencies that preclude alternative ways of thinking and acting. All of these actors are related to the act of understanding and naming the Oak Ridges Moraine and constructing it as a conservation object. An understanding of any phenomenon or policy does not take place in a vacuum but rather under the influence of a wide range of surrounding factors that need to be considered in unison.

The tools of the environmental historian of the *longue durée* inspire an exploration of different landscape representations over time (Gold and Revill, 2000; Mitchell, 2002). Human representations of any phenomena can assign a particular meaning to a landscape that shapes its understanding, study, and management. Human representations of non-human nature and landforms over time are also instructive in informing us about the stability of terms and images in the short term, yet their character is likely to change over the long term (McGreevy, 1994;

Cronon, 1996; Osborne, 1998a; Castree, 1995, 2001; Braun and Castree, 1998; Castree and Braun, 2001; Demeritt, 2001). The Oak Ridges Moraine, for example, has been represented in many ways over the centuries, and it is only in the last 30 to 40 years, when the Moraine has been increasingly surrounded by encroaching development, that it has been socially constructed as unique and worthy of conservation.

Students of the history of science similarly argue that scientific facts and legislative acts are historical and contingent representations that may take on the role of actors when humans accept them as given and natural. Such representations may then confine policymakers' strategies, actions, and goals within stipulated frames. Michel Foucault (1980; see also Haas, 1992) refers to epistemes and epistemic communities and discourse to delineate and identify a common set of metaphors, phrases, and words that are used by experts to understand a particular phenomenon and process. Technologies, such as the techniques employed by natural scientists to measure and trace hydrological dynamics or ecosystem change, can take on an important role when they become central elements of inquiry and contention in determining the approval of developments.

Critical planning theorists likewise identify the use of the concept of rationality by planning practitioners to understand and mediate the balance between growth and conservation (Flyvbjerg, 1998; Forester, 1989; Friedmann, 1998). Such a rationality operates through a "commitment to science, efficiency, and public administration" (Shutkin, 2000: 95). In this situation, land-use planning policies and laws become the sacred texts, and the planners and lawyers the expert mediators through which contestants have to seek resolutions. Citizen activists often learn and use the language and concepts of planning to challenge planning processes and outcomes or to propose their own alternatives (Bäckstrand, 2003, 2004; Jasanoff, 1997).

The role of aesthetics is related to the concept of rationality in a contested terrain where exurban and resource values compete. Duncan and Duncan (2004) have shown that environmental aesthetics of biodiversity can serve as an actor to maintain a privileged community that excludes others. The insights of the Duncans suggest that the ecological restorationists' proclamation that a win-win environmental aesthetics can accommodate both growth and conservation in rural and exurban landscapes is suspect. We propose to explore the idea and agency of a socially privileged and win-win aesthetics in the context of the Oak Ridges Moraine.

Seeing the world through a political ecology of actor networks has implications for the way in which we present the Oak Ridges Moraine and the debates that surround it. The naming of the Moraine, the attribution of traits to describe it, and the positioning of the landform against other physical and human geographies are not innocent activities. These activities are all part of the construction of the Moraine as unique and spectacular – a reputation, we argue, that needs further exploration.

The Oak Ridges Moraine: A Unique Phenomenon?

In the Toronto region the struggles to preserve the Oak Ridges Moraine from development have been lauded as an exceptional success story for conservation forces. Yet contestations over land use pressures on nature conservation at the rural-urban periphery are neither new nor exceptional. Throughout the 1960s and 1970s environmentalists and suburbanites challenged the despoliation of natural areas and farmlands by accelerated urban development (Rome, 2001). In response, local growth-control measures were enacted in cities across North America, especially in California and Oregon (Walker, 2007; Walker and Hurley, 2011). Since the mid-1990s, challenges to sprawl development have proliferated in urbanized regions in the United States as settlements expanded into sensitive natural areas (Hurley and Walker, 2004; Feldman and Jonas, 2000; Chapin, Connerly, and Higgins, 2007; Mason, 2004).

In Canadian cities, battles over sprawl, urbanization, and a consequent decline in the overall quality of life are often hidden by their framing as contestations over highways, infrastructure, or aggregates or the protection of a rural or small-town way of life or of First Nations land rights, or a combination of these issues. However, at base, these are often land use conflicts over the pace of urbanization and its impacts on nature and the quality of life in rural or exurban areas. They interleave a concern for the fate of a particular place with wider invocations for urban sustainability, smart growth, and the preservation of nature. For example, protests over new highway development – such as the four-lane highway completed in 2007 that runs through the Red Hill Valley (Ontario's largest urban green space) near Hamilton, Ontario (Oddie, 2009; Mulkewich and Oddie, 2009) – can combine the claims of Indigenous activists and white, middle-class, environmentalist groups for attention to urban ecology, the design of sustainable cities, and Indigenous land rights. In British Columbia, near Victoria, First Nations have challenged a resort development of a golf course, residential sub-divisions, roads, and strip malls on the grounds that it will threaten sacred places as well as degrade the rainforest ecosystem and watersheds (Wonders, 2008). By focusing primarily on contention over Indigenous land rights, we often forget that major Canadian confrontations were prompted by land use change: in Oka, Quebec, the attempt to develop an Indigenous burial ground as a golf course incited a major protest; in Caledonia, Ontario, there is an ongoing confrontation over Indigenous lands designated for a suburban development (DeVries, 2011).

Citizens are increasingly challenging infrastructure projects that serve urban growth, claiming that they will deplete and contaminate large and pristine aquifers (Walther, 2011; Lee, 2009). Resistance to large aggregate operations near major cities, such as the proposed (2011) but now defeated megaquarry in Melancthon, north of Toronto, challenges the values that elevate economic growth and urban development over other regional priorities such as preservation of farmland (Shuff, 2011b). In all these instances, citizen resistance to market-based growth in urbanized areas has called into question the privileging of economic growth over the conservation of nature, cultural values, human well-being, and social equity.

In a confluence of environmental politics and land use conflicts there is new attention being paid to the ways in which environmentalism engages with urban growth politics. In Canada, environmentalists have turned their attention to contentions in urbanized areas that threaten farmland, aquifers, and sensitive natural areas (Mulkewich and Oddie, 2009; Walther, 2011; Wekerle, Sandberg, and Gilbert, 2009a).

In cities across North America the emphasis on growth management at a regional scale constitutes "an ongoing territorial struggle" (Dierwechter, 2008: 4) among municipalities and regional and provincial governments, as well as between interests that favour economic development and others that support an approach that addresses quality-of-life and conservation goals. New regional policies and structures, as Andy Jonas and Stephanie Pincetl (2006: 487) claim, "incorporate a variety of political rationalities relating to everyday material struggles around planning, growth, fiscal flows, economic development, land use and environmental protection, which are fought out in specific urban and regional settings." Despite the prevailing neoliberal focus on less state intervention, new forms of political mobilization at a regional scale and citizen challenges to development proposals interrogate prevailing planning regimes and politics around land use change by calling for more state regulation (Brenner, 2004).

In this book we focus on a particular chapter in Ontario's environmental politics: the struggles to preserve the Oak Ridges Moraine that unfolded over several decades but came to a crisis point and resolution at the turn of the twenty-first century. We examine the tensions in exurban development that precipitated widespread public debate on a land-use planning system predicated on continued sprawl development, and the ensuing search for alternatives. The book focuses on the changing environmental and land use politics in the Toronto region. It also illuminates larger stories and issues: the power of the conservation narrative to challenge the prevailing economic growth paradigm of large city regions; the conditions for the formation of a regional movement that supported regional land use plans as a means to the conservation of nature and the management of growth; and the re-emergence of the provincial government as a strong regional actor attempting to reconcile the goals of economic growth and conservation.

Growing out of Bounds: The Oak Ridges Moraine within a Sprawling Region

The terms, definitions, and metaphors that frame the debates surrounding the Oak Ridges Moraine are specific and by no means self-evident. In the following chapters we describe the way in which insiders typically write and talk about the Oak Ridges Moraine, its perceived threats, and the policy options available for its conservation. In literally hundreds of popular tropes in government and environmental organizations' publications and websites, the Oak Ridges Moraine is above all described as a valuable and special landform, an irregular ridge of porous sand and gravel created during the Wisconsinan glacial period 12,000 years ago by advancing and retreating glaciers. Although the ice melt flowed easterly from the Niagara Escarpment cuesta to form four sediment wedges, Albion Hills, Uxbridge, Pontypool, and Rice Lake, these wedges have since come to be seen as one continuous landform (Barnett et al., 1998). The Moraine is reported to extend 160 kilometres from the Niagara Escarpment in the west to beyond Rice Lake and the Trent River in the east, averaging 13 kilometres in width, spreading officially over 190,000 hectares, and being 90 per cent privately owned. It crosses 32 municipalities, three regional municipalities (Peel, York, and Durham), four counties (Dufferin, Simcoe, Peterborough, and Northumberland), and the City of Kawartha Lakes. Sixty-five per cent of the Moraine lies within the boundaries of the Greater Toronto Area. All these jurisdictions typically claim ownership and advertise their connection to the Moraine.

The Moraine has also become something more than a landform; it is now considered a provider of so-called ecosystem services for humans (that is, ecosystems such as water, air, pollination, timber, and stone being unquestionably used as fundamental resources by humans). Below ground, the Moraine's sand and gravel deposits are assigned importance as recharge areas for groundwater in their absorption of rain and snow melt. The Moraine's thick sequence (up to 150 metres) of stratified sand and gravel deposits is often portrayed as the filter for the water, though in terms of monetary value these deposits are more valuable as a source for the aggregate industry serving the Greater Toronto Area. Aquifers, it is reported, slowly feed 65 river systems and streams flowing south to Lake Ontario and north into Georgian Bay, lakes Simcoe and Scugog, and the Trent River; 35 of these river systems are located in the Greater Toronto Area (City of Toronto, 2001). Moraine conservationists also boast that the Moraine supplies drinking water to more than 250,000 people, though this is a small number in comparison to the millions of Toronto residents who rely on chemically and mechanically treated water from Lake Ontario. The concentration of valuable ecosystem services in the form of hydrological and geological features is today considered to be part of one of the most distinct and vital landscapes of southern Ontario.

Above ground, the Moraine is celebrated for ecosystem services in the shape of streams, woodlands, wetlands, kettle lakes, and bogs, the natural habitat for many species of flora and fauna; some sensitive and threatened species are not found elsewhere in the Greater Toronto Area. The Moraine, being 30 per cent forested, is also presented as one of the last continuous corridors of green space left in south-central Ontario and one of the last refuges for forest birds in all of southern Ontario (City of Toronto, 1998). Forests and green spaces host hiking trails, century farms, land trusts, golf courses, and long-established hamlets and villages. There are fewer statements about the fact that the Moraine's marginal development potential and record in the past is what has made it into a conservation area today.

The Moraine is also made special by its representations in maps that are widely publicized in the media and on the Internet. Maps both reveal and conceal the nature of any particular area. In figure 1.2 we created a map of the Moraine that is similar to many other maps seen in public discourse. The outer boundaries of the Oak Ridges Moraine are

Figure 1.2: The Oak Ridges Moraine and the Greenbelt in the Greater Toronto Area

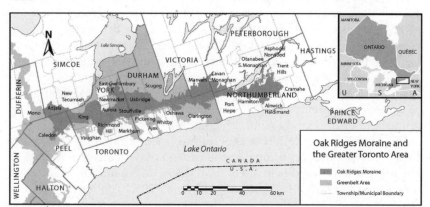

The map depicts a standard representation of the Oak Ridges Moraine and the Greenbelt in the Greater Toronto Area. It exaggerates the distinction between conservation and development areas. The boundary between the two areas is often unclear when one is travelling across the Moraine. Source: Rajiv Rawat; the authors, 2012

displayed. The conservation areas appear homogeneous and impressive in size. However, the map gives a false impression of the state of development within the Moraine. There are extensive resource, settlement, and infrastructure developments on the Moraine, and some of the restrictive development provisions are highly permissive.

The Oak Ridges Moraine story is also made special by its context, the tremendous growth of the Greater Toronto Area. The greenfield development of residential, commercial, industrial, aggregate, water resource, and recreational lands has typically been labelled as urban sprawl in the Oak Ridges Moraine debate. Sprawl is seen in a negative light and characterized by development on farmlands and green space at the outer edges of urban communities. The negative aspects of the sprawl narrative suggest that urban expansion destroys farmlands, wildlife habitats, and natural ecosystems and contributes to deforestation and soil erosion. Sprawling land use development is typically labelled low density with a strong separation between residential, commercial, and industrial functions. The sprawl narrative often resorts to statistics to support its position. Commentators lament that between

1976 and 1996 the Greater Toronto Area lost 60,703 hectares of prime farmland to urbanization (Hare, 2001; see also Miller, 2005a: 47). Over the last 50 years the urbanized fabric of the Toronto region grew six to seven times as a result of a suburbanization process driven by increases in population, income, land consumption per capita, and pro-development agendas (Bourne, 2000). If such a development pattern prevails, the critics state, it is anticipated that, with the projected population increase, 43 per cent of the land in the Greater Golden Horseshoe will be urbanized by the year 2031, of which 92 per cent will be located on prime agricultural land (Winfield, 2003: 2).

The growing population of the Toronto metropolitan census area is a particularly referenced topic in the urban sprawl narrative (table 1.1). The population tripled from 1.8 million in 1966 to 5.6 million in 2009 and is expected to reach a total of 7.45 million by 2031. The region has a 20 per cent growth rate, which ranks the Toronto region as one of the fastest-growing large cities in North America, and is presented as a "threat" to the Oak Ridges Moraine (GHK Canada, 2002).[1] Despite recent provincial policies of encouraging intensification in existing urban areas, population growth has intensified in the lower density suburban and exurban areas of the region. In the period 2006–2011, population growth in Toronto was 4.5 per cent, below the national average of 5.9 per cent. In the Greater Toronto Area the 2006–2011 growth rate was 9.0 per cent. However, in the regions that border or encompass the Moraine, populations now outnumber the number of residents in the City of Toronto (Statistics Canada, 2006; 2012). Between 2006 and 2011, York Region had a growth rate of 15.7 per cent, compared with the city of Vaughan at 20.7 per cent and Markham at 15.3 per cent. Halton Region had a growth rate of 14.2 per cent, and Durham Region a growth rate of 8.4 per cent (City of Toronto, 2012; Statistics Canada, 2012).

The population in the surrounding regional municipalities is growing more than three times faster than is the population in the City of Toronto. Cities like Markham, Brampton, Vaughan, and Richmond Hill are among the fastest-growing and the most diverse municipalities in the Greater Toronto Area and in Canada (Statistics Canada, 2006). Markham's population more than quadrupled in the last 30 years, growing from 77,000 in 1981 to 301,709 in 2011 (Statistics Canada, 2006, 2012). Vaughan's demographic growth has been even more significant, growing almost 10 times, from 29,041 residents in 1981 to 288,301 residents in 2011 (Statistics Canada, 2012). The economic mobility of earlier European immigrants moving out of the city and the arrival of highly skilled newcomers (targeted by Canadian immigration policy) predominantly

Table 1.1 Population projections for the Greater Toronto Area

Population	2001	2011	2021	2031
Toronto	2,584,000	2,765,200	3,040,400	3,265,200
Durham Region	527,600	628,900	751,500	909,400
Halton Region	390,900	519,900	673,700	854,100
Peel Region	1,032,100	1,364,800	1,681,700	2,020,200
York Region	762,700	1,061,700	1,299,000	1,565,600
Greater Toronto Area	5,297,400	6,335,200	7,446,400	8,614,500

Source: Ontario Ministry of Finance, 2011

account for this phenomenon of the suburbanization of immigration in the Greater Toronto Area.

The growth of the Greater Toronto Area is often portrayed in the context of the relative growth of a foreign-born immigrant population. However, this phenomenon is seldom mentioned in the context of the development pressures experienced on the Moraine. The foreign-born population in the Toronto Census Metropolitan Area[2] accounted for 45.7 per cent of the total population in 2006, the largest number of any metropolitan area in Canada. Most of the growth in the foreign-born population occurred in the municipalities surrounding Toronto, with suburban cities attracting specific immigrant populations. In Brampton, for example, the foreign-born population comprised 47.8 per cent of its total population in 2006, representing an increase of 59.5 per cent since 2001 (Statistics Canada, 2009). At the same time, visible minorities[3] accounted for 57 per cent, and residents of South Asian descent 32 per cent, of the city's population (Statistics Canada, 2006). With 56.5 per cent of its total population in 2006 having been born outside of Canada, Markham had the second-highest proportion of foreign-born residents among Canadian municipalities, after the city of Richmond, British Columbia (57.4 per cent) (Statistics Canada, 2009). Markham's visible minorities population accounted for a larger percentage (65 per cent) of the total population, of which 34 per cent came from the People's Republic of China (Statistics Canada, 2006). Vaughan also saw an increase (44.9 per cent) in its foreign-born population between 2001 and 2006, but only 26 per cent of its population identified as visible minorities in 2006 (Statistics Canada, 2009, 2006).

In stark contrast, the growth, or the absence of growth, of a foreign-born population is hardly mentioned in the context of the communities on the Oak Ridges Moraine. On the Moraine, people in the visible-minority category are basically invisible. Table 1.2 identifies the percentage of people in the visible-minority category for a number of census divisions that cover significant parts of the Moraine. The Moraine is largely an enclave for white English-speaking Canadians. The percentage of visible minorities remains considerably lower than the average both for Ontario and for the Metropolitan Area of Toronto.

The sprawl narrative contains a more fundamental contradiction that extends beyond the Oak Ridges Moraine. In a capitalist society, growth is understood as something positive when it generates economic activity and prosperity. The province of Ontario is no exception. Land development and construction industries account for over 10 per cent of Ontario's gross domestic product, that is, approximately $45 billion (Urban Development Institute of Ontario, 2004). Government incentives have favoured urbanization and urban sprawl through homeownership subsidies, highway programs, infrastructure subsidies, and tax deductions. In Canada, post–Second World War federal housing programs subsidized home building by ensuring that mortgages could be obtained on easy terms for the purchase of new homes in the suburbs (Tindal and Tindal, 2003). Sprawl was enabled by land speculation, a rise in property values, limited municipal powers, and a robust economy that was triggered in part by a booming real-estate and construction industry (Boudreau, Keil, and Young, 2009; Sewell, 2009). Automobile dependence associated with suburbia has justified an increasing expansion of highways, which, in turn, has justified more sprawling development (ibid.; Harris, 2004). As a result, Toronto's daily commuter-shed now extends approximately 80 kilometres (Blais, 2003).

Urban sprawl has been enabled by land policy and social values that seem to consider rural and "natural" lands as *terra nullius*, that is, lands waiting for building, development, and capital investment. Sprawl has also been facilitated by the three-level structure of governance: the Province, which dictates the objectives; the regional municipalities, which set growth targets, develop official plans, and provide services to residents and businesses; and local municipalities, which are required to conform to and implement provincial policies. Disputes over the appropriate use of the land, presided over by the Ontario Municipal Board, have typically favoured sprawl in appeals on matters relating to

Table 1.2 Visible minorities on the Oak Ridges Moraine, 2006

Select Census Division	Visible Minority %
Caledon	7.2
King Township	4.6
Aurora	13.1
Whitchurch-Stouffville	7.4
Uxbridge	2.3
Alnwick-Haldimand	0.9
Province of Ontario	22.8
Metropolitan Area of Toronto	42.9

Source: Statistics Canada, 2006

official plans, land use zoning, development applications and permits, subdivisions, and site plans.

Many exurban or rural communities that are in need of more revenue have welcomed growth and the prospect of new residential and commercial developments stimulating economic growth because development charges on each newly built dwelling unit contribute to municipal coffers, pay for needed services, and help to keep property taxes down. At the same time, many municipal governments have very limited capacity to regulate environmental protection. Growth and conservation management, therefore, represent more than a bureaucratic challenge of land use regulation. For suburbanites and exurbanites seeking closeness to "pristine" nature, there are struggles over competing values, claims, and production regimes. The contradictory elements of the term *urban sprawl*, criticized in the public debate, yet accepted in everyday practice, are a subject that we strive to understand more fully in the chapters that follow.

The Oak Ridges Moraine: A Place of Uneven Development

Most references over the last 20 years acknowledge that urban sprawl has gradually encroached on some of the Oak Ridges Moraine's most environmentally sensitive ecosystems (Pim and Ornoy, 2002; Sewell, 2009). In these references the Moraine is typically presented as an

Figure 1.3: Humberland Drive at Bathurst Street

Lou Wise, a former Royal Canadian Air Force pilot, has taken aerial photographs of the Oak Ridges Moraine for conservation authorities and environmental organizations over three decades, which have been an important influence in the efforts to conserve it. In 2007, then 86 years old, Wise received the Latornell Conservation Pioneer Award. In the above photo, subdivisions can be seen north of Humberland Drive (moving horizontally across the middle of the photo), east of Bathurst Street (in the lower left-hand corner), in the settlement area of the Moraine. Subdivisions have since encroached on the green space south of Humberland Drive. In the lower right-hand corner, land has been cleared for a new subdivision. Ironically, perhaps, the Humber Flats EcoPark, established to provide trails and a wildlife corridor as well as to improve the aesthetics and the storm water absorptive capacity of the area, is located in the middle of the photo. Source: Lou Wise for Toronto and Region Conservation Authority, c. 2002. Additional materials available at York University Libraries, Clara Thomas Archives and Special Collections, Lou Wise fonds, F0539

undifferentiated landform that is identified primarily by its name and border. The forests, open spaces, habitats, and aquifers on the Moraine have been increasingly threatened by aggregate extraction, road extensions, and housing subdivisions (figure 1.3). Hamlets and towns on the Moraine have faced proposals to build new housing that would double and even quadruple their populations. Such events made the Moraine a flashpoint for local struggles over urban growth, environmental conservation, and threats to the rural way of life in the 1990s.

The Moraine, however, is a highly diversified place consisting of sub-urbs, small towns, exurbs, and rural settlements surrounded by forests and agricultural fields. In this mix, the suburbs – though not necessarily those that already exist – are typically seen as the villains of sprawl. The exurbias, by contrast, are often seen as the bulwarks against sprawl, where the residents fight the proposed housing subdivisions, roads, sewers, sandpits, and now wind farms. They are a global phenome-non that comprises small towns and large tracts of land developed into hobby farms, country estates, and low-density subdivision tracts. They may also contain some suburbs but only where they appear as islands in a larger sea of countryside and rural estates. Exurban areas play a significant role in both promoting and resisting sprawl. Exurbanites are often city people, living in exceedingly low-density areas, who "commute by cars, trains, planes and internet to one (or more) cities in the sub-urbs for work, shopping and entertainment" (Taylor, 2011: 324). Exur-bias are thus not bounded places but "networks" of "social relations" that demand a "no boundaries" approach (ibid.). Exurban areas typi-cally harbour migrants in search of amenity where "natural" values fig-ure prominently and where exurbanites express a close attachment to the countryside and to nature, scenery, and aesthetic, recreational, and other consumption-oriented values.

People who have moved to exurban areas often have an idealized version of rural life and cherish a landscape aesthetic of open spaces and low densities (Rome, 2001). Jeff Crump's (2003) empirical study comparing the reasons that people move to exurbia or suburbia finds that exurbanites desire to live in a rural environment, and suburban-ites are attracted by the lower housing cost and access to highways. Gerald Walker (2000: 110) notes that exurbanites often seek "a superior residential environment" that combines "the twin values of romantic ruralism and anti-urbanism." The perception of "living in nature" is, therefore, at the heart of the exurbanite attraction to the countryside, and unsurprisingly the defence of such an environment and its associ-ated lifestyle (including property) becomes a key value of exurban liv-ing (Rome, 2001; Schmidt and Paulsen, 2009).

The exurbanite battle to conserve the Moraine is often portrayed as operating in the general public interest. It is seldom acknowledged that issues of land use and correlated aspects of private property and property rights have been a driving force in the development of urban, suburban, and exurban patterns of living. Exurbia epitomizes an individualized, private, and exclusive living in an idealized nature. It is that individualized living that lies at the basis of many efforts to defend exurban spaces. It is often an exclusionary landscape where municipal by-laws that stipulate minimum floor space and setbacks shut out poorer people. Restrictive covenants on how to construct buildings and on the types of vegetation to conserve and grow also may confine the exurbs to wealthy residents (Duncan and Duncan, 2004). Besides newly arrived affluent residents, exurban places may also include long-time residents such as farmers, people dependent on resource industries, and those living in hamlets or villages, often resulting in conflicts between them and newcomers intent on pursuing an amenity-based lifestyle (Walker and Fortmann, 2003).

The sprawl narrative is also prone to neglecting the negative environmental impacts of exurban development. Conservation biologists have identified low-density exurban sprawl development as a threat to biodiversity, habitat, and species at risk (Theobald 2004). In the United States, Brown et al. (cited in Taylor, 2011: 327) warn that 25 per cent of the development in mainland United States (excluding Alaska) has been built at exurban densities (from one unit per 0.4 hectares to one unit per 16.2 hectares) with dire consequences. These consequences include a decrease in native species, increases in exotic plant species, increased fragmentation of landscapes, a decrease in farming and forestry, increased impermeable surfaces, and more intensive use of energy, water, and chemicals (Cadieux, 2011). Municipalities and upper tiers of government experience increasing pressure from exurban residents and environmentalists to preserve relatively undisturbed open space and habitat in exurban areas (Schmidt and Paulsen, 2009). As Schmidt and Paulsen note, this is often "an attempt by middle-class property interests to use the rhetoric of environmentalism to protect and further their own amenity and landscape consumption values" (96).

Data assembled specifically on the Moraine by the Oak Ridges Moraine Technical Working Committee in 1991 illustrate the highly variable settlement pattern of exurbia. These are the only easily available demographic and socio-economic data that correspond to the then-existing boundaries of the Moraine; they are still likely to give a representative picture of the settlement pattern today.

The population numbers and densities at the time show high concentrations of people in the central parts of the Moraine, in the city of Vaughan, Newmarket, Aurora, and Richmond Hill, with respective

Table 1.3 Population and population densities on the Oak Ridges Moraine, 1991

Region	Jurisdiction (west to east, north to south)	Population	Hectares	Population density (per ha)
Peel	Caledon	8,950	69,650	0.1
York	King Township	5,510	21,900–22,200	0.3
	Vaughan	4,560	3,100–3,190	1.4
	Newmarket	1,600	380–400	4.0
	Aurora	14,600	2,900–2,950	5.0
	Richmond Hill	13,900	5,300–5,420	2.6
	East Gwillimbury	1,600	5,000–5,080	0.3
	Whitchurch-Stouffville	13,000	16,600–16,800	0.8
Durham	Township of Uxbridge	4,100	18,750	0.2
	Pickering	1,190	3,310	0.4
	Township of Scugog	1,280	8,750	0.1
	Whitby	690	2,030	0.3
	Oshawa	430	2,480	0.2
	Clarington	1,990	17,550	0.1

Source: Oak Ridges Moraine Technical Working Committee, 1994b

densities of 1.4, 4.2, 5.0, and 2.6 persons per hectare. These areas can be largely classified as exurban, but they are moving towards suburban concentrations, where residents have since been shown to be particularly prone to resist development and call for conservation measures. Caledon, King Township, East Gwillimbury, Whitchurch-Stouffville, and the Township of Uxbridge, with low existing densities at 0.1 to 1.2 persons per hectare, represent the typical exurbias, with rural estates as a dominant feature. The remaining parts of the Moraine comprise rural areas of relatively low existing densities, at 0.1 to 0.5 persons per hectare. This is also true for the parts of the Moraine that extend to the east of Durham Region, an area that comprises 35 per cent of the Moraine but which is not included in table 1.3 (Ontario Ministry of Municipal Affairs and Housing, 2008a). The initial conservation interest in the Moraine started and remains concentrated in the suburban and exurban regions of the Greater Toronto Area of the Moraine, while the rural eastern sections are under considerably less development pressure. Indeed, in the eastern jurisdictions, development is largely sought by local politicians, though there is also a growing number of professional exurban in-migrants who oppose this trend.

Land assessments across the Oak Ridges Moraine in 1994, presented in table 1.4 below, provide further evidence of regional differences and the centrality of private property and exclusive living. Land assessments and zoning restrictions and allowances reflect the presence of exurban estate developments (or extensive landed properties in the countryside) in the western parts of the Moraine, in the Region of Peel's Caledon area, and in the western parts of York Region along Sixteenth Side Road and Keele Street. At the time, land assessments stood at $43,750 to $185,000 per hectare, and there were generally no allowances for severances on the large parcels that were available for purchase. Along the Yonge Street corridor in Richmond Hill the land values stood at $500,000 to $700,000 per hectare for serviced land and $150,000 to $200,000 per hectare for raw land. The potential for severances in the area reflects the presence and potential for higher-density suburban subdivisions. It was along the Yonge Street corridor that a modern sewage system traversed the Moraine to provide services to the growing and relatively dense (in comparison to estates) subdivisions (White, 2003). Finally, in the Newcastle-Scugog area located in Durham Region, land values dropped considerably from a high of $125,000 to a low of $18,750 per hectare. This area was, and in large part remains, rural in character, though it has recently come under considerable exurban development pressures.

Tackling Sprawl: State Interventions in Growth and Conservation

In 2001 and 2002 the provincial government passed the *Oak Ridges Moraine Conservation Act* and more particularly the *Oak Ridges Moraine Conservation Plan* to protect the ecological and hydrological integrity of the 190,000 hectares of Moraine area in the face of continuous urban sprawl in the Greater Toronto Area (Ontario Ministry of Municipal Affairs and Housing, 2001a, 2002a). The Oak Ridges Moraine legislation built on the *Niagara Escarpment Planning and Development Act* of 1973 and the *Niagara Escarpment Plan* of 1985 (Government of Ontario, 1973, 1985) and provided the impetus for the provincial government to extend further into more wide-ranging policies to manage growth in the Toronto region.

Table 1.4 Land value assessment across the Oak Ridges Moraine, 1994

	Caledon area (Region of Peel)			Yonge Street corridor in Richmond Hill (York Region)			Newcastle and Scugog (Durham Region)	
Estate residential	Highway 50			16th Sideroad and Keele Street	Bathurst to Dufferin and Teston Road (southern Moraine)	In proximity to Bathurst Street between Bloomington and Stouffville Roads	Not specified	
Size of site (hectares)	0.8 no potential for severance	4.0 no potential for severance	20.0 no potential for severance	4.0 no potential for severance	0.5–0.7	1.6–4.0 raw land with potential for severance	0–0.8	0–4.0
Value per site ($)	150,000	175,000–225,000	1 million	250,000–350,000	350,000		75,000–100,000	75,000–125,000
Value per hectare ($)	185,000	43,750–56,250	50,000	62,500–87,500	500,000–700,000	150,000–200,000	93,750–125,000	18,750–31,250
Agriculture	Class 2	west of highway	east of highway		along Yonge Street	Bayview Avenue and Leslie Street	South Scugog and Northern Newcastle	
Value per hectare ($)	6,100–9,800	6,000–7,000	8,000–9,000		50,000	15,000–25,000	4,000–6,000	
Park conservation Value per hectare ($)	5,000–6,000				25,000–50,000	15,000–25,000	3,000	

Source: Oak Ridges Moraine Technical Working Committee, 1994b

In 2005 the *Places to Grow Act, 2005,* and the *Greenbelt Act, 2005* (respectively Ontario Ministry of Public Infrastructure and Renewal, 2005a, 2005b), were passed to reconcile the tensions between growth and conservation in the sprawl narrative. The *Greenbelt Act* and the *Greenbelt Plan* (2005) seek to protect 728,434 hectares across the Greater Golden Horseshoe region as countryside, ecologically sensitive areas, and natural heritage systems. The "countryside" designation is intended to protect prime agricultural lands and rural and small towns and to contribute to the economic viability of farming communities. The *Greenbelt Act, 2005,* along with the *Niagara Escarpment Planning and Development Act, 1973,* and the *Oak Ridges Moraine Conservation Act, 2001,* thus establish a network of countryside and open space areas and represent the commitment of the current provincial government to conserve environmentally sensitive lands and landscapes.[4]

However, the *Greenbelt Plan* also identifies lands on which urbanization will be allowed, and therefore it is considered to be "a strategic response to the politics of sprawl," reflecting the competing interests that speak both for and against development at the urban fringe (Pond, 2009). The *Places to Grow Act, 2005,* and the *Growth Plan for the Greater Golden Horseshoe, 2006* (Ontario Ministry of Public Infrastructure and Renewal, 2005a, 2005b, 2006) dictate how and where growth will occur in the region. Building on other key initiatives including the *Greenbelt Plan,* the *Planning Act,* and the *Provincial Policy Statement, 2005,* the *Growth Plan* seeks to manage growth by sustaining a robust economy, building strong communities, and conserving natural and healthy environments. The *Growth Plan* proposes to accommodate the forecasted population increase of 4.0 million by 2031, for a total of 11.5 million by increasing the intensification of provincially designated existing and newly planned urban growth centres, corridors, and transit areas, as well as brownfield and greyfield redevelopment. Intensification serves, "in the interest of promoting economic prosperity," as the driving principle for the development of "healthy, safe and balanced communities" by addressing issues of transportation, infrastructure planning, land use planning, urban form, housing, and natural heritage and resource protection (Ontario Ministry of Public Infrastructure Renewal, 2006: 6, 12).

The contradiction in the growth and conservation management strategy surrounding the Oak Ridges Moraine and the Greenbelt is well illustrated in figure 1.4. We have produced a map of the so-called protected areas of the Greater Golden Horseshoe, based on provincial data.

Figure 1.4: Protected areas of the Greater Toronto Area and Golden Horseshoe

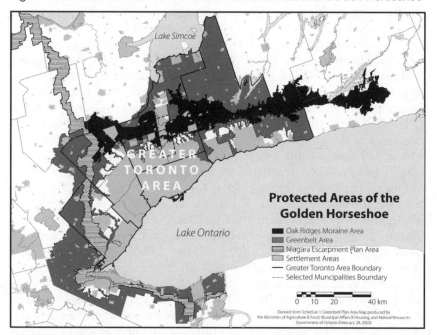

In contrast to the map in figure 1.2, this map complicates the distinction between development and conservation areas. It shows extensive settlement areas within the Moraine. There are also prospective building sites, in the so-called white belt, located to the south of the Moraine and the Greenbelt, which accommodate development for the next 20 years. Source: Rajiv Rawat and authors, 2012

The map tells a story. It shows the Ontario Greenbelt, which incorporates the Oak Ridges Moraine and the Niagara Escarpment, and all three areas are shown in the three darkest shades on the map. But we also show settlement areas inside and outside the Greenbelt in the lightest shaded colour. Note that the Moraine is interspersed with settlement areas, especially along Yonge Street where the Moraine is almost cut in half. The white-coloured areas are rural areas open to settlement. Note in particular the white areas north of the settlement areas of the Greater Toronto Area and south of the Greenbelt. These areas can accommodate more than 20 years of settlement growth.

The combined growth and conservation policy intervention in the Greater Toronto Area has allegedly resulted in the implementation of one of the strongest sets of growth management legislation in North America, reminiscent of and comparable with greenbelt legislation on other continents, such as Europe (in cities like London, Amsterdam, and Stockholm) where the regulatory powers of central states and the presence of extensive land areas in public ownership have enabled the shaping and regulating of urban development (Carter-Whitney, 2008). The Ontario greenbelt legislation can also be compared with examples in the United States, such as the City of Portland, Oregon, which has implemented a regional growth plan to limit exurban sprawl and promote densification, integrate residential and commercial uses, and build up public transport (Song and Knaap, 2004). Portland constitutes an exception rather than a rule, however, and it is facing stiff opposition from the ideologies of individual liberty and from free market proponents who endorse and view "urban sprawl" as desirable (Bruegmann, 2005; O'Toole, 2009). The San Francisco greenbelt, much larger than the typical nature conservation area, is more typical of the U.S. experience. It is largely a private initiative in which the state government has played a marginal role (Walker, 2007). Both the *Greenbelt Plan* and the *Oak Ridges Moraine Conservation Plan* have received prominent planning awards and praise in international circles for tackling the negative consequences of sprawl. It is on this point that the Oak Ridges Moraine constitutes a unique phenomenon that may provide wider lessons.

Research Approach

We draw on our diverse interdisciplinary backgrounds of sociology, geography, landscape and planning studies, and environmental history to employ a set of conceptual tools to interrogate development, sprawl, and conservation in the Toronto region. We do not begin from the assumption that the Oak Ridges Moraine represents a best practice of conservation or development. Instead, we critically examine the social and environmental assumptions and conditions that have transformed the Moraine from a rather unnoticed glacial feature to a hotspot of environmental politics and activism. We follow a methodological approach that examines the historical, discursive, material, ecological, sociocultural, and institutional context of environmental mobilization on the

Moraine in order to provide a more complex understanding of the tensions and contradictions between growth and conservation.

Our study is based on seven years of research and thinking about the environmentalist challenges to sprawl on the Oak Ridges Moraine. The entry point of our research was an interest in environmental and resident activists with whom we conducted 25 interviews. We also interviewed 40 officials: mayors and councillors; planners from municipalities, regions, the Ministry of Municipal Affairs and Housing, and the Toronto and Region Conservation Authority; former officials from the Ministry of Natural Resources; representatives of land trusts; and members of the Oak Ridges Moraine Advisory Committee. We also solicited insights from developers, lawyers, local scientists, and spokespersons and members of environmental organizations who played an active role in formulating, interpreting, and implementing the conservation legislation. We conducted a series of formal interviews and had many informal conversations during 15 public consultations and other meetings. Some interviews were conducted by the authors (one, two, or the three of us), some were done collaboratively with graduate students, and some were organized by students under our supervision. We also conducted participant observation at public meetings during the *Oak Ridges Moraine Conservation Plan* and *Greenbelt Plan* consultations, at council meetings and public hearings, and at meetings organized by environmental organizations. Other sources include draft and final provincial legislation documents, legislature debate transcripts, and a growing production of growth management and regional planning reports, policy, and position papers produced by different levels of governments, environmental organizations, and lobby organizations of aggregate producers and developers. Our research was constantly fuelled by extensive coverage of the Moraine in daily newspapers, community papers, and other media (such as radio and television). We collected and archived articles on a daily basis and relied also on the database searching system Factiva to access additional print media articles. We also spent a considerable amount of time in diverse areas of the Moraine, taking photographs, talking to residents, visiting sales offices of housing developments, and occasionally joining in protest events. We amassed housing magazines and developers' promotional brochures on various subdivisions. We also used and compiled census data to gather a demographic and socio-economic profile of the many regions and municipalities on the Moraine and in the Greater Toronto

Area. We greatly benefited from secondary research conducted by our students for course assignments and theses. At the height of the Moraine battles in 2001 we organized a panel at York University on the Moraine, to which we invited activists and guest speakers from the province and the Toronto and Region Conservation Authority. We invited key Moraine actors to speak to our classes. We ran a graduate planning studio on the Moraine, including substantial field visits and interviews with local officials.

In response to the volume of data, the speed with which regional growth management and policy changes have taken place in the Greater Toronto Area and the Greater Golden Horseshoe Area, the range of actors involved, and the complexity of relationships, we compiled an extensive chronology and organized our evidence thematically in the construction of our written work, integrating them with the secondary sources (see the appendix). Our themes were loosely constructed as we were interested in multiple meanings, interpretations, and representations through the enactment of conservation discourses, policy, and partnership relationships. Our analyses ranged from the interpretation of images to repeated and close reading of a specific document to the complex and intricate review of discursive expressions, rhetoric statements, and stylistic constructions of print media. Over our research period the discourses of different actors were actually changing and evolving, so we also consider the position of power that people and their institutions hold and develop. In the end, we recognize that given our theoretical frameworks and our methodology, our representation of environmental politics on the Oak Ridges Moraine is only one of many in the field of possible meanings.

Outline of the Book

In the next chapter we explore various human representations of the Moraine. The main message is that representations of landscapes generally, and the Moraine specifically, are moving targets that are socially and naturally co-produced and therefore change over time. As with any other landscape, the Oak Ridges Moraine is not a landform that should be taken as given. At one point it had no name and no identifiers, and its inhabitants probably saw it as part of a wider socioeconomic and spiritual place. No doubt, the Moraine has had its own agency during its evolution. However, it has also been represented differently by a range of actors, including First Nations peoples, European settlers (both loggers and farmers), geologists, archaeologists, restoration professionals, planners, developers, aggregate producers, recreation seekers, naturalists, and conservationists. Such an analysis helps to put the current suburban and exurban conceptions of the Moraine into perspective.

In chapter 3 we examine the most recent and now dominant representation of the Moraine as an object of conservation and planning. We explore the historical precedents, dating back to the 1960s and leading to the Oak Ridges Moraine legislation, when various individuals, including civil servants, planners, and natural scientists, promoted the Moraine as a conservation object; we also look at the construction of the common ideas about it and the way in which these elements evolved over time. Throughout this chapter we examine both the Moraine itself – its materiality, flora, and fauna and how it has presented itself and influenced conservation planners – and the concept of the Moraine as a distinct object as imagined by conservation planners. In the end, we convey the resulting Oak Ridges Moraine legislation itself as an actor that shapes, determines, and constrains conservation measures.

In chapter 4 we explore the role of residents on the Moraine as actors promoting the landform as a bioregion and a place of attachment and belonging that touches the mind, emotions, and desires of people towards place and nature. We conclude that statements of a sense of loss and of a general "above and below the ground" attachment to the Moraine, as well as the media frenzy that both fed off people's protests and contributed to them, were instrumental in the realization of the Moraine as a conservation object. However, such attachment was part of a particular landscape vision expressed by certain privileged groups, which left the positions of other groups either marginalized or obscured.

In chapter 5 we examine the story of activists as actors in protesting runaway growth and sprawl and promoting the conservation of the Moraine. We recount the initial, separate, place-based battles on the Moraine, battles that eventually produced a common sentiment and strategy around the Oak Ridges Moraine as a unified concept and then the formation of the Moraine legislation. The chapter suggests that the Oak Ridges Moraine is part of a recurrent story of suburban and exurban environmentalisms and rural movements. It examines the dynamic and changing relationship between these movements and the state in its jurisdiction over land use and environmental policies in the region. We examine the emergence of a networked movement on a regional scale that crafted a Moraine-wide identity, and the consequences of legislation implementing initial demands and of new agencies, in partnership with the state, engaging civil society in monitoring the Moraine.

In chapter 6 we investigate the agency of the rationality of planning to which conservation groups have come to subscribe and the fundamental and deep-seated procedural biases that have resulted. Growth in alternative and greener built forms has been subordinated to economic considerations and current real-estate and construction institutions. Both development and conservation efforts are linked to a progressive ideology of the technocratic management of natural resources and a planning rationality in organizing space. We identify several flaws in the Oak Ridges Moraine legislation that favour growth and development.

In chapter 7 we identify and explore a hybrid aesthetic that contains both consumption-oriented and production- or extraction-focused elements that may seem contradictory but which, in fact, complement each other. We illustrate this point through the use of two examples: the exclusive housing associated with recreational (primarily golf) nature and its aesthetic values; and the aggregate industry sector. These examples show how the Oak Ridges Moraine is emerging as an increasingly private and exclusive landscape where wealthy exurban living jostles and nestles with aggregate pits and where a nature rhetoric serves as a cornerstone for both. Exurbanites favour rural qualities such as the proximity of "nature," open space, privacy, and recreational amenities, while expressing a strong anti-urban ethos that repudiates crime, congestion, and pollution. In our account of the aggregate industry we examine the rationalities that argue for its continued presence in conservation areas. The Moraine, we suggest, is part of a growing number of hybrid elite landscapes that are premised on both attractive and extractive foundations.

The concluding chapter discusses more generally the implications of our study for nature conservation studies. We reflect on the position of the Oak Ridges Moraine with regard to other greenbelt legislation and on the lessons that its experience can teach us about political ecology.

Chapter Two

The Surfacing of a Landform: Historical Representations of the Oak Ridges Moraine

At the turn of the twenty-first century, contestations over land use change and growth focused on a particular landform in the Toronto region: the Oak Ridges Moraine, a landscape feature that was seen as unique from an ecological and geological perspective. Before then, over centuries, the Moraine had taken on many different meanings as a First Nations' homeland, a settler frontier, a failed agricultural area, a wasteland, a planning headache, a valuable financial asset, a sensitive habitat, a water resource, and a place in which to build houses (see figure 2.1). Erich Zimmerman (1951) once famously wrote that resources never are; they become. The same applies to landscapes and landforms and the other categories of nature that they embody. They are not; they become or they are in many ways constructed or produced by people. We may, therefore, think of individual landscapes "as being compromised, partial, contested and only provisionally stable as modes of ordering the world and our engagement with it" (Gold and Revill, 2000: 15). Landscapes and natures change as they are manipulated by people. They also change in the minds of people, in how people think and form mental maps and representations of them and expect certain functions to flow from them. We are, of course, also mindful that landforms and natures have agency, sometimes independent of humans, and that human representations of natures are complicated by the dynamics of non-human natures (Mortimer-Sandilands, 2009).

In this chapter we consider the representations of the Moraine as landscape, tracing the history of the region before its present dominant form as suburbia and exurbia. The lesson from this exercise is to point to the ephemeral nature of the Moraine as a distinct phenomenon; it was not there yesterday, and while it is there today, it may not be there

Figure 2.1: Yonge Street and Bond Lake in Richmond Hill

Yonge Street, moving northwards, is located to the left in the photo. Bond Lake is one of the many kettle lakes on the Moraine. Another kettle lake, Lake Wilcox, is seen in the distance. Since the aerial photo was taken, subdivision development by Lebovic Enterprises, a prominent builder, has occurred north of Bond Lake. The photo illustrates the Moraine as a place for suburban expansion along the Yonge Street corridor that is also served by an extensive sewer line. Source: Lou Wise for the Toronto and Region Conservation Authority, ca. 2002. Additional materials available at York University Libraries, Clara Thomas Archives and Special Collections, Lou Wise fonds, F0539

tomorrow. The precedents of the landscape are thus present and influential in the current dynamics of the Moraine. To be sure, the Moraine is a cultural construct, but it is also a nature or materiality that matters, it has its own dynamic and clock that remain unpredictable and elusive to human actions and understandings, and it will likely remain present in some form in a post-human world. We trace the Moraine's material-cultural enactments as a physical home to Indigenous peoples, an object of study by twentieth-century archaeologists, a resource frontier for European loggers and farmers, a geomorphologic feature identified and labelled by nineteenth-century geo-scientists, a "failed" farming frontier, and a forest regeneration and watershed protection initiative for conservation professionals in the 1930s and 1940s. We also explore the Moraine as a recreational haven in the growing post-war, car-bound society and as an ecological preserve in more recent years. In the present, representations of the Moraine as a farming area, an aggregate source, a wind-farm site, recreational land, a planning unit, a scientific object, an ethnic and class enclave, a bioregion, and a protected area compete with and sometimes complement and support each other. The key argument is that the Moraine as a distinct landscape is a social construction that has been determined not only environmentally (that is, by its physical attributes) and locationally (through its closeness to the city of Toronto) but also socially and historically by various interest groups pursuing, protecting, and rationalizing specific functions or goals.

Do Moraines Listen?

In her seminal book *Do Glaciers Listen*, Julie Cruikshank (2005) explores conflicting descriptions of glaciers and how they are not only caught up in different cultural histories but also "objectively entangled" in biophysical processes. Glaciers, in other words, have their own dynamic that is independent of human action. Cruikshank's account does not translate into a crude environmental determinism where the physical environment, as in Ellsworth Huntington's (1971) climate determinism, decides the fate of the mental brainpower and the brawn of humans. Instead, it constitutes a situation in which the physical environment, by its mystique and agency, serves as one actor in a complex web of human and non-human interactions.

Sarah Whatmore (1999) has suggested that physical geography or non-human nature provides a "creative presence" that is a powerful actor in human and non-human interactions. A set of flora, fauna, or landscape features may have material attributes that speak to human sentiments and can come to be perceived as valuable, attractive, spectacular, sublime, and worthy of conservation (Buller, 2004). As Whatmore (1999: 26) states, "non-human nature is a co-constituent in shaping growth, where nature's agency is a 'relational achievement,' involving the creative presence of organic beings, technologies and discursive codes." The creation of so-called mega-fauna and mega-flora and their role in shaping conservation efforts may perhaps be seen as a relational achievement. So may the creation of the weed-free and chemically fed lawn, to which North American suburbanites and exurbanites have become enslaved in spite of being fully aware of its negative consequences for human health and the environment (Robbins, 2007). However, non-human nature may be part of not only "relational achievements" but also what may be called a "relational failure," a situation in which human interventions and non-human reactions combine to create dystopic environments, a climate that changes, a landscape eroded of vegetation, a forest devoid of animal populations, and soils pregnant with toxins (Whatmore, 1999). Timothy Mitchell (2002) points to one such relational failure, the modernity project in post-war Egypt. In a telling chapter called "Can the Mosquito Speak," he argues that the mosquito combined with human changes to cause the death of so many people that the number far exceeded the toll of the German invasion of Egypt during the Second World War. In the case of the Moraine, biophysical phenomena, such as salamanders, deer, coyotes, oaks, forests, rivers, ravines, geology, hydrology, and climate, play active roles in shaping human and non-human destinies. Such actors can take on dynamics that are unpredictable and often do not conform to the modelling and manipulative efforts of scientists and managers.

Moraines, like their originators, the glaciers, do listen, speak, and respond. To the first human settlers, the Indigenous people who once lived and moved through it, the Moraine offered subsistence as well as tradable resources. To the European settlers it offered forests to be cut, game to be hunted, soils to be sowed, and sand to be mined. And to current residents and visitors the Moraine offers a unique nature, scenery, and escape from the ravages of modern life. But the relationships are complicated. At one time and in certain places of the Moraine the soils did not listen to the intentions of the farmers' ploughs or the standards of an emerging industrial agriculture that were set by state bureaucrats, resulting in farm abandonment over extensive areas of the Moraine (Watson, 1947). At other times, abandoned sandpits left sterile wounds that have not healed (a relational failure), while on other occasions they turned into habitats for a biodiverse flora and fauna (a relational achievement).

Erik Swyngedouw (1999: 445) urges us to think of socio-nature relationships to understand better the way in which nature is intentionally and unintentionally produced, by suggesting that "the actually existing socio-natural conditions are always the result of intricate

transformations of pre-existing configurations that are themselves inherently natural *and* social." We thus propose a situation where the
human and non-human are co-mediated, co-constituted, and co-produced
to form unique and constantly new human geographies, where old values are rejected and new ones take their place. Nature's alleged destruction and conservation are co-constructed and co-produced by human
actions and non-human processes (Robbins, 2004; Forsyth, 2003). Nature is thus made, unmade, and remade and constantly materially
reconstituted.

Indigenous People and the Moraine

The archaeological record speaks primarily of the Indigenous peoples
who settled and inhabited the Moraine prior to the arrival of Europeans (Heidenreich and Burgar, 1999). They were hunters of large animals, seasonal hunters and gatherers of a more diverse flora and fauna,
and settled agriculturalists. For them the Moraine was likely not seen
in the stark and precise spatial terms outlined in the current debate; it
was rather seen as one integral part of a larger socioecological system.
It was a lived place, a livelihood space, and a spiritual realm that was
a constant in people's very existence. The Moraine both set constraints
and provided opportunities for human actions.

After the last glacial period, 10,000 years ago, the partially submerged
Moraine slowly emerged as the land rebounded from the pressure of
the ice sheets and the extensive glacial lakes shrank. The exposed lands
were gradually vegetated and forested, and inhabited by wildlife, and
Indigenous groups moved into the territory to take advantage of these
resources. Over time, Indigenous groups changed in numbers and in
their activities, as did the composition and type of species of flora and
fauna. During what Western archaeologists call the Palaeo, Archaic,
and Early and Middle Woodland periods (9000 BC to AD 800), Indi-
genes were nomadic, and their camps were set up locally for the hunting and gathering of specific flora and fauna, among them caribou and
spawning fish (Oak Ridges Moraine Technical Working Committee,
1994c; Heidenreich and Burgar, 1999).

During the Late Woodland Period (AD 800–1600), Indigenous groups
introduced maize and other cultigens and developed various forms of
agriculture. The population increased, and communities became permanent with specific-purpose seasonal camps. Two main groups, the
ancestors of the Huron to the north and the Iroquois to the south, are

likely to have inhabited the area surrounding the Oak Ridges Moraine, with the Moraine itself constituting a dividing line and a natural barrier between them. Some evidence suggests that certain Indigenous sites were strategically located on the Moraine to take advantage of the trade and movement across it (Oak Ridges Moraine Technical Working Committee, 1994c). Overall, the Moraine appears to have been continuously occupied by humans since the last glaciation.

At the time of European contact a tall prairie-and-oak savannah with mixed softwoods existed, the red oak being the species that gave the Moraine its name. The forest was part of the sustenance of the Indigenous communities. The bark of the white birch and the slippery elm was used to make canoes and teepees; sugar maple yielded syrup; and the bark of the white elm was used for utensils and rope. The roots of the white spruce were used to make rope for canoes and baskets (Puck's Farm, 2006). At the time of contact with Europeans in the sixteenth century, the fur trade complemented previous trade and subsistence activities of the Indigenous groups in the area. The Huron were able to take best advantage of the fur trade, given their strategic location by Lake Ontario. However, their previous skirmishes with the Iroquois intensified during the fur trade and the exploration activities of the Europeans. As a result of European diseases and the shifting of the fur trade to the west and north, the area was vacated. In time, the Huron and Iroquois were replaced by the Mississauga who moved into the area in the mid- to late-seventeenth century from their traditional hunting grounds in the Georgian Bay area and the southern edge of the Canadian Shield. The Mississauga were the last Indigenous peoples to occupy and use the area on their own terms and on an extensive scale, though their physical presence and use of the land have now been largely eliminated owing to European encroachment. During the winter the Mississauga roamed their hunting grounds from Lake Ontario to the watersheds on the Oak Ridges Moraine. In the early spring they collected maple sap to make maple sugar. During the summer they caught salmon at the river mouths, and in the late summer the Indian women harvested corn on the river flats. In the fall the small villages broke up into family hunting groups that returned by foot or by canoe to their inland ranges. The Mississauga between Toronto and the Trent River travelled to Rice Lake where they harvested the abundant crop of wild rice (Smith, 1991: 28).

Trails have continuously passed through the Moraine, perhaps the most famous one being the Carrying Place Trail, also a portage route, which crossed the Moraine to link the Humber and Holland rivers. But there are others. Between Woodbine Avenue and Kennedy Road in Whitchurch-Stouffville an old native trail connected the Holland River over the crest of the Moraine to the Little Rouge River. In Hamilton County in the east, several native trails climbed the Moraine from Lake Ontario to Rice Lake. The First Nations community on Georgina Island in Lake Simcoe maintained traplines on the Moraine into the 1930s that now form the Oak Ridges Moraine Trail (Oak Ridges Trail Guidebook, 2006). Written accounts typically suggest that there are only remnants of Indigenous settlements throughout the Moraine. These remnants are typically described as ancient and dead and are often re-enacted through displays and reconstructed Indian villages such as at Crawford Lake (figure 2.2). Indigenous oral accounts of the presence of First Nations on the Moraine may convey a different story (Johnson, in press).

There is only one formally recognized First Nation community that partially occupies the Oak Ridges Moraine, the Alderville First Nation Reserve. It is located at the southern end of Rice Lake in the eastern part of the Moraine. The (Mississauga) Anishinabeg of the Ojibwa Nation that occupies the reserve illustrate, from an Indigenous perspective, the arbitrariness of singling out the Moraine as a distinct and significant landscape feature. For the Ojibwa, the Alderville community constitutes the eastern edge of a larger cultural context that is now centred in the northeast around Lake Simcoe, Georgian Bay, Manitoulin Island, the northern shores of Lake Huron, and various parts of the central United States (Schmalz, 1991). In addition, the Anishinabeg were relocated to this site in the 1830s after their lands at the Bay of Quinte had become an area of settlement for United Empire Loyalists. At that time, under the pressure of the European invasion, the Anishinabeg adopted Christianity, primarily Methodism, and became subject to various other assimilationist policies. However, as the Anishinabeg themselves put it, "the Methodist experience amongst the Mississauga can best be described as a hybrid, or a mixed composition of traditional and western values and spiritual world view... For ensuing generations this resistance toward their complete assimilation existed and it has become the basis upon which the cultural survival of the people has been maintained" (Alderville First Nation, 2006).

Given the oral tradition of Indigenous communities, the tendency for the colonizers to write their history, and the apparent absence of First Nations communities on the Moraine, it is perhaps not surprising that written historical representations of their lands are sparse and selective.

Figure 2.2: A Huron-Iroquois village

Part of A PALISADED HURON-IROQUOIS VILLAGE

This is an illustration of a seventeenth-century Huron-Iroquois village that is frequently used as a possible representation of a First Nation's community on the Oak Ridges Moraine. Such Western-based representations and associated archaeologies of First Nations on the Moraine are more frequent than those representations that are based on First Nations peoples' own oral accounts and histories. Source: Jefferys, 1953

The consultants who explored the First Nations on the Moraine for the Oak Ridges Moraine Technical Working Committee in the mid-1990s wrote that this presence "held and may still hold significance on a spiritual or cultural level for the people who used the area" (Oak Ridges Moraine Technical Working Committee, 1994c: 10).

There may also be a basis for First Nations' claims to lands on the Moraine, given previous occupancy, though such claims have not been articulated formally so far. In 2006, for example, David Sanford, "an individual of First Nations heritage," claimed on account of several First Nations groups that in its exchange of the Seaton lands south of the Oak Ridges Moraine for developers' lands on the Moraine, the Province of Ontario failed to consult with First Nations groups that had an interest in the Seaton Lands. The evidence submitted by Sanford and various witnesses challenged the ownership of the Seaton lands, the different groups that retained an interest in them, and what one witness called the "archaeological doctrine" used by the government to justify its actions (Ontario Divisional Superior Court of Justice, 2006). For Sanford and the First Nations groups, the Seaton lands still constitute a "traditional territory" that is closely interconnected with their history, presence, and future. The recent protests in Caledonia, just west of the Moraine, illustrate one example of an Indigenous community asserting its claims to 20 hectares of land that were slated for residential development and may forebode similar events on the Moraine. In March 2006, members of the Six Nations people occupied the Haldimand Tract located at the entrance to Douglas Creek Estates, a 71-lot subdivision being constructed by Henco Industries Ltd. on Six Nations territory (as part of the 1784 Haldimand Deed) (DeVries, 2011). There has been an intensification of the assertion of First Nations' rights over lands and resources throughout Canada in the last three decades. Incidents over land claims in Oka, Adams Lake, Ipperwash, Burnt Church, and Caledonia are part of the First Nations' challenge to the assimilationist policies of the past, including residential schools, band councils, and reserve systems. In reaction, there are now initiatives to assert Indigenist systems of education and governance based on nationhood and self-governance.

In the built-over and European-settled central and western parts of the Moraine, where no reserves exist, the Indigenous presence and visions of the Moraine are less prominent. To Western-trained archaeologists and to the provincial state, these First Nations sites represent "prehistoric cultural heritage resources" that are subject to "assessment," "interpretation," and "archivization." Such inventories do not, however, always happen as historic settlements often represent obstacles, delays, and additional costs to development projects. Thus, many historical Indigenous settlement sites (including bones and artefacts) have been wiped out by bulldozers (Dewar, 1997). Other sites become the subject of hasty investigations by archaeological consultants who work for the developers of the sites. With lax regulations and decreasing funding for provincial archaeologists, artefacts are stored by private consultants and the government in inadequate facilities, consultants' reports are jealously guarded and not shared, and an informal market in artefacts is thriving (ibid.).

It is perhaps not surprising, therefore, that First Nations' elders frequently recommend that remains should stay where they are found

(Gabe, 2006). For them, the sites represent something sacred that deserves to be left alone. For the science of archaeology, by contrast, the historical site and artefacts represent a way to "learn" more about the past, though that learning often turns into an *ex situ* commodification of the past and its artefacts. On some occasions, Moraine residents and environmentalists, some say cynically, draw on archaeology as one strategy to challenge development projects and protect their lands on the Moraine.

The Alderville First Nation nestles on the shores of Rice Lake, and a substantial part of it rests on the Moraine. The history of the reserve resembles that of many other First Nations' communities: poverty, unemployment, and substance abuse. However, along with other efforts to advance its status, one of its most recent initiatives is focused on restoring the natural region of the area known as Rice Lake Plains, composed of tallgrass prairies and oak savannahs dominated by large black oak (*quercus velutina*), white oak (*quercus alba*), two-metre-high grasses, and a diverse range of wildflowers (Alderville Black Oak Savanna, 2006, 2009).

These restoration efforts are largely funded by external environmental organizations (figure 2.3). They are also marketed heavily to relatively affluent urban ecotourists. One experience of ecotourism is known as "Portage through the Past": "Spend two days exploring the aboriginal settlement and natural heritage of Rice Lake. Your journey begins at Victoria Inn, a charming century-old lakefront inn on beautiful Rice Lake – 90 minutes east of Toronto. Settlement history is brought to life on the shores of the rivers, lakes and canals of the Kawarthas with a living history experience on the banks of the Indian River or an evening listening to a shoreline reading about Catherine Parr Traill and her part in the settlement of the Kawarthas. Visit the sacred Indian burial grounds at Serpent Mounds Park or the nearby Canadian Canoe Museum" (Great Ontario Outdoor Adventure, 2006).

The Oak Ridges Moraine is here represented as a tourism commodity, a restored original landscape, complete with flora and fauna and Indigenous guides, which also provides all the modern conveniences for the colonial visitor. Some critics may suggest that this scenario obscures the possibility of the growth of a self-sustainable and locally focused development strategy. However, it may represent the First Nation's adoption of a new development strategy – biodiversity promotion and its use in ensuring cultural survival. The contemporary partners include Nature Conservancy of Canada, Environment Canada, and Ontario Nature (Alderville Black Oak Savanna, 2006, 2009). Regardless of which representation we favour, First Nations' visions of the Moraine

Figure 2.3: Alderville black oak savannah

A publication by the Alderville First Nation describes the black oak savannah and the tallgrass prairie on the Oak Ridges Moraine as the largest remnant of an endangered ecosystem found in central Ontario. Source: the authors, 2009

are clearly entangled in the interests of the dominant colonial society, this time in response to the aspirations of ecological restorationists and wealthy outsiders in search of a biologically diverse ecosystem and a culturally unique ecotourism experience.

The Moraine as a Re-settler Frontier

The first Europeans to arrive in North America are typically referred to as *pioneers*, *early settlers*, or *colonists*. These terms imply that they were the first to settle the land. This is, of course, not true. Indigenous peoples initially settled the Moraine and surrounding lands. Cole Harris (1997) has, in a different context, coined the term *re-settlers* for European settlers to acknowledge the original settlement of Indigenous groups in North America, their gradual displacement, and the resettlement of their lands by Europeans. The Moraine was thus resettled by loggers and farmers in the late eighteenth, the nineteenth, and the early twentieth century. They saw the land as a timber and agricultural frontier. The oak forest was both an asset and an obstacle to the re-settlers. On the one hand, re-settlers established hundreds of sawmills that crudely sawed and sold lumber locally and for export (figure 2.4). On the other hand, they also cleared the forest by other means to establish farming. In some areas of the Moraine, along the north and south slopes, where re-advances of the ice lobes deposited a thin layer of till material, the desired type of farming was and has remained relatively viable (Save the Oak Ridges Moraine [STORM] Coalition, 1997: 16). However, on large parts of the Moraine the predominant soils, sandy grey-brown luvisols, have developed on the glacial outwash. These soils are highly sensitive to erosion and degradation when cleared of forests and used for farming (Wood, 1991). The relatively poor agricultural soils of the Moraine, though, constituted only one factor in the failure of farms and in farm abandonment. At the time capitalist forces and bureaucratic decrees affected farmers beyond their control. Thus, the farming attempts of the poorest farmers largely failed, leading to soil erosion and farm abandonment (Watson, 1947). Wealthier farmers remained where suitable soils were present.

Farmers continue to exert influence on the local politics of the Oak Ridges Moraine. In the Town of Caledon, in the western part of the Moraine, for example, which is known as the green capital of Ontario, where environmental initiatives go beyond the requirements of the *Oak Ridges Moraine Conservation Plan* (Gilbert, Wekerle, and Sandberg, 2005), there are powerful farming interests that promote a more resource-extractive agenda. This point is illustrated in the Town's ambivalent and spotty support of a bylaw that is aimed at banning the use of pesticides for aesthetic purposes. Professional groups initiated this measure, while local farmers, well represented on the council, have opposed it and substantially watered down its effectiveness (Lee-Macaraig and Sandberg, 2007). It is also reflected in the continued accommodation of aggregate extraction on a large scale throughout the township. Many local farmers hold lands that contain aggregate resources (Chambers and Sandberg, 2007).

The Oak Ridges Moraine also emerged early as a source of aggregate material. Indeed, sand and gravel pits represented for many farmers

Figure 2.4: Tyrone Mills, 1846–

Saw and grist mills served the re-settler communities across the Oak Ridges Moraine. Tyrone Mills is still milling flour and sawing lumber. Source: the authors, 2011

what woodlots constituted for others – places to turn to from time to time to extract resources for cash to complement income on the farm or to seek capital for farm investment. Since the 1970s the ownership and operation of aggregate extraction have been concentrated in the hands of a few large operators – including transnational companies that operate on a huge scale – in specific areas of the Moraine. To aggregate operators and consumers, including the provincial government, which is a major buyer of aggregates, the Moraine constitutes an essential resource both for sand and gravel for building purposes in the Greater Toronto Area, and for the provincial economy as a whole. But there are also more recent "farming activities" that are welcomed with mixed feelings. Residents are strenuously opposing the proposed wind farms at Bethany, Manvers, Millbrook, and Pontypool. And at Oak Heights Winery local residents are protesting the loud bangs that are given off by propane-powered cannons to scare off the birds that are eating the ripening grapes. Although there are restrictions and regulations on the extent and nature of economic activities on the Moraine, the legislation also clearly acknowledges their existence along with some of their negative environmental, amenity, and social effects.

The Moraine as a Scientific Object

A moraine refers to an accumulation of boulders, stones, and other debris carried and deposited by a glacier. The term *moraine* derives from the French language, meaning "a mound of earth." The Oak Ridges Moraine is classified as an interlobate moraine, that is, a moraine formed by sand, gravel, and stone sediments that accumulated and were deposited in layers by the flows of meltwaters between two massive ice sheets. The Oak Ridges Moraine is now defined literally by a line drawn in sand that follows certain physical attributes. The 2002 *Oak Ridges Moraine Conservation Plan* that established the Moraine as an object of conservation states:

> The outer boundary of this Moraine area ... is based on a number of topographical, geomorphological and geological attributes, including the 245 metre (above sea level) contour along the southern boundary of the Moraine from the Town of Richmond Hill to the eastern boundary of the Municipality of Clarington. It has been more precisely defined in Ontario Regulation 01/02 by the Surveyor General employing a method of survey which uses UTM (Universal Transverse Mercator) coordinates. The Plan of the Boundary of the Oak Ridges Moraine Area provides the information for establishing the boundary on the ground by a Licensed Ontario Land Surveyor, under instructions for the Surveyor General for the Province of Ontario. (Ontario Ministry of Municipal Affairs and Housing, 2002a: 6)

These measures are highly technical and precise, yet arbitrary since the Oak Ridges Moraine continues as a physical and ecological unit beyond these specific physical geographic criteria. At the moment, however, the Moraine encompasses the Oak Ridges Aquifer Complex (Oak Ridges Moraine Research Group, 1995: 19–20). When people travel through the Moraine, it is impossible for them to know when they leave or enter unless there are signs that tell them. The present definition is simply the end point that has crystallized from the imprecise observations and research of geoscientists of different orientations over nearly two centuries.

Initially it was primarily its topography that invited scientific interest in the Moraine. In 1833, J.J. Bigsby provided the first identification of the Moraine as a "bold continuous line of heights running east and west ... breaking into confused ridges and hummocks (quoted in Duckworth, 1975: 9). In 1863, Sir William Edmond Logan (who had established the Geological Survey of Canada in 1842) identified an approximate full length of the Moraine, though he felt that a limit in the east was difficult to discern (ibid.). In 1913, F.B. Taylor conducted a more in-depth study of the western parts of the Moraine for the Bureau of Ontario Mines (ibid.). The next major study on the Moraine and other glacial landforms in Ontario was conducted by Chapman and Putnam (1951) and published in their seminal *Physiography of Southern Ontario*. Chapman and Putman used the contour line at the height of 274 metres (or 900 feet) above sea level to demarcate the boundaries of the Moraine. To them, this contour line was the most suitable since it "approximately defines the break in slope between the hilly surface of the moraine and the more gentle slopes to the north and south" (quoted in Duckworth, 1975: 3). The Moraine was thus defined by its visible morphology, that is, by the hummocky, ice-contact deposits that make up its central geographic core and separate it from the more gently undulating till and clay deposits on its flanks. As a consequence, Chapman and Putnam's Moraine was substantially smaller in extent than recent reincarnations that use the 245-metre contour line as a definitional criterion.

Science and scientists alone did not drive the identification of the Moraine; instead they were part of a nationalist quest to map minerals and soils for industrial inputs and agricultural outputs across Canada. As Suzanne Zeller (1987) has put it, Canada had to be invented, and the inventory science of geology was one key element in mapping and redefining landforms and in locating mineral resources to forge a transcontinental nation (see also Braun, 2002). The Oak Ridges Moraine was part of that invention and inventory project. And as part of such a larger project, the Moraine was but one of many glacial features identified. When viewing Chapman and Putnam's (1951) account of the hundreds of glacial features in southwestern Ontario, it is perhaps difficult now to fathom the reason for the Oak Ridges Moraine being singled out as special, because there are numerous moraines in southern Ontario (figure 2.5).

Figure 2.5: Moraines in southern Ontario

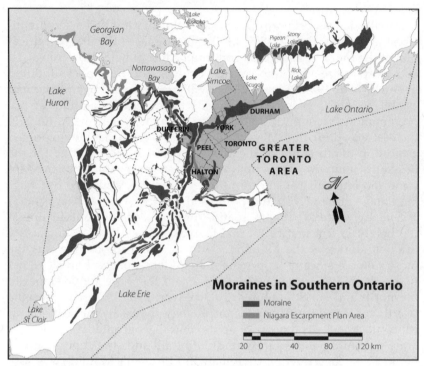

The map shows the numerous glacial formations in southern Ontario and calls into question the uniqueness of the Oak Ridges Moraine. Source: Rajiv Rawat and the authors, 2009

The scientific explorations of the Oak Ridges Moraine remained, until very recently, superficial and surficial, that is, focused on the surface. The bowels of the Moraine or its function as a retainer, filter, conduit, and expellant of water is the new research frontier for scientists. As late as 1975, Duckworth (1975: 3) noted that any precise estimates of sediment thickness (never mind the composition of those sediments) were difficult to make because very few boreholes had been drilled into the bedrock that forms the foundation of the Moraine. However, once again it was not only science that paved the initial path for the development of these insights. It was concern for the impact of development, through uncontrolled and unregulated urban sprawl, on water quality

and quantity that sparked the recent investigations. And, paradoxically, it was the scars of development – the aggregate pits and the road
cuts in the Moraine – that provided science with its first opportunity to
explore the inner composition of sediments and the hydrological flows
of water along the sediments inside the Moraine.

The most powerful impetus for natural science-based research on
the Moraine occurred in the spring of 1993. Led by the Geological Survey of Canada, a collaborative multi-agency, multidisciplinary project
was launched as "a response to the need for a better understanding
of the regional geology and groundwater resources in an area of intense urban growth" (Russell et al., 1996). The research was precipitated by the absence of data in light of the controversial Interim Waste
Authority's search for waste disposal or landfill sites in the Greater Toronto Area, and the quest of the Oak Ridges Moraine Technical Working Committee of the Ontario Ministry of Natural Resources to provide
some basic hydrogeological data on the Moraine.

Geoscientists have since become increasingly interested in the origin, retention, destination, quality, and quantity of the water that flows
through the Moraine. Their objective is to understand and document the
"seismic facies and regional architecture of the Moraine area" (Pugin,
Pullan, and Sharpe, 1999). The one-dimensional common map and the
sometimes two-dimensional relief map have given way to three-dimensional depictions showing the sediments and bedrock of the Moraine
and the water that is cycling through it.

Geoscience and geoscientists represent the Moraine in different ways.
Their pictures depend not only on the state of knowledge at any given
time but also on the scale, context, and personal predilections and judg-
ments of the scientists involved. Geoscientists, as other scientists, tell
stories that are open to the same kind of scrutiny as is any other type of
facts or information. However, the Moraine itself is also an actor. It has
proven difficult to map comprehensively and definitively, especially
since the continuing building and development likely change the hydrological flows as quickly as they are mapped. The perpetual change
then calls for perpetual study. We shall have occasion to explore the co-
production of hydrogeological truths and consequences by human and
non-human agents in more detail in later chapters.

The Moraine as a Landscape of Restoration

While the soils of the Moraine were judged to have "failed" farmers
in the late nineteenth century into the 1930s, the Moraine was remade

Figure 2.6: Reforestation on the Oak Ridges Moraine

Extensive areas of the Moraine were reforested in the 1920s, 1930s, and 1940s with coniferous pine plantations in anticipation of harvesting for sawlogs. These forests have since been transformed into primarily recreational forests. The planted forest now constitutes the major portion of the natural core areas of the Moraine. Extensive areas of York Regional Forest are shown in the above aerial photo, which was taken from the north looking south. Highway 48 traverses the view and intersects with Cherry Street in the lower half of the photo. To the left of Highway 48 is the Hollidge Tract, with the York Region Forest headquarters visible in the clearing in the middle of the forest. To the right of Highway 48 are the Eldred King Hall and Patterson Forest tracts. The thin winding clearing through the latter tracts was formerly part of a railway line that extended to Jackson's Point on Lake Simcoe. Source: Ministry of Natural Resources, undated; kindly supplied by Leonard Munt, 2012

and constructed differently. In many places, but at different times, the Moraine was reconstructed as a barren inhospitable land and deemed an object of restoration. It became the focus of major reforestation measures in the 1920s and 1930s, when extensive pine plantations were established with the anticipation of supplying wood to the sawmilling industry (figure 2.6). The Moraine, stripped of trees only a century before, was to be resettled by trees again. Durham Regional Forest, a publicly owned and managed forest of 4,000 hectares, was assembled from abandoned farmlands in the 1920s and 1930s. It was then planted with white pine, Ontario's provincial tree, and black spruce to restabilize soils and restore abandoned and degraded blow-sand areas (McPherson and Timmer, 2002). Other areas of the forest were left to regenerate naturally to a mixed deciduous composition.

In the Regional Municipality of York, York Regional Forest was established in 1924. At the time, much of its maple and pine forests had been cut down, and the soil extensively ploughed for farming. The forest was managed by the Department of Lands and Forests (renamed the Ministry of Natural Resources in 1972) from 1924 to 1998, a function that was taken over by York Region in 1998. The forest is officially described as one of the most successful restorations of a degraded landscape in North America (York Region, 2006a).

Subsequent to the 1920s, reforestation efforts occurred on a more formal basis in the 1940s and beyond. In 1941 six organizations formed the Guelph Conference on the Conservation of the Natural Resources in Ontario. A 1944 report recommended an integrated resource management planning study of one watershed in Ontario, the Ganaraska watershed, which covers large areas of the eastern parts of the Moraine. Written by A.H. Richardson (1944: vi), the report labelled the Oak Ridges Moraine headwaters of the Ganaraska River as a "barren waste." The farmers were studied and classified into wealthier and poorer groups, with predictable recommendations on who should stay and who should leave their lands. The report recommended reforestation of 8,000 hectares in the northern section of the watershed and agreed to buy, reforest, and manage degraded lands in the watershed. It also recommended the formation of so-called conservation authorities across Ontario (ibid.). The Ganaraska Region Conservation Authority was formed in 1946 (ibid.). These conservation authorities were seen as state agents that would proactively manage natural resources and create work for returning veterans. The vision of a future Ganaraska watershed was seen to contain a carefully maintained landscape where forest plantations, reforestation efforts, erosion dams, agricultural activities, camping, hunting, and fishing were nestled together in close and supportive harmony (figure 2.7).

In 1947 the first trees were planted on 640 hectares of the future Ganaraska forest. By 1991 the total amount of land acquired was 4,200 hectares. Reforestation was considered to be necessary on 50 per cent of this

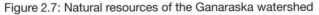
Figure 2.7: Natural resources of the Ganaraska watershed

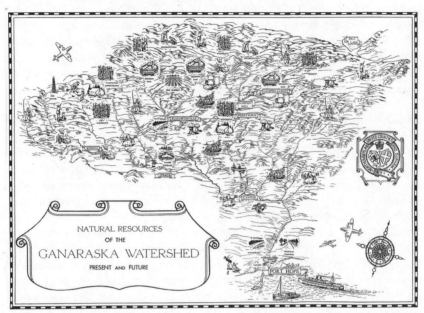

In 1944 the federal government published an in-depth study of the Ganaraska watershed with the aim of managing the watershed efficiently for human use. The map represents a vision of rational resource management of multiple use that includes woodlots (lumber and maple syrup), recreational activities (hunting, fishing, and skiing), flood control, and agriculture (dairy, tobacco, and field and truck crops). There is no mention of the current emphasis on protecting ecosystems and natural heritage sites. The current southern boundary of the Moraine runs in an east-west line through Campbellcroft on the map. Source: Richardson, 1944

land and took the form predominantly of red pine (*pinus resinosa*) plantations to provide sawlogs for the future. In 1997 the Ganaraska Region Conservation Authority became solely responsible for the management of the Ganaraska forest (Ganaraska Regional Conservation Authority, 2012).

The Ganaraska Region Conservation Authority was but one conservation authority established in Ontario in the 1940s. Others were developed throughout the province to not only reforest the land but also

manage the whole watershed for other purposes, including prevention of the flooding that is inherent on natural flood plains and exac-
erbated in watersheds where the forest has been cut extensively. A.H.
Richardson (1944) carefully documented the floods emanating from the
Ganaraska River watershed that caused severe damage in Port Hope.
Hurricane Hazel, which hit the Toronto area in 1954 and caused extensive flooding, killing 81 people and leaving 4,000 homeless, later reinforced the urgency of protecting forests on the headwaters of the rivers
that flowed from the Moraine and preventing settlements on their natural flood plains.

There is some farming that also fit into the restorative theme. Organic
farms, based on animal products, vegetables, fruits, and grains do exist,
some catering to local niche markets. The Friends of the Greenbelt
Foundation (2006) provide grants for farmers to support and improve
environmental practices on their land. The grant money is particularly
directed to protecting soil and water resources, as well as wildlife, and
to reducing the use of pesticides.

There is a long tradition of envisioning the Moraine as a restoration
area, efforts that first stemmed from the colonizers' failure to commer-
cially and profitably employ modern farm methods in its poor and
flighty soils. Only a century after the area had first been resettled, it
was re-envisioned as a desolate and infertile land and therefore subject
to massive reforestation efforts. Decades later, natural scientists have
explored the positive effects (Hill, 1976; Buttle, 1995; McPherson and
Timmer, 2002). This concept of restoration has since been a prominent
part of a conservation agenda and is acknowledged and supported in
the *Oak Ridges Moraine Conservation Plan* and *Act*.

The Moraine as a Recreational Landscape

In the post-war boom of industrial development, road building, and
automobile manufacture and travel the Oak Ridges Moraine first
emerged as a recreational landscape, along with its role as a working
landscape. Its forest plantations, intended to supply sawmills, were
reconceptualized and transformed into recreational forests for hiking,
birding, cross-country skiing, and snowshoeing, among many other
activities. Rural places previously based on sawmilling, like Musselman's Lake, established a big dance hall in 1929 where locals and city
dwellers gathered on the weekends and during summer vacations for
mutual enjoyment and summer activities. In other places, children's

and church camps sprang up to accommodate the need for recreation in the increasingly congested and polluted city. The railways provided the initial means of transportation to these venues, transferring thousands of weekend recreationalists for daily outings on the Moraine. Buses and cars followed in their wake. Conservation authorities have similarly taken on a greater role as providers of recreational services, even to the extent of compromising their initial focus on watershed management (Cardwell, 1996). The focus on recreation on the Moraine in the post-war period has thus transformed the ways in which all interests present their visions of its use.

Within the last 20 years, however, the recreational and other activities on the Oak Ridges Moraine have taken another direction, namely, an ecological turn. All actors now portray themselves as environmentalists and conservationists who appreciate and respect nature's way and ecology's processes. Yet, as we shall see in subsequent chapters, major battles have characterized and continue to shape this interaction.

Conservation authorities, regional forests, and various levels of government jurisdictions all use the language of ecology to represent their activities. In York Regional Forest, efforts are now made to operate forest operations on a sustainable basis that takes into account both ecological and social concerns. These efforts include the establishment of a twenty-year management plan, the formation of a Regional Forest Advisory Team, and the adoption of a forest certification scheme developed by the Forest Stewardship Council. So-called natural heritage features and values are acknowledged through an ecosystem-based approach in which environmental values are prioritized: "Forest users must keep in mind that the health and integrity of the Regional Forest will override all other concerns, whether recreational, aesthetic, social or economic" (York Region, 1998: 7). The Ganaraska Region Conservation Authority (2012) describes its forest as "a living example of how the principles of integrated resource management can be used to balance many different uses of forested lands on a sustainable and ecologically sound basis."

Golf courses on the Moraine similarly advertise themselves as operating in an environmentally friendly and unique natural context (Webb, 2002). In the promotional literature of one golf course, the Heather Green in Durham County, the potential visitor is told that "the environmentally-concerned will appreciate how the 76 acre [30 hectare] course is woven through [a] breathtaking natural setting of mixed forest fringes [and] pristine undulating meadows" (Heather Green Golf Course, 2006). In 2000 several "cash-strapped" conservation authorities were targeted by a company called EnviroGolf to establish ecologically sensitive golf courses on the Moraine (Paul, 2000).

The building of a linear hiking trail, the Oak Ridges Moraine Trail, is a central feature of the recreational agenda (Cowles, 1995; Jacob, 2003). Run by the Oak Ridges Trail Association, which is managed by volunteers but sponsored by a variety of organizations, the trail now extends for 250 kilometres along the Moraine (Oak Ridges Trail Association, 2006). Its precedent goes back to 1973, when the Ontario Trail Riders' Association established the Equestrian Great Pine Ridge Trail for horseback riders, which was primarily located along existing roads. In 1991 the current emphasis on hiking along a system of public recreational trails was identified by a group of volunteers who worked in cooperation with Save the Oak Ridges Moraine Coalition, the then Metro Toronto and Region Conservation Authority, and Hike Ontario. The following year the Oak Ridges Trail Association was formed (ibid.)

The recreational representations and functions of the Moraine are clearly varied. This is especially evidenced by a tension in recreational activities between the use of mechanical devices, such as snowmobiles, dirt bikes, and all-terrain vehicles – often associated with a rural population involved in productive activities, such as farming, forestry, and aggregate extraction – and more nature-oriented forms of recreation, such as hiking, bird-watching, bicycling, and nature appreciation, which are associated with a professional class of commuters, retirees, and second-home residents.

This tension between motorized and non-motorized forms of recreation is apparent across the Moraine. One area of the eastern part of the Oak Ridges Moraine known as Test Hill or East Cross Forest in the Township of Scugog, for example, was until recently a privately owned, unsupervised, and abandoned sandpit that was used intensively by recreational drivers of off-road motor vehicles. In 2002, however, a task force was established in the township to provide "solutions" to "problems" plaguing the area. The problems were listed as trespassing (particularly by motorized vehicles), environmental degradation, and waste dumping (Kawartha Regional Conservation Authority, 2006). Vilifying these activities, the task force also referred to the dangers of off-road vehicle traffic. The accident statistics supported such assertions. According to the Provincial Health Planning Database, the rate of off-road motor vehicle injuries in Durham Region is far higher than the provincial average (Durham Regional Police, 2012). The explicit task was to remake the area into an ecological preserve for passive recreation. By 2005 the East Cross Forest had become part of Kawartha Conservation, a cross-jurisdictional, semi-public conservation group promoting watershed management in the surrounding area. Kawartha Conservation had at this point assigned not only a new name but a new descriptor to the area, featuring its connection to the Oak Ridges Moraine as central (Kawartha Regional Conservation Authority, 2006).

The East Cross Forest illustrates the tension between motorized and non-motorized forms of recreational activities. The latter recreationalists prescribe environmental and aesthetic values associated with a biodiverse flora and fauna. However, these values do not necessarily correspond with the nature and recreational aspirations of the segment of the population that supports and derives its livelihood from production activities and that cherishes motorized forms of recreation (Foster and Sandberg, 2004).

The exurban shadow has an effect on the level of tolerance of off-road vehicles in local areas across the Moraine. Opposition is less intense the further one travels from the city of Toronto. In the nearby Durham Forest off-road vehicles are prohibited, in the more distant Ganaraska Forest they are accommodated in special zones, but in the remote Northumberland Forest they are left more or less free to reign (though there is mounting opposition). There may also be a stronger tradition of a romance with the combustion engine in the eastern parts of the Moraine, perhaps fuelled by the history of the automobile-manufacturing industry in places like Oshawa and by international car racing at Mosport, a race track on the Moraine that was opened in 1959.

The Moraine as an Ecological Landscape

The ecological turn in the planning of the Oak Ridges Moraine has a history. However, the interest in the early years was not in the Moraine as a coherent landscape. Interest focused on its disparate parts – flora, fauna, kettle lakes, and surface geology in specific geographical areas. The first historical explorations of the Moraine's ecology came from the same inventory sciences that plotted its geoscientific origins. Scholars and students at the University of Toronto, for example, made regular research trips to the Moraine to explore its unique biology and ecology. Toronto field naturalists have similarly made treks to the Moraine. On the Moraine itself the Federation of Ontario Naturalists, now Ontario

Nature, established a branch in Richmond Hill in the mid-1950s. However, well into the 1990s, its members were primarily concerned with birding, parks, and beautification initiatives within the town.

This approach has changed. While its surroundings have been urbanized, the Moraine as a coherent and cohesive unit, or as a landform and an ecosystem, has emerged, resulting in a vision of an uninterrupted bioregion and a continuous landscape feature that is seen as accommodating the movement of flora and fauna along an east-west axis. The field of landscape ecology is central to a study of ecological connectedness across space. The Moraine is here presented not only in isolation but as one ingredient in a larger, imagined, ecological network. This representation is now a common position held in the popular debate, as well as among civil servants, planners, scientists, environmentalists, residents, and even industry representatives. The concept of the Moraine as an integrated and continuous landscape was first given coinage officially in the late 1980s under a Liberal government, was shelved by the Progressive Conservatives of Premier Mike Harris that gained power in June 1995, and then was revitalized by the same government under pressure from environmentalists and residents. The *Oak Ridges Moraine Conservation Act* and *Plan* were consequently developed and passed in 2001 and 2002.

Environmentalists and resident activists make considerable use of the ecological sciences to promote the conservation of the Moraine. As we shall see later, scientists in the environmentalist community or scientists solicited by the environmentalists have positioned the Moraine in an ecological network called "the Niagara Escarpment to Oak Ridges Moraine to the Algonquin Park/Adirondack Park Axis Heritage System," known under the acronym of NOAH. This concept, expressed by local environmentalists, fits in with the previously developed "Algonquin Provincial Park to Adirondack Park (A2A)" scheme, which links the United States and the much grander Wildlands Project in an imagined ecological network that covers the whole North American continent (Noss, 1992).

Ecology is also a notion embraced by the infrastructure and extraction industries, industries that are highly active in operating the highways, sewers, and aggregate pits that traverse and disturb the surface of the Moraine. The Ontario Ministry of Transportation, which is responsible for provincial highway building and maintenance, for example, claims to be in the process of improving the way it "assesses environmental risk and controls the environmental impacts resulting from its activities by developing a consistent, systematic approach to environmental management" (Ontario Ministry of Transportation, 2006). The Ontario Stone, Sand and Gravel Association (2012a), the major lobby and interest group of Ontario aggregate producers, similarly embraces a conservationist and ecological mantra, arguing that its activities are compatible with and may in fact improve on natural and ecological processes.

In spite of such large-scale ecological conceptions of the Moraine, the contestations over and celebrations of its ecological values still occur largely on a site-by-site basis. There are struggles over the ecological impact of landfills, subdivision developments, and highway and sewer extensions at specific sites, sometimes referred to as hot spots. Similarly, the Moraine is celebrated at often discrete and bounded places, many of them donated by wealthy individuals. The book honouring the Oak Ridges Moraine that is published by the Save the Oak Ridges Moraine Coalition (1997), for example, contains mostly chapters on distinct forests, trails, and conservation and wildlife areas.

The Oak Ridges Moraine, then, is represented on different ecological scales that can contain potential tensions. On the one hand, the Moraine is scaled as a bioregion that fits into a larger continental natural framework. On the other hand, the struggles over, and the celebration of, its ecological uniqueness are often focused on particular sites. In later chapters we will more fully explore the implications of these conceptions for the Moraine's internal ecological integrity as well as for the broader ecological network of which it is a part.

Conclusion

All landscapes or landforms, including the exurban landscape on the Oak Ridges Moraine, are material and cultural enactments that are naturally and socially constructed, produced, recognized, and maintained. People define, demarcate, and give specific names to landscapes that change over time. The Moraine is something that is in constant flux not only physically but socially. Thirty years ago, for example, the Oak Ridges Moraine was not a recognized landscape feature in the local and popular debate. The media mentioned the Moraine infrequently, and most local residents did not know or care that they lived on it.

The Moraine has only relatively recently been categorized as an ecologically significant landform that is deemed worthy of environmental conservation. Provincially and locally, it is held up more or less as a success story that has inspired even wider conservation legislation in the shape of the *Greenbelt Act* and *Plan* of 2005 (Wekerle et al., 2007). Sometimes places beyond the Moraine's current official boundaries are made part of it, such as the town of Walkerton in the north and the ravines of the city of Toronto to the south (Schuurman, 2004; Young and Keil, 2005). In other cases the Moraine is imagined as the potential centre of the Greater Toronto Area, for example when Young and Keil (2005) use the epithet "Morainetown" to describe one option for the region's management of water resources.

There is diversity across the Moraine that is shaped by its history. Representations of the Moraine differ in time and among groups and individuals. The Moraine also means different things in different regions across the Moraine. We thus caution against seeing the Moraine as a homogeneous phenomenon. It is as fractured and diverse socially, politically, and perceptually as it is geologically and ecologically.

Chapter Three

Nature Conservation Planning in South-Central Ontario: A Flashpoint

In 2000 a petition recommending a moratorium on development on "the ridge north of Toronto known as the Oak Ridges Moraine" was presented to Ontario's premier, Mike Harris. Signed by 465 science luminaries, including David Suzuki and Pollution Probe's founder, David Chant, the petition argued that the Moraine, though still reasonably intact, was at serious risk of quick decline without a plan to prevent the development that would destroy water quality and wildlife habitat (Immen, 2000a). The signing of the petition was organized by the Federation of Ontario Naturalists, whose representative declared it to be a milestone in the efforts to conserve the Moraine. In the past, the representative suggested, mere environmentalists had spoken up for its protection, but now scientists added their voice of attachment and belonging to the Moraine: "It's easy for politicians to say, 'Oh yeah, it's just a bunch of environmentalists,' but now to get scientific specialists on board carries a lot of more weight" (ibid.: A17). Silenced scientists were also prominent at an OMB hearing in 2003 (figure 3.1). Five years later, at the conclusion of the Monitoring the Moraine conference in Richmond Hill, the organizers praised the Oak Ridges Moraine legislation and the plan as natural science based, naming it "an unprecedented conservation success, marking one of the first pieces of land use legislation in North America to embed conservation biology and landscape ecology principles" (Oak Ridges Moraine Foundation, 2007: 3). The prominent position of natural scientists and natural science in these instances gives the impression that the natural sciences entered the debate late and only at the urgings of local residents and environmentalists. However, the natural sciences, such as ecology, biology, and hydrogeology, were part of a long-term

Figure 3.1: Silenced scientists

As activists in support of the Oak Ridges Moraine, natural scientists appeared late in the media, though they did provide a well-established nature conservation architecture for the Moraine legislation. Source: *Toronto Star*, 17 November 2003: A21; Rick Eglinton, GetStock.com

planning process dating back to the 1970s. The Oak Ridges Moraine conservation legislation rested on a long tradition of building on the information provided by the natural sciences.

Complementing the mobilization and pressure of residents and environmentalists, the subtle information and seemingly apolitical findings supplied by the natural sciences were embraced by provincial environmental planners in order to identify the Oak Ridges Moraine as a conservation object to be governed under a specific conservation policy, the *Oak Ridges Moraine Conservation Act* and *Plan*. In the process, planners, policymakers, and natural scientists favoured certain concepts and terms over others, with significant consequences for both people and the physical landscape. Resident suburbanites, exurbanites, and environmentalists as citizen scientists (which we shall see in subsequent chapters) then drew on the natural sciences to make their claims legitimate and count in the policy debate.

In this chapter we trace the emergence of a nature conservation planning policy in Ontario by using a historical approach to explore not only what is included but also what is excluded or lost in such a policy. The development and conservation of the Oak Ridges Moraine did not reach full convergence until the passing of the *Oak Ridges Moraine Conservation Act* and *Plan* in 2001 and 2002. We use the metaphor of a flashpoint to describe the convergence. A flashpoint is the point at which a vaporizing liquid ignites; it is preceded by a necessary build-up in temperature to make the ignition possible. In a similar way, we argue that there was a steady build-up of nature conservation planning concepts, beginning in the 1960s, before these were embraced fully by the *Oak Ridges Moraine Conservation Plan*. The actors who sparked the passing of the Plan were the residents and environmentalists who rose in protest at the time. The environmentalists also prompted scientists to take on the role of activists and pose in media stunts to communicate their message more effectively. We focus on the precedents and unique characteristics of nature conservation planning in the *Oak Ridges Moraine Conservation Plan* and their inclusions, exclusions, and implications for both people and the physical environment.

Writing in 1981, environmental planner Paul Eagles suggested that most policies involved with nature protection in Ontario had revolved around park designations, the application of fish and game laws, point-source pollution programs, and endangered species legislation. Eagles (1981: 313) identified, by contrast, the presence of a new set of public policies and programs based on science and "upon a broad systems approach involving an increasingly sophisticated ecological understanding of landscape productivity, processes and dynamics." This ecological approach, Eagles averred, had "a better appreciation of the importance of 'scale,' i.e., the hierarchical relationship of environmental issues from continental to local significance in size and importance" (ibid.). Eagles pinpointed the kernels of the wider adoption of a multitude of ideas and concepts, such as sensitive areas planning, ecosystem management, biological conservation, and landscape ecology (Soule and Wilcox, 1980; Noss and Cooperrider, 1994; Norton, 2003). One common feature of all these concepts was the notion of a spatial strategy to nature conservation, that is, the identification of specific nature reserves or natural areas and the creation of so-called natural cores and corridors designating viable ecosystems and their interconnections and interdependencies at the wider provincial, national, and continental landscape level. Many conservation biologists now argue that conservation management should not be confined to reserves but take account of places beyond the patches; however, the reserve system is still very much in place in everyday practice (Robin, 2009).

There are multiple ways to practise and think about planning for nature and nature conservation and about the science and scientific concepts that inform conservation practices. Michel Foucault's notion of an episteme provides a useful framework. Foucault (1980: 197) defines an episteme as "the strategic apparatus which permits of separating out from among all the statements which are possible those that will be acceptable within ... a field of scientificity, and which it is possible to say are true or false. The episteme is the 'apparatus' which makes possible the separation, not of the true from the false, but of what may be from what may not be characterised as scientific." Drawing on Foucault, only specific select statements of nature conservation planning may be acceptable within the professional community. The concept of episteme prompts us to ask numerous questions related to conservation. What are the precedents for ecological conservation thinking in Ontario? What are the dominant elements of conservation policy in the province? How have they evolved over time? How are they expressed today? How has the Oak Ridges Moraine been invoked as a conservation object? How has the Moraine been constructed over time in reports and legislation? What are some of the salient features of conservation in the *Oak Ridges Moraine Conservation Act* and *Plan*?

Haas's (1992: 3) definition of an epistemic community is also useful in thinking about the human actors who have promoted, have come to accept, and now conduct their debates within the conceptual frames of ecosystems planning. According to Haas, an epistemic community is "a network of knowledge-based experts or groups with an authoritative claim to policy-relevant knowledge within the domain of their expertise. Members hold a common set of causal beliefs and share notions of validity based on internally defined criteria for evaluation, common policy projects, and shared normative commitments" (ibid.). Haas's concept suggests that a group of ecological planners has played a prominent role in shaping the type of nature conservation that prevails in the *Oak Ridges Moraine Conservation Plan*. This group has promoted ecosystem management thinking as well as the creation of the policy and the legal conservation framework for the Moraine. This epistemic community promoting nature conservation is not, however, limited to individuals of the provincial bureaucracy; it includes specialists from the academic and private spheres, as well as a broader community of international actors and peers who communicate similar world views. Indeed, environmentalists and residents typically also aspire to be part of this community because such participation legitimizes their claims. The epistemic community concept provides a way of thinking about a group of experts in the lead of formulating and pushing for a nature conservation policy in the province. It also offers a means to question experts, laying bare the assumptions, and the concepts and metaphors that are taken for granted, which guide their understanding of conservation and the alternatives that they have marginalized or rejected in the process (Bocking 1997, 2004).

In this chapter we explore the acceptance of a spatial way of thinking about ecology, a practice that eventually resulted in the identification of the Oak Ridges Moraine as a distinct and identifiable space bound up and submerged in a specific set of spatial arrangements and attachments. This spatial perspective contrasts with a conservation policy that would touch all spaces and places equally, a conservation policy that makes no distinction between development and conservation. In making our case, we rely primarily on key policy documents and the ideas they contain, as well as some of the secondary literature on environmental and nature conservation. These policy documents and ideas not only serve to identify the episteme directly but also serve as proxies for an epistemic community. We point to the emergence of environmental planning perspectives as a key precedent shaping actor or agent in the identification and maintenance of the Oak Ridges Moraine as a conservation object.

The Emergence of a Nature Conservation Episteme in South-Central Ontario

The Oak Ridges Moraine as we know it today is part of what Sarah Whatmore (1999) has called a "relational achievement," that is, a landform co-produced by biophysical processes and human actors. The Moraine was seen as marginal land during the latter part of the nineteenth century and the earlier part of the twentieth century owing to its unsuitability for agriculture. Paradoxically, the agricultural marginality created by sandy soils and stark topography was what later made the Oak Ridges Moraine attractive to suburban and exurban migrants looking for a rural retreat in the countryside that was close to the city of Toronto.

The emergence of a nature conservation episteme in the Greater Toronto Area was closely connected to the multitude of ravines containing streams and rivers that originate on the Oak Ridges Moraine and end up in Lake Ontario (Richardson, 1974). These ravines are both relational failures and achievements in the history of the Greater Toronto Area. Initially, they were considered hazard lands because they were prone to flooding and erosion that periodically caused damage to human activities and settlements. It was only much later that they emerged as landforms appreciated by recreation seekers and nature lovers. An epistemic community of planning experts with knowledge of flood management emerged to regulate the ravines and their watersheds as distinct and bounded conservation lands. The ravine lands were thus conceived of as linear systems, which aimed to accommodate and control the movement of water and prevent flooding. Such developments both emulated and reinforced a pattern for the subsequent planning of roads, sewers, recreation, and wildlife control. Following a pattern identified by Evans (2007: 138–9), the wildlife corridors that were deemed necessary in Ontario required no fundamentally new approach to planning because linear features, such as roads, railways, and trails, formed the basis for plan making and had a long history in urban planning. The management of conservation lands or wildlife corridors very much resembled the linearity involved in the planning of road and sewerage networks.

Early Origins of Nature Conservation, 1940s to 1972

Stephen Bocking (2006) has written on the construction of an epistemic community of urban expertise in Toronto's professional and political authority spheres from 1940 to 1970. He refers in particular to the similarities among three forms of expertise: the engineering of urban services (for example, water supply, sewers, and highways), the planning of new communities, and the conserving of watersheds. It is particularly out of the last area, watershed conservation, that ecosystem management emerged as a key subject of conservation in subsequent years. Watershed protection arose in the 1940s as a central area of concern for the whole province, as well as the Greater Toronto Area. The cutting of vast tracts of forest on the Oak Ridges Moraine, for example, resulted in the erosion and flooding that threatened to affect Toronto's built-up areas to the south. In response, the Province created the so-called conservation authorities in 1946, whose mandate is to control flooding through reforestation and the building of retention dams and channels for streams and rivers. The approach was fundamentally technocratic, using expertise and technology to wrestle the natural environment into engineered submission.

The role of the conservation authorities was reinforced in 1954 when Hurricane Hazel, the most famous hurricane in Canadian history, struck southern Ontario. Category four in magnitude, it pounded the Toronto region with winds that reached 110 kilometres per hour and left a record 285 millimetres of rain in forty-eight hours, causing major flooding. Bridges spanning the Humber River were washed out, and a whole subdivision (thirty-two houses) on Toronto's Raymore Street on the banks of the river was washed into Lake Ontario. Thousands were left homeless, and eighty-one people died in the floods. The total material destruction was estimated at $100 million. The control measures of the conservation authorities up to that point proved deficient, and additional but insufficient efforts were made to rectify the situation in subsequent years. Hurricane Hazel mobilized the need for managing watersheds on a regional basis (Toronto and Region Conservation Authority, 2004a).

The development of a sewerage infrastructure and road networks closely followed the storm-water management pattern. Sewer systems were at first local, reliant on small sewage treatment plants and local water bodies. Local systems were then consolidated into centralized systems, one of which reached the Oak Ridges Moraine, the extensive York Durham Sewage System; it had a central sewage treatment plant in the town of Pickering (White, 2003). The road network similarly grew from a grid system of smaller roads to the development of larger arterial routes that cut across the grid to move traffic efficiently across the landscape. Following the tradition of parkways developed in the United States during the New Deal era, green areas were sometimes established along the highways to accommodate the increasingly automobile-dependent society after the Second World War. Many of these green areas were, in fact, created and maintained by the Department of Highways. In all these instances, as Bocking (2006) has shown, technocrats worked to move storm water, sewage, or traffic efficiently across space through different forms of corridors, be they pipes or highways, in order to accommodate a growing metropolis.

The concept of providing for nature, ecology, and biodiversity has also been met by the establishment of linear greenways to accommodate nature and natural processes (Fischer et al., 1991; Howard, 1991; Reid, 1991). One key precedent for the designation of the Oak Ridges Moraine was the establishment of the Niagara Escarpment as a green corridor in the late 1950s and 1960s. It started with efforts by the Bruce

Trail Committee to create a 780 kilometre hiking path across the spine of the escarpment from Queenston in the south (near Niagara Falls) to Tobermory in the north (the tip of the Bruce Peninsula). The initiative was spearheaded by recreational hikers in the southern parts of the Niagara Escarpment who embarked on negotiations with property owners along the escarpment to gain access for the trail. The Bruce Trail, completed in 1967, is now Canada's oldest and longest trail and provides the only public access to the Niagara Escarpment. Today it is administered by the Bruce Trail Conservancy, a charitable organization committed to establishing a conservation corridor along the Niagara Escarpment "in order to protect its natural ecosystems and to promote environmentally responsible public access to this UNESCO World Biosphere Reserve" (Bruce Trail Conservancy, 2008).

Members of the public were also concerned about the destructive activities of aggregate firms on the escarpment in the 1960s. At the time, the aggregate-extraction scars that could be seen from the major Highway 401 were particularly identified as a call for action. The Dufferin Gap, a breach in the escarpment created by Dufferin Aggregates to gain access to its quarry operations, provided the impetus for protests over aggregate operations on the escarpment, and the common conception that such operations posed a threat to the escarpment as a continuous landform (figure 3.2).

In 1966, the *Toronto Star* reported that "the evidence of man-made destruction is already quite noticeable. Quarry operators in the Milton area were leaving raw and unsightly gashes in the side of the towering cliffs" (*Toronto Star*, 1966: 6). The newspaper thus called for a greenbelt in southern Ontario, and the Hamilton and Halton Region Conservation Authorities urged the government to buy land along the Niagara Escarpment.

Members of an embryonic epistemic community of conservation professionals soon joined the chorus of protesters. In 1966, Norman Pearson at the University of Western Ontario estimated that an additional 70,000 hectares of parkland would be needed to meet the recreational needs of southern Ontarians over the next ten years (ibid.). Pearson, a founding member of the Bruce Trail Committee, thus called for the government to buy land for conservation purposes. This is a significant point because Pearson identified the role of the government as a central interventionist agent in the land market to promote nature conservation.

The provincial government began to take an interest in the Niagara Escarpment in the 1960s. On 11 March 1967, Ontario premier John

Figure 3.2: The Dufferin Gap

The Dufferin Gap in the Niagara Escarpment, visible from Highway 401, first called attention to the importance of maintaining the continuity of natural landforms. A footbridge that is part of the Bruce Trail provides a way for hikers to navigate the gap. Source: the authors, 2004

Robarts reported that the escarpment would be saved for recreation, especially its "scenic potential" (*Toronto Star*, 1967: 13). The premier then appointed Leonard Gertler of the University of Waterloo to chair a wide-ranging study of the Niagara Escarpment with a view to protecting it as a "continuous landform," a concept that was central in the *Niagara Escarpment Conservation and Recreation Report* released by Gertler in the summer of 1967 (Whitelaw, 2005: 76).

In 1973 the Province passed the *Niagara Escarpment Planning and Development Act*, which was aimed at maintaining the escarpment as a continuous landform, and appointed the Niagara Escarpment Commission, a seventeen-member body representing the public at large and upper-tier municipalities associated with the escarpment. Backing these commissioners was a group of full-time policy analysts and natural scientists who occupied permanent offices in two communities along the escarpment. Their role was to develop a large-scale environmental land use plan for the escarpment and to provide the scientific foundations on which the commissioners could take their decisions on development proposals. The Niagara Escarpment Commission was founded on the notion that the state and its bureaucrats had a crucial role to play in the fate of the escarpment. The efforts to protect the Niagara Escarpment took place in spite of a significant number of rural landowners and their political representatives protesting the infringement on their private property rights by the Act and then delaying the formation of the *Niagara Escarpment Plan* until 1985. Along the way, these landowners successfully lobbied for the reduction of the Plan area by 63 per cent (Whitelaw, 2005: 77).

The Niagara Escarpment experience is noteworthy as a point of comparison to the subsequent *Oak Ridges Moraine Conservation Plan* and *Act*. The conception of the escarpment was rendered an important epistemic characteristic – landscape continuity – that was considered worth conserving, a conception that is also central in the *Oak Ridges Moraine Conservation Plan* (Foster, 2006). The threatened disruption of the continuity of the Oak Ridges Moraine is represented by subdivision development at Richmond Hill (figure 3.3). In addition, a public body, in the shape of the Niagara Escarpment Commission, with a full-time staff of scientists well versed in natural science and ecology, was mandated to administer a conservation act. An additional aspect of their mandate was the task of buying lands to add to the public land bank as an important means of nature conservation. These features are rooted in a government model of conservation policy, which is based on regulation and government bureaucracy and is substantially different from the governance model of markets and volunteerism that informs the *Oak Ridges Moraine Conservation Plan* (Sandberg and Wekerle, 2010).

The *Toronto Centred Region Report*, issued in the early 1970s and one of the first significant attempts to plan the development of the Greater Toronto Area, constitutes another conservation policy precedent to the Oak Ridges Moraine legislation. As with the Niagara Escarpment, the focus of the report was the efficient integration of human and natural processes through a spatial corridor concept (figure 3.4). Agricultural and recreational lands were identified and mapped at the periphery of the city of Toronto. The objective was to limit growth northwards by a so-called parkway. The parkway was supposed to

Figure 3.3: The "choke point" at Richmond Hill

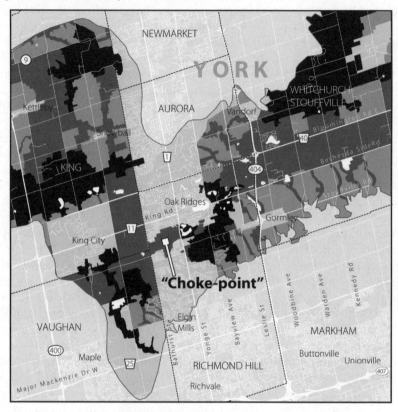

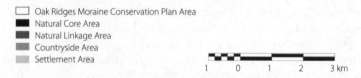

The "Choke-point" at Richmond Hill

☐ Oak Ridges Moraine Conservation Plan Area
■ Natural Core Area
■ Natural Linkage Area
■ Countryside Area
■ Settlement Area

During the height of the Oak Ridges Moraine controversy, activists often pointed to a critical choke point in Richmond Hill where development threatened to cut the Oak Ridges Moraine in half. The map shows the thin natural linkage area in dark grey in a sea of light-grey settlement areas to the north and south. The linkage area consists largely of the Bathurst Glen Golf Course. Source: Rajiv Rawat and the authors, 2008

Figure 3.4: Toronto Centred Region concept

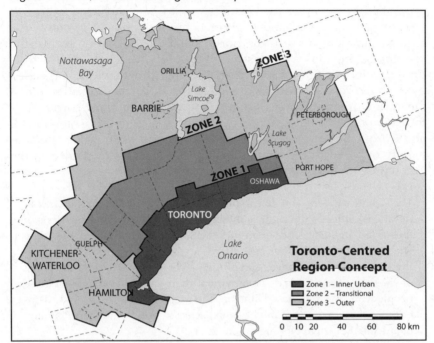

The Toronto Centred Region concept provides an early example of the application of a spatial plan with cores and corridors to organize the human and non-human spaces of the Greater Toronto Area. The concept did not, however, "name" the Oak Ridges Moraine as a landform worthy of separate planning measures. The Moraine was, instead, intended as a transitional agricultural area interspersed with smaller settlements. Dense urban settlement was intended for the inner urban zone, while the rural landscape was relegated to an outer area. Source: Central Ontario Lakeshore Urban Complex Task Force, 1974; Rajiv Rawat and the authors, 2011

contain an arterial highway that would ease the connection of settlements extending along the shores of Lake Ontario from Hamilton in the west to Coburg in the east. To the immediate north of the greenway the report envisaged an agricultural preserve and a commutershed extending to Lake Simcoe and flanked by recreational lands in the form of the Niagara Escarpment to the west and the Muskoka region to the north.

It has been recognized by many that the Toronto Centred Region concept failed as a plan for the Greater Toronto Area. Aspiring to growth and being closely tied and supported by development interests, the regional municipalities to the north lobbied successfully against the concept, paving the way for a surge of tract subdivisions and infrastructural development moving northwards. This growth was spearheaded by the building of highways, as well as the anticipated construction of the York Durham Sewage System along the Yonge Street corridor, effectively punching a hole in the Oak Ridges Moraine at Richmond Hill and Aurora. Some of the towns and cities north of Toronto were adamantly opposed to the restrictions on development contained in the Toronto Centred Region concept.

> The Province is very, very late in producing a suggested plan, and one can rightly ask if it has the right to inhibit or even destroy the aspirations of those who, in the absence of a proposal, planned and invested. For those who have made ridiculous speculative investments, we have no sympathy, but for those who have been prudent over the years to carefully select on the basis of trend, we do have sympathy. In Vaughan we think of those people who have purchased land around Maple, Woodbridge, and Kleinburg – urban nodes that might be expected to grow (Vaughan Planning Board, cited in Town of Vaughan, 1972: 2).

Nevertheless, the visions of a well-planned and state-regulated Toronto region remained alive and well and continued to strengthen in the epistemic community of nature conservationists. The identification of spatial belts of agricultural, estate, and suburban residential and recreational uses identified in the Toronto Centred Region concept was an attempt to rationally balance and acknowledge the importance of the competing sectors in the region. The concept showed the embryonic notions of a landscape ecology where swathes or corridors of recreational and natural areas accommodate non-human actors and organisms. The emerging epistemic community of planners and scientists imagined natural corridors as a rational way of managing growth and nature in the region.

The Toronto Centred Region concept, however, did not contain any reference to the Oak Ridges Moraine and did not identify the Moraine as a distinct landform in its various maps. Instead, it emphasized the importance of maintaining the areas north of Toronto as agricultural lands and as a commutershed for the city.

Early Warning Signals on the Moraine

The first identification of the Moraine in planning documents occurred in 1972. At that time the planning department of the Regional Municipality of York issued an interim report on rural-residential development. It urged the adoption of a philosophy that would preserve the unique, rural character of the landscape; minimize the urban use of agricultural lands; integrate residential, agricultural, recreational, and open space uses in the most satisfactory manner; maximize the development of natural resources for recreational, open space, and conservation purposes and provide for increased public access to the countryside; and ensure that non-farm, residential development in the rural areas was economically self-supporting (Regional Municipality of York, 1972: 6). The Oak Ridges Moraine was specifically mentioned by name and included as an example of a place in which rural residential and open space concepts could be combined. The planning department indicated, however, that the policy did not constitute a development plan but rather a set of policy guidelines for the rural regions. This observation was made in the general climate of enormous development pressures being put on the Region.

In 1974 the planning department followed with an interim policy approach to development on the Oak Ridges Moraine (Regional Municipality of York, 1974b). Both the planning department and the council of the Regional Municipality once again expressed a concern over the increasing number and scale of development applications affecting the Oak Ridges Moraine. The objective of the report was to document the physical resource information relating to the Oak Ridges Moraine and to assess the Moraine's ability to accommodate certain types of outdoor recreational activities for the Greater Toronto Area (ibid.).

In addition, the planning departments of the Peel and Durham regions were also concerned about the natural integrity of the Moraine. In a study from 1978, Chris Gates conducted interviews with major actors (Gates, 2009). When he worked in two planning departments, Gates observed a grave concern among planning staff with regard to the invasion of exurban estate developments on the Moraine and their impact on the landscape. At the time, the pressure was more intense on the Moraine than on the surrounding agricultural lands, a situation resulting from the Province's concern to preserve agricultural lands as well as the desirability of the Moraine for estate development. Yet planners had few means to stop the development process. The studies conducted by the Regional Municipality of York (1972, 1974a, 1974b), for example, were ignored, and the advice and recommendations of planners were routinely overridden by municipal councils that were interested in revenue-generating growth. There was also considerable influence exerted by developers on individual councillors. Gates (2009) quit the land use planning profession because he felt it was "too political"; far too often the credible ecological interventions by planners were ignored by town councils.

The Moraine was also identified in the provincially based *Central Ontario Lakeshore Urban Complex Plan*, a plan that succeeded the *Toronto Centred Region Plan* and received extensive local and regional input (Central Ontario Lakeshore Urban Complex Task Force, 1974). The 1974 plan followed closely the 1968 *Toronto Centred Region Plan* in laying out a series of spatially delineated "landscape areas" (figure 3.5). The core was an urban area extending from Hamilton to Toronto to Oshawa. A "parkway belt" with linear functions related to agriculture, amenity, recreation, resource extraction, and some urban areas followed. The parkway belt was then enveloped by an extensive area of different degrees of agricultural use, an area that dominated the *Central Ontario Lakeshore Urban Complex Plan* area in spatial extent. Two special zones of "waterfronts" were identified as recreational, environmental protection, and fishing areas. Finally, the plan contained "upland landscape areas and other areas of diverse resource potential" (ibid., no page). These areas were dominated by the Niagara Escarpment and the "Oak Ridges Moraine–Great Pine Ridge." The resource imperatives for the Moraine were stated as follows: "enhance rural amenity; adopt and implement scenic area, environmental protection area and near-urban recreation policies; create linear recreation corridors; extract mineral early and rehabilitate; manage for outdoor recreation, conservation, timber, wildlife, agriculture; and divert rural residential pressure" (ibid., no page). As we will note later in this chapter, the emphasis on rural amenity, scenic, environmental, and recreational values was significant for the wider socio-economic status of the Moraine in 1974.

The *Central Ontario Lakeshore Urban Complex Plan* followed the fate of the Toronto Centred Region concept: it was never realized. Exurban estate housing spread out over the northern reaches of Toronto, and subdivision tract housing along the Yonge Street corridor. Gerald Walker (1987: 143) has written extensively about the spread of an elite exurbia on the Oak Ridges Moraine. He asserted that the *Central Ontario Lakeshore Urban Complex Plan* sought to consolidate the Moraine's

Figure 3.5: The Central Ontario Lakeshore Urban Complex

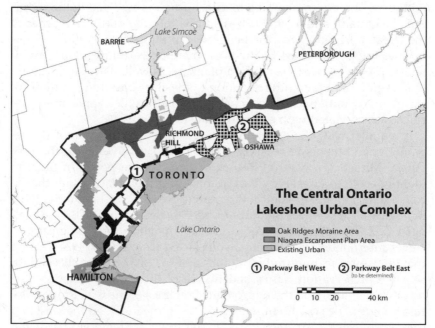

The complex first identified the Oak Ridges Moraine (or, as it was also called, the Oak Ridges Moraine–Great Pine Ridge) as a conservation object, in a wider attempt to manage nature and growth in the Greater Toronto Area. As in the previous Toronto Centred Region concept, the growth of the Greater Toronto Area was imagined to be confined to the shores of Lake Ontario. A parkway belt moving from the east to the west was intended to prevent urban development from encroaching on the agricultural lands, the Niagara Escarpment, and the Oak Ridges Moraine to the west, east, and north. Source: Central Ontario Lakeshore Urban Complex Task Force, 1974; Rajiv Rawat and the authors, 2011

position as living space for "several of the more prestigious exurban communities of central Ontario" (ibid.). In his view, "the agenda called for the fringe to fill in. The ragged edges of development, in the early 1970s, were to be rounded out. Agriculture and urban residential uses were anticipated in much of the Peel Plain. Finally, the open country uplands were largely reserved for the elites of Ontario" (1993: 211–14).

Toronto's former mayor John Sewell lamented the failure to adopt the initiatives of modern planning to direct urban growth along the shores of Lake Ontario and to stall urban sprawl into the northern reaches of the Greater Toronto Area. He believed that the plans were lost opportunities for the province, a situation where powerful development interests prevailed over the modern planners (Sewell, 1993: 211–15; 2009). However, Sewell paid little attention to the class-based foundations of the planning initiatives and did not question the elite character and social costs associated with exurban estate development.

In parallel with the efforts of the planning departments of the regional governments to identify ecologically sensitive areas, the provincial Ministry of Natural Resources had its own policy in place to identify ecological reserves. Part of this effort took place under the so-called International Biological Program (Gates, 1978). The International Biological Program was organized under the leadership of British ecologist C.H. Waddington to coordinate an inventory of ecological preserves internationally. The endeavour lasted from 1964 to 1974. During that time, over six hundred candidate sites in Ontario were checked for possible preservation status, and twelve of those were either located on or closely linked to the hydrological regimes of the Oak Ridges Moraine (ibid.). The sites identified on the Moraine included the west and east sections of the Jefferson Forest in the Town of Richmond Hill; Sand Point Marsh and Millvalley Hill Forest in Northumberland County; and Manvers Fleetwood Creek Valley in Victoria County in the eastern part of the Moraine (ibid.). By 1978 the Ministry maintained and periodically updated a list of biologically sensitive areas as part of a *Strategic Land Use Plan* of the Ministry's Land Use Coordination Branch. Its Parks Planning Branch was also studying candidates for potential acquisition as provincial parks, though their list was confidential to avoid possible land speculation (ibid.).

The policy paper of the planning department of the Regional Municipality of York, the *Central Ontario Lakeshore Urban Complex Plan*, and the inventory programs of the Ministry of Natural Resources thus provided some attention to the Moraine, though it was still not a landform that warranted formal provincial recognition and protection from the rapid urban sprawl that characterized the region. The policy paper, the *Central Ontario Lakeshore Urban Complex Plan*, and the Ministry of Natural Resources' designations of natural areas, like the *Toronto Centred Region Plan*, were ignored, though the ideas behind them continued to thrive and develop. Chris Gates (1978: 2) noted that the Moraine, in comparison to the Niagara Escarpment, was "another equally significant, if less visible, landform in Southern Ontario which is currently experiencing unprecedented pressures from expanding residential, recreational and industrial development." The study noted, in particular, the pressures on the western half of the Moraine, from the Town of Caledon in Peel Region to the Township of Uxbridge in Durham Region, where conflicts over resource-related land use were endemic, ranging from "soil and water conservation, mineral aggregate extraction, wildlife, recreation development, urbanization and agriculture" (ibid.: 7). The eastern part of the Moraine was under less development pressure, though one study in Northumberland County had noted the rapid increase in non-farm residential development related to recreational and second-home development in that region (ibid.).

The 1970s, nevertheless, saw an increased interest in the Oak Ridges Moraine as a conservation object by the regional municipal governments, the provincial Ministry of Natural Resources, and conservation authorities. Studies noted the significance of the Moraine and the detrimental effects of the clearing of its forests and the building of housing and industrial developments. In particular, the quality and quantity of stream flows had an impact on native trout populations, which are highly dependent on cold-water streams. Various agencies were also involved in inventorying fauna and flora on the Moraine. The Ministry of Natural Resources' Land Use Coordination Branch, and its offices in the suburban communities of Maple (in York Region) and Lindsay (in Durham Region), though hampered by a lack of clear definitional criteria, was in the process of locating the sensitive areas in its districts.

In the 1980s the trend towards the recognition of ecologically significant areas was fuelled by the provincial reorganization of county governments into regional governments (Eagles, 1981). The provincial legislation made land use planning mandatory and set limits on the development of regional plans. The legislation also included provision for environmental management principles and the identification of environmentally sensitive areas (ibid.: 316). Such areas were defined as "natural landscapes that contain features such as: aquifer recharge, headwaters, unusual plants, wildlife, vital ecological functions, rare or endangered species, or combinations of habitat and landforms which could be valuable for scientific research or conservation education" (ibid.: 315).

By 1981, Eagles indicated, all the major jurisdictions covering the Moraine, including the regional municipalities of Peel, York, and Durham and the counties of Northumberland and Peterborough, had completed or had underway environmentally sensitive area studies. The implementation of regional governments was a controversial decision, but they did provide employment to a cadre of young scientists who embraced ecosystem management and a sympathetic outlook towards sensitive area planning. As Eagles (1981: 317) states, "the planning staff members tended to be young and recent university graduates, often with resource planning backgrounds. The importance of the role of environmental planners within the regions at the time that all programs were formulated must be emphasized."

Paul Eagles himself, following in the footsteps of Leonard Gertler, was part of this epistemic community, being an assistant professor and a coordinator of the outdoor recreation–resource management stream in the Department of Recreation at the University of Waterloo, while also operating his own private planning practice. Indeed, one of Eagles' doctoral students, Graham Whitelaw (2005: 23), notes that the environmental planners and academics at the University of Waterloo played a significant role in promoting the ecosystem management approach in the province at the time.

The Oak Ridges Moraine as a Prominent Nature Conservation Object

In the late 1980s and the 1990s the Oak Ridges Moraine as a "bounded space" grew in stature in the presence of a strong cadre of ecosystem management thinkers provincially, federally, and internationally. An epistemic community of "ecopreneurs" – policy entrepreneurs and natural scientists with an ecological specialization – was firmly in place within the provincial bureaucracies, academy, and non-governmental organizations and within private consultancies that served not only the government and the non-governmental organizations but also the development and extractive industries that had to respond to the growing demands of ecosystems thinking and practice.

By the 1990s scientific statements and studies on the Oak Ridges Moraine had become an industry, where federal, provincial, and local authorities and non-governmental organizations jockeyed to obtain funds, conduct research, and share their findings. Several sets of documents stand out in identifying the Moraine as a significant conservation object in the late 1980s and early 1990s. The first is a statement of the Environmental Assessment Advisory Committee in 1989 that pointed to, for the first time, the negative cumulative environmental impact of development on the Ganaraska River watershed of the Moraine (Ontario

Ministry of the Environment, Environmental Assessment Advisory Committee, 1989; Guselle, 1991).

Two years later, in 1990, Liberal Member of Provincial Parliament Ron Kanter (1990) produced a 164-page report entitled *Space for All: Options for a Greater Toronto Greenlands Strategy*, identifying the Moraine as a significant, sensitive, and foundational feature of the natural system of the Greater Toronto Area. Kanter focused on conservation and governance of the headwaters of the rivers that connected the Moraine with the Toronto waterfront (ibid.).

Between 1990 and 1992 the Royal Commission on the Future of the Toronto Waterfront (1992), led by former Toronto mayor David Crombie, identified the Moraine as key to an integrated approach to the conservation of natural systems in the Greater Toronto Area. The Royal Commission, sponsored as it was by the federal government, and hearing hundreds of concerned individuals and groups, was particularly influential in pushing the bioregional and ecosystem form of thinking as a focal point of its investigation and recommendations. It was a testament to the strength and impact of the ecosystem form of thinking that the Royal Commission's initial mandate to centre on the waterfront ended up looking at the greater Toronto bioregion (Cooper, 1999; Laidley, 2011). The Oak Ridges Moraine was a central component of that bioregion. A map produced by the Royal Commission provided a new identity for the region and the millions of people living in its urban-rural interface (figure 3.6). As Aberley (1993: 22) remarked, "people began to understand that they didn't just live in a city."

Finally, the provincial government declared an interest in the Moraine, which led to the generation of a set of guidelines for development of the Oak Ridges Moraine area within the Greater Toronto Area. The appointment of the Oak Ridges Moraine Technical Working Committee in 1991, its mandate to commission fifteen studies on the Moraine, and the delivery of its final report in November 1994 formed a significant part of this initiative (McClean, 2001). The technical working committee commissioned studies on various aspects of the Moraine, which now occupy over a foot of shelf space in libraries. They were key elements in engaging a large cadre of government scientists and private consultants in the investment of time, energy, and interest in the Moraine (Tomalty et al., 1994; Riley and Mohr, 1994).

As a result of the background studies, the Oak Ridges Moraine Technical Working Committee (1994a) identified three interconnected natural systems on the Moraine. These included a natural heritage system that

Figure 3.6: The Greater Toronto Bioregion

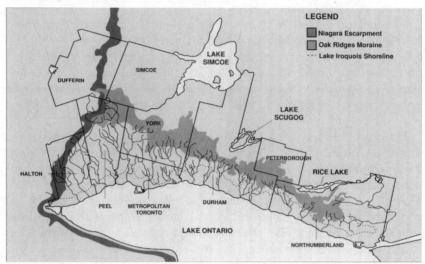

The Royal Commission on the Future of the Toronto Waterfront first articulated the presence of the Oak Ridges Moraine as the central part of a broader bioregion. The map turns the viewer's attention to the importance of the areas south of the Moraine, which include the rivers and watersheds originating on the Moraine. At the same time, the map renders invisible the rivers that flow northwards from the Moraine and the bioregions that they feed. These bioregions are now receiving development that is leapfrogging the Moraine and the Greenbelt. Source: Royal Commission on the Future of the Toronto Waterfront, 1992: 22

was divided into core and corridor areas. The core areas were the most significant from an ecological point of view, containing areas that were environmentally sensitive and of natural scientific interest: kettle lakes, wetlands, old-growth forests (over 100 years of age), and forests in excess of 30 hectares in size. Corridors were defined as being the means to enhance the opportunities of plant and animal species to move between core areas. The natural heritage system of core areas and corridors represented about 25 per cent of the Moraine. The second interconnected natural system identified by the technical working committee was a water resource system. The identification of this natural system acknowledged the Moraine as an important source of surface and ground water. The committee recommended that the headwaters of the rivers and streams on the Moraine, as well as the recharge areas (where water percolation occurs in permeable soils) and related aquifer systems, be protected and that regional governments develop comprehensive aquifer management plans. The third natural system named was a landform conservation system. It referred in particular to the visual character of the Moraine, such as its hummocky terrain and areas of steep slopes, forests, and streams. The areas were classified into significant landscape features, visually attractive areas, vistas, and panoramas.

Don Alexander's "Planning as Learning: The Education of Citizen Activists" (1994) is a participant-observer study of the environmental organization Save the Oak Ridges Moraine, based on his own membership in the organization; it positions activists as social learners of planning in the late 1980s and early 1990s. Alexander argues that through empowerment, teamwork, and the assertion of citizenship rights, activists became important members of the epistemic community that thought about and identified the Moraine as a significant conservation object. The central point is that the environmentalists were not teachers; they were learners of an already existing planning system into which they inserted their own efforts and initiatives.

Graham Whitelaw's study "The Role of Environmental Movement Organizations in Land Use Planning: Case Studies of the Niagara Escarpment and Oak Ridges Moraine Processes" (2005; see also Whitelaw et al., 2008, and Puric-Mladenovic and Strobl, 2006) similarly situates environmental groups as key actors in the development of an epistemic community of conservationists. Whitelaw describes the Oak Ridges Moraine policy process as a case of collaborative planning in which an interactive partnership among government, interest groups, major sectors of the community, and the public, all identified as stakeholders, worked towards consensus on problem solving, direction setting, and implementation (Whitelaw, 2005: 16). He further shows that these groups held common assumptions and frames for action, sharing "intellectual capital including agreement on data or analysis, definitions of a problem or objective, and mutual understanding of each other's interests" (ibid.: 17). Scientists and bureaucrats in the civil service are very much part of Alexander's and Whitelaw's epistemic community, frequently supporting, feeding information (often clandestinely), and professionally advocating for the environmentalists' agenda. Their studies also provide prominent examples of environmentalists moving in and out of the state structures to advise and take part in setting a conservation planning and science agenda for the Moraine.

The attention paid to the Oak Ridges Moraine from the late 1980s to 1995 occurred during the reigns of supportive Liberal and New Democratic provincial governments. From 1995 to 2002, however, a sympathetic provincial policy climate was initially suspended during two terms of Progressive Conservative governments. It was to be revived later under pressure from residents and environmental groups and, perhaps, the greening of the provincial Tories themselves. It helped too, no doubt, that half of the seats in the provincial legislature came from the "905" belt[1] of northern Toronto that encompasses large parts of the Moraine. Nevertheless, during the dark years of the Tory terms the conservation community continued its work. Planners in the regions of Peel, York, and Durham produced a document on the Oak Ridges Moraine in 1998 (Regions of York, Durham, and Peel, 1999). Civil servants in the provincial government bureaucracy compiled additional documentary material for the identification of the Moraine as a conservation object (Doyle, 2004). In fact, a virtual cottage industry composed of government bureaucracy, environmental consultancy, and environmentalist sectors, which grew in the 1990s and early 2000s, busily produced and reproduced studies on the Oak Ridges Moraine that fed the landform's significance in the public discourse.

In the context of the development of these and associated conservation plans, an expanded epistemic community of not only ecosystems scientists, consultants, and bureaucrats but also environmentalists and developers came to identify, accept, and defend the Moraine as a conservation object. The Oak Ridges Moraine was constituted as an unquestioned (yet questionable) spatial unit set aside as a natural area. It thus joined a series of other conservation areas that now exist on a similar principle: the Niagara Escarpment; the provincially designated Greenbelt established in 2005 that surrounds the Greater Toronto Area; the Province of Ontario's and Nature Conservancy's network of "natural heritage areas"; the Toronto and Region Conservation Authority's Terrestrial Natural Heritage System; environmental groups' Niagara Escarpment to Oak Ridges Moraine to the Algonquin Park/Adirondack Park Axis Heritage (NOAH) concept; and Reed Noss's Wildlands Project (1992; see also Whitelaw and Eagles, 2007).

There is also a growing *oeuvre* of published scholarly articles that now accepts and identifies the Oak Ridges Moraine as a distinct bounded area of conservation. Many of these accounts acknowledge the problems of a fixed boundary for the Oak Ridges Moraine. They also share a concern over leapfrog development, the exemptions to growth in the Oak Ridges Moraine legislation, the increasing housing costs, the lack of support for agriculture, and the poor regard for existing municipal plans, including the lack of support for implementation of the *Oak Ridges Moraine Conservation Plan* (Gilbert, Wekerle, and Sandberg, 2005; Fung and Conway, 2007; Hanna, Webber, and Slocombe, 2007; Wekerle et al., 2007). Yet, these studies consider the problems to be anomalous oversights that can somehow be addressed in future policy documents if only policymakers and governments would provide the proper input and support.

The problem with these statements is that none considers sufficiently the space-based assumption that forms the foundation of many nature conservation practices. Robin (2009: 203) reviews recent challenges by conservation biologists of the space-based assumption. The scientists argue that the areas outside the conservation reserves play a key role in maintaining ecological patterns and processes. Yet Robin notes that the research in the most well-resourced places of the earth (Europe, North America, and Australia) "is strongly biased towards areas designated as 'reserves' or national parks" (ibid.). The spatial approach to nature conservation remains attractive, probably because it offers simplistic and purportedly self-evident solutions to very complex problems that deserve deeper reflection and action (Hintz, 2007).

There are five interrelated ways in which the spatial approach of conservation, or the tendency of seeing nature as being "something out there," plays a contradictory and compromising role in the protection of the natural environment (Leopold, 1949; Cronon, 1992). First, the notion obscures any position that sees conservation as a common enterprise relevant to all areas across space. In this alternative way of viewing nature conservation, humans are seen as part of nature, and land is thought of as one unit that can and should accommodate multiple functions simultaneously. Bioregional conceptions of space, for example, conceive of an ecological area, typically a watershed, as an integrated planning unit in which the economy is planned within the area's ecological limits (Carr, 2004; Gilbert, Sandberg, and Wekerle, 2009; Robin, 2009). Development is not seen as separate from nature; it is instead held up to scrutiny as a human activity that is considered part of combined natural and cultural processes. Second, spatially delineated preserved areas such as parks may have compromised histories as social constructs that yield benefits to some but costs to others. This is the history, for example, of the creation of many federal and provincial parks as national natures for the Canadian public at large. Their establishment often took place at the expense of local residents and resource users, both European settlers and First Nations peoples (Osborne, 1998b; McEachern, 2001; Sandlos, 2008; Thorpe, 2012). Third, the conception of specific conservation areas as sites of scientific study may have compromised histories. Adams (1997) argues that the designation of specific areas for nature conservation was actively supported by an emerging society of ecologists in the 1930s. They were then interested in conserving representative areas of what were thought to be stable but predictably changing ecosystems. Such special areas were thought to provide places to study ecological processes without human impact and were therefore closely monitored for scientific investigation. This situation has, in large part, survived in the ecological sciences where humans are not seen as integral but as external to ecological processes and areas. As Cronon (1992: 1369) suggests, ecologists "more often than not treat people as exogenous variables that fit awkwardly if at all into the theoretical models of the discipline." This conception marginalizes the alternative position that humans are integral parts of ecosystem dynamics and that ecosystems may be inherently unstable. Fourth, the spatial approach to conservation may come to constitute a screen rather than an obstacle to development. In this situation, the development projects themselves escape scrutiny, and the question about the kind of human interaction with nature remains unexamined. The emergence of conservation areas as offsets provides an example. These areas may be located at long distances from development areas, yet compensate for the carbon emissions and biodiversity losses at those sites (Masden, Carroll, and Moore Brands, 2010). Finally, the focus on a spatially based conservation limits the struggle between development and preservationist factions to the placing of boundaries, rather than questioning the common enterprise of boundary-setting itself. Such boundary-setting exercises inevitably leave, whether intentionally or unintentionally, the land for development and boundaries subject to negotiation in the future. Indeed, with growth or development being in the default position, nature conservation is typically fighting a rearguard action. These shortfalls of the spatial assumption of nature conservation are endemic to the concept itself, be it the Oak Ridges Moraine or any other conservation area.

Conservation and Growth Provisions in the Oak Ridges Moraine Legislation

The documentation provided by the Oak Ridges Moraine Technical Working Committee of the early to mid-1990s and the additional work done by the provincial bureaucracy in the late 1990s form the basis of the formal and legal identification of the Oak Ridges Moraine in the *Oak Ridges Moraine Conservation Act* and *Plan* of 2001 and 2002, respectively. The Moraine became formally and legally conceptualized as a conservation area that covers 190,000 hectares and internally divided into four land use designations of varying sizes: "natural core areas," "natural linkage areas," "countryside areas," and "settlement areas" (table 3.1).

The spatial separation of conservation implies a spatial separation of its antithesis – growth or development. If "nature" is conserved in one space, development or growth has to occur elsewhere. The ensuing patchwork of conservation and growth necessitates the building of means to connect the various patches. People who live in a suburban development, for example, may need to connect to their workplaces that may be located in a commercial development area some distance away; this necessitates the building of transportation corridors. Similarly, flora and fauna need corridors to realize seasonal migration patterns or to maintain species vitality through genetic exchange. There is thus strong pressure to accommodate nature within growth but also to make room for growth within nature.

In the Oak Ridges Moraine legislation there are strong legal restrictions on the actions of private landowners on the Moraine, though they are varied and complicated. The *Oak Ridges Moraine Conservation Plan* contains an apparently strong prohibition stating that "no person shall, except as permitted by this Plan, (a) use land or any part of it; (b) undertake development or site alteration with respect to land; or (c) erect, move, alter or use a building or structure or any part of it" (Ontario Ministry of Municipal Affairs and Housing, 2002a: 29).

The "except as permitted by this Plan" provision is remarkably permissive. The most restrictive provisions are contained in the natural core areas. However, they are by no means absolute. All developments are restricted, but there are allowances for fish and wildlife management, conservation and flood control projects, agricultural uses, transportation, infrastructure and utilities if needed, home businesses, home industries, bed and breakfasts, farm vacation homes, low-intensity recreational uses, unserviced parks, and any accessory activities to these uses (ibid.: 33–4). In natural linkage areas, mineral aggregate operations, wayside pits, and accessory uses complement these activities. In countryside areas, the permitted activities are even more liberal. Agriculture-related activities, small-scale commercial, industrial, and institutional establishments, major recreational uses, residential

Table 3.1 Land use designations on the Oak Ridges Moraine

Land use designation	Percentage of area	Provisions/restrictions
Natural core areas	38	• Lands with the greatest concentrations of key natural heritage features that are critical to maintaining the integrity of the Moraine as a whole. • Only existing uses and very restricted new resource management, agricultural, low-intensity recreational, home businesses, transportation, and utility uses are allowed in these areas.
Natural linkage areas	24	• Protect critical natural and open space linkages between the natural core areas and along rivers and streams. • The only uses allowed are those that are allowed in natural core areas, plus some aggregate resource operations.
Countryside areas	30	• Provide an agricultural and rural transition and a buffer between the natural core areas and natural linkage areas and the urbanized settlement areas. • Prime agricultural areas as well as natural features are protected. Most of the uses typically allowed in agricultural and other rural areas are allowed here. • The lands also contain rural settlements, or existing hamlets or similar small, generally long-established communities, that are identified in official plans.
Settlement areas	8	• Reflect a range of existing communities planned by municipalities to reflect community needs and values. • Urban uses and development as set out in municipal official plans are allowed.

Source: Ontario Ministry of Municipal Affairs and Housing, 2002a

development, and accessory activities are allowed. Residential development is, however, restricted to the Palgrave Estates residential community in the Town of Caledon as well as the City of Kawartha Lakes and the counties of Peterborough and Northumberland. Finally, in settlement areas, liberal provisions are made for both settlement and other activities. The settlement areas are confined to Caledon East in Peel Region; the northern part of Nobleton and prominent parts of King

City, Vaughan, Richmond Hill / Oak Ridges / Aurora (the Yonge Street corridor), Newmarket, Ballantrae, and Stouffville in York Region; and Uxbridge in Durham Region. No settlement areas are assigned east of Uxbridge in Durham Region, an area that encompasses over half of the Moraine. However, the liberal concessions to development in country-side areas in the eastern parts of the Moraine indicate that those who constructed the legislation are amenable to such an option.

In the eastern parts of the Moraine the support for development values is more sanguine. Some provisions for housing subdivisions are made in the conservation legislation, though many local politicians feel that these are still too strict and consequently resent the legislation. In the Township of Alnwick/Haldimand in Northumberland County, for ex-ample, Warden Bill Finley protested the pending Oak Ridges Moraine legislation in 2001, proclaiming that "we need growth to survive ... If you tell us we can't develop here, what you are going to do is shut this part of Ontario down" (quoted in Swainson, 2001c: NE25). Finley also stated that "the eastern municipalities don't want anyone from the big city telling them how and where to place development" (ibid.). Councillor Dalton McDonald also warned that rural municipalities in the eastern part of the Moraine need growth to help foot the bills "or we'll die." McDonald continued: "If you want to take our land by telling us we can't grow, then you'll have to give us compensation ... We have to survive somehow" (ibid.). Finley has since become mayor and has more recently expressed regrets over the presence of the Oak Ridges Moraine occupying so much of the township, resulting in the loss of property tax dollars; he is arguing for the extraction of alterna-tive Moraine resources, such as spring water, as compensation. The town council has thus provided solid support for both local water bot-tling and aggregate extractive schemes in the face of widespread com-munity protests (Valley Voices Residents Association, 2006). In Mill Valley, for example, a natural spring water operation provides local customers with bottled water and ice, but the operation also supplies more distant markets. An exclusive brand of spring water, 1 Litre, is supplied by the Mill Valley operation. It uses an exclusive and con-servationist message to market its product, describing its bottles as having won awards for their functional yet chic design, and its water as coming from the unspoilt Northumberland Forest in the heart of Canada. As of September 2011, the brand was only distributed in the United States.

The *Oak Ridges Moraine Conservation Plan* puts the onus on the developer or landowner to ensure "the integration of environmental and land use planning in order to maintain, and where possible improve and restore, the ecological integrity of the Plan Area" (Ontario Ministry of Municipal Affairs and Housing, 2002a: 43). Protection areas include key natural heritage features, hydrological features, and landform conservation areas. These protection areas are extensive. The Ministry of Natural Resources has identified over one hundred natural areas on or in proximity to the Oak Ridges Moraine. Most of these are wetlands (bogs, headwaters, swamps, and marshes), but there are also forests and savannahs as well as various unique landforms associated with moraine deposits (uplands, rolling hills, sand plains, drumlin till plains, drumlin supraglacial till, and kame mounds) (Ontario Ministry of Natural Resources, 2010b).

The *Oak Ridges Moraine Conservation Act* and *Plan* are complemented by a series of on-the-ground instructions, the *Oak Ridges Moraine Technical Papers* (table 3.2). Developed by technical experts in the Ministry of Natural Resources and the Ministry of the Environment to aid municipalities and townships, these instructions set out the procedures for implementing the plan. The technical papers address seventeen different, albeit overlapping, topics worked out by different experts in two government ministries. The Ministry of Natural Resources typically handles natural and ecological matters while the Ministry of the Environment deals with hydrological issues.

The identification and regulation of the Moraine as a continuous landform and a complex set of ecologies, hydrogeologies, and topographies is a powerful basis for its present conservation status. However, these different classifications of the Oak Ridges Moraine are not absolutes but are socially constructed. They are therefore open to debate and contestation when development projects are proposed. The Oak Ridges Moraine legislation thus serves as a disciplinary measure that both promotes and challenges conservation.

Local municipalities have the responsibility to inspect and approve development applications on the Moraine. In most instances, local landowners and developers probably decline to develop their properties through their own reading of the Oak Ridges Moraine legislation or through advice from local planning offices. But sometimes, when landowners' development proposals are turned down by a local municipality or when a third party contests the development, there may be a hearing at the Ontario Municipal Board (OMB). OMB hearings to date

Table 3.2 *Oak Ridges Moraine Technical Papers*: Themes and sponsors

Technical paper	Themes	Sponsoring ministry
1	Identification of key natural features	Ministry of Natural Resources
2	Significant wildlife habitat	Ministry of Natural Resources
3	Supporting connectivity	Ministry of Natural Resources
4	Landform conservation	Ministry of Natural Resources
5	Identification and protection of vegetation protection zones for areas of natural and scientific interest	Ministry of Natural Resources
6	Identification and protection of significant portions of habitat for rare, threatened and endangered species	Ministry of Natural Resources
7	Identification and protection of significant woodlands	Ministry of Natural Resources
8	Preparation of natural heritage evaluations for all key natural heritage features	Ministry of Natural Resources
9	Watershed plans	Ministry of the Environment
10	Water budgets	Ministry of the Environment
11	Water conservation plan	Ministry of the Environment
12	Hydrological evaluations for hydrologically sensitive features	Ministry of the Environment
13	Subwatersheds (impervious surfaces)	Ministry of the Environment
14	Wellhead protection – Site management and contingency plans	Ministry of the Environment
15	Recreation plans and vegetation management plans	Ministry of the Environment
16	Sewage and water system plans	Ministry of the Environment
17	Stormwater management plan	Ministry of the Environment

Source: Ontario Ministry of Municipal Affairs and Housing, 2008b

have established some precedents and indications of the strengths and limitations of the *Oak Ridges Moraine Conservation Plan.*

Promoting Conservation on the Oak Ridges Moraine

In 2005 planner David Burnett made several observations on disputes resolved by the OMB in which the conformity of the *Oak Ridges Moraine Conservation Act* and *Plan* with local development proposals was at issue. Burnett observed that in an early decision with regard to the grandparenting of a housing development in an abandoned gravel pit in a countryside area, the OMB applied a very liberal interpretation of the legislation. "Applications for subdivision and zoning submitted after the *Oak Ridges Moraine Conservation Act* was passed [were] to be treated as if they had been submitted before the deadline on the grounds that the policy direction had already been established in an OPA [*Official Planning Amendment*] approved before the Act came into force" (Burnett, 2005: 19). This precedent was later used in other OMB decisions but was struck down in an amendment of the *Oak Ridges Moraine Conservation Act* in June 2004 (ibid.). In a second decision, Burnett noted the confirmation that no transportation, infrastructure, and utilities that infringe on key natural heritage features can be undertaken by a private landowner on the Moraine. In a third decision, he noted the denial of the establishment of a bed and breakfast (though such an activity is allowed) as an additional dwelling on a lot in a natural core area. In this case, the board stated that the construction of the extra dwelling was against the Plan, adding that "the clear intent of the Conservation Plan is to limit uses and the intensity of uses within the whole of the Conservation Plan area, but particularly to do so within the Natural Core Area" (ibid.: 20). In yet another decision, the board allowed the infilling of a wetland in an industrial park in a settlement area, but only after the proponent had shown conclusively, using the *Oak Ridges Moraine Conservation Plan* implementation guidelines, that the area was not a key natural heritage feature (ibid.: 21–2). In a final decision, Burnett noted that in a contestation between Dreamworks Property Inc. and the City of Vaughan over a subdivision development located partially in a settlement area and partially outside the Moraine, where two key natural heritage features were affected, the OMB, with input from the Toronto and Region Conservation Authority, ordered a revision of the subdivision plan that accommodated one of the heritage features (ibid.). Burnett argued that the *Oak Ridges Moraine Conservation Plan* gives planners more clout to negotiate subdivision designs that preserve natural features (Wekerle et al., 2007). Burnett also concluded that, at the time, the Province had taken an increasingly active role in amending the Oak Ridges Moraine legislation and supplying staff resources to ensure that developments on the Moraine were compliant with the Moraine legislation and consistent with its conservation objectives.

Perhaps reflecting the continuation of this trend, the OMB recently denied the development of a housing development in a settlement area east of Bathurst Street and south of Mulock Drive in Newmarket, where Mademont Investment Limited had sought to build a 448-home subdivision. The board upheld the Town of Newmarket's assignment of a higher level of protection for the area, and the Province's approval of the assignment (Persico, 2008a, 2008b, 2008c). The decision was based on a clause in the *Oak Ridges Moraine Conservation Plan* that allows for municipalities to upgrade the conservation of the Plan as long as they are not "prohibited by the Plan" (Ontario Ministry of Municipal Affairs and Housing, 2002a: 78). In Newmarket the proponents of the successful rejection of the subdivision referred to it as "an important precedent for other municipalities seeking to protect greenspace within their borders" (Persico, 2008c).

Conclusion

This chapter points to the presence of a largely unquestioned episteme of natural conservation planning based on the ecological sciences (including landscape ecology and conservation biology); a space-based or land-use-based form of conservation; and an epistemic community of ecosystem thinkers and managers of sensitive natural areas who have been instrumental in promoting and producing the Oak Ridges Moraine as an object of conservation. Planners, ecologists, and scientists, whether in the private or the public sector, have been central in introducing the concepts of ecosystem management and natural heritage planning in the province, concepts that were put to use in developing the *Oak Ridges Moraine Conservation Plan* and *Act*.

The significance and ramifications of the presence of an episteme and an associated epistemic community have not been recognized fully in the literature. Most observers have emphasized the important role played by civil society groups in creating the trigger or turbulence that has pushed or allowed sympathetic civil servants and planners to develop and implement conservation policies. Of less relevance and interest have been the conceptual frames that the civil service and ecological episteme have provided in the shape of a template for policy, legislation, and conflict resolution. Most members of the epistemic community have shunned a critical exploration of the shortcomings of the environmental planning, the ecological sciences, and the nature conservation, or what these fields refuse to consider; instead they have emphasized the progressive steps taken towards conserving nature and especially the Oak Ridges Moraine.

This chapter made the argument that an episteme of landscape ecology and conservation biology and an epistemic community of environmental planners and ecosystem thinkers and managers have become firmly entrenched in the way in which nature conservation is formulated and imagined in south-central Ontario, including the efforts to protect the Oak Ridges Moraine. The spatial separation of nature conservation, though questioned in the most recent iterations of conservation biology, is still a dominant concept that obscures both thinking about nature and culture as interrelated and inseparable and planning for biodiversity as an enterprise that includes human beings.

Chapter Four

Residents Speak for the Moraine

I am very upset that they are cutting down the trees in this fragile environment. In our world today, so many natural environments are being destroyed, and it's sad to think that it's happening here in our town. I thought we were smarter than to destroy such a rare piece of land. With every forest and Moraine we destroy, the more we lose our identity as a suburb, the reason so many of us came to live here … As I grow up I fear that there will no longer be any natural land for me to enjoy, and no trees to clean our air. I will have to live in this world after you leave it.

(Richmond Hill Council Public Hearing, 2000: no. 46)

By the turn of the twentieth century many suburban and exurban residents who lived on or had a particular interest in the Oak Ridges Moraine had articulated a place-based environmental consciousness and a shared emotional attachment to the landform (figure 4.1). Such a consciousness was constituted by local knowledge, natural science, and ecological metaphors and tropes and expressed by a sense of urgency to protect the distinctiveness and uniqueness of the Moraine. In this chapter we investigate residents' roles as actors who filled the Moraine landscape with memories, meanings, and attachments. We particularly explore residents' efforts to construct a sense of emotional and symbolic belonging to the Oak Ridges Moraine bioregion. We are also mindful of the possibility that place attachment and bioregional belonging can be ephemeral phenomena or that they can change in intensity and quality as media coverage and land use controversies subside.

Places can be actors. Writing about emotional geographies, Davidson and Milligan (2004: 524) argue that emotions "have tangible effects

Figure 4.1: Pastoral landscape on the Oak Ridges Moraine

The Moraine is often portrayed by this type of rural scene, with hills, trees, and a horse farm. Such depictions erase the settlement areas, roads, subdivisions, golf courses, and aggregate operations that are also found on the Moraine. Source: the authors, 2007

on our surroundings and can shape the very nature and experience of our being-in-the-world. They can clearly alter the way the world *is* for us, affecting our sense of time as well as space." Escobar, Rocheleau, and Kothari (2002: 320) contend that place is "the ground where body, home, community and habitat are joined in everyday experiences as well as in history." Place is about not only various spatial scales but also scales of class, gender, race, or institutional(ized) exclusion. Place identity refers to the "symbolic importance of a place as a repository for emotions and relationships that give meaning and purpose to life" (Williams and Vaske, 2003: 831).

In theories of bioregionalism, emotions are linked to the meanings *of* a place and also *for* a place (Parsons, 1985). One can identify with a place through emotion, interaction, experience, and attachment. This situation corresponds to Peter Berg and Richard Dasmann's (1977: 399) position that a "bioregion refers both to the geographical terrain and a terrain of consciousness." Bioregionalists believe that "to live is to live locally, and to know is first of all to know the place one is in" (Casey, 1997: 18). Doug Aberley (1999: 37) contends that place attachment and bioregionalism are stories "best learned from listening to many voices." There may thus be competing emotions and desires that inevitably sanction some voices while silencing others (Cronon, 1992: 1350). In the increasingly suburbanized and exurbanized rural-urban fringe, some of the silenced voices often include those of resident farmers and older communities based on resource extraction. Members of these communities frequently see themselves as threatened by local concerns for amenity and environmental values. Environmental discourses may thus contain discourses of inclusion as well as exclusion (McElhinny, 2006).

Local newspapers, television and radio news programs, numerous Internet sources, and public hearing submissions provide the sources for our documentation. Their importance is expressed in a reader's letter to the *Toronto Star* that stated: "I am thankful to the *[Toronto] Star* for not losing sight of how important it is that the Oak Ridges Moraine does not get developed. Every day there is an article concerning this issue and it is how I keep myself apprised of this situation that has become so important to me" (Calnan, 2000). We employ a content analysis of 130 articles published in the *Toronto Star* and the *Globe and Mail* from September 1986 to October 2004. We complement this analysis with public hearing testimonies, the most extensive being the more than 200 letters sent by residents to Richmond Hill Council in February 2000 prior to its making a decision on an official plan amendment to add housing for 25,000 more people in the township. The confrontations with developer-friendly local governments provided residents with a widened platform to present their ideas through environmental discourse. We organize the opinions and information under various key discursive themes representing particular emotions (for example, anger, surprise, worry, or deception), socioecological concepts (for example, sustainability, interdependence, stewardship), particular ecosystems (for example, wetlands, wildlife, farmlands), specific locations (for example, Town of Caledon, Northumberland County, City of Toronto), or political relations (for example, local governments, tax increases, activism events). We find that people's concerns converge around two predominant themes: attachment to local ecosystems and attachment to the so-called "rural character" of the Moraine. This convergence is very reminiscent of the values of exurban communities in other parts of the world. Throughout the chapter we refer to residents as our principal subjects of inquiry. These residents, however, do not necessarily represent all residents on the Moraine. They were, nevertheless, part of the hundreds of citizens who felt compelled to voice their views in various public forums.

In what follows we examine the ways in which place and place attachment are constituted, and we show the residents' ability to express a commitment and connection to hydrological and terrestrial ecosystems. Such attachments and testimonies demonstrate the exurban residents' ecological literacy and ability to situate themselves in the ecosystem management episteme and to draw on its metaphors and tropes to advance their interests. In addition, we examine different forms of visions, what we label *ruralities*, suggesting that the dominant conservation values may marginalize voices that articulate different ruralities of the Moraine.

Place and Place Attachment

Place attachment designates an emotional bond between people and place. This bond, connection, or sense of belonging has been described as a sense of place and rootedness (Relph, 1976; Shamai, 1991) or topophilia (Bachelard, 1958; Tuan, 1980). Such sense of place varies in intensity from immediate sensory delight to long-lasting and deeply rooted attachment. Place attachment can be expressed by the smell of pine forests, a vista that moves us, a cherished landscape of childhood, a sacred place to which one goes to think or remember, a favourite fresh produce stand, a weekend hideaway, or an everyday appreciation for the landscape around one's home. Place attachment addresses the place consciousness of people because it communicates an emotional, experiential, and physical connection (Altman and Low, 1992; Williams and Roggenbuck, 1990). At the most basic levels, place describes residents' involvement in their local neighbourhood and the degree to which that neighbourhood meets their needs. Home ownership, length of residence, stage in the life cycle, and local social relations explain the development of such attachment through people's economic and social investment in place. But place attachment is not something innate or predetermined; it is something that people construct by using different words, metaphors, and concepts.

Familiarity, expressed in length of residence or intensity of use, was associated positively with residents' building a sense of place attachment on the Moraine. This is clearly expressed in the words of many exurban residents on the Moraine. One Richmond Hill resident stated: "We have lived in Oak Ridges for 16 years, and my three children are growing up here. I want a future place for them that is not just tract housing, gridlocked transportation and no parkland or concern for the environmental impacts of unrestrained development" (Richmond Hill Council Public Hearing, 2000: no. 68). A similar intergenerational attachment was expressed by another Richmond Hill resident who stated that he "chose this neighborhood because we felt it had several natural conservation areas we assumed would be protected for our children and future grandchildren to appreciate and enjoy" (ibid.: no. 66). Such statements confirm Mesch and Manor's (1998: 506) contention that "those who express a high level of satisfaction with the physical and social attributes of the local environment also might tend to express a higher level of attachment, regardless of the extent of their involvement in locally based social relationships."

For many individuals and families on the Oak Ridges Moraine, home ownership as an economic investment and asset was also presented as the basis for a profound attachment to place. This position is well expressed by one frustrated resident who, in watching the cutting down of a forest adjacent to his property, stated that "this is the ugliest thing I've ever seen ... We put our life savings into this property to escape the city and now they're ramming [a] road up beside and destroying my retirement fund" (quoted in Swainson and Mahler, 1999). Place attachment can, therefore, be created through mobilization against development.

The construction of place attachment may not be limited to physical boundaries; it may extend to surrounding natures and residents. One resident of Toronto remarked that "a couple of months ago I was fortunate enough to meet a few members of STORM [Save the Oak Ridges Moraine Coalition] and since then I have been concerned with the issue [of the Moraine]" (Calnan, 2000). Many advocates for the conservation of the Oak Ridges Moraine, though not living on the Moraine per se, expressed concerns over the bioregional impacts of the Moraine's destruction or conservation. Such claims confirm that "it is not the possessors of meanings that are local, but the meanings themselves" (Williams and Stewart, 1998: 19). For example, residents mobilizing around the particular conservation of the Lynde marsh and creek (flowing from the Moraine to the shores of Lake Ontario in Whitby) defended it with the argument that "this is the only remaining Class One wetland on Lake Ontario between Hamilton and Cobourg." Residents imagined the Lynde valley, a prime nesting and resting area for migrating birds, as having "the potential to be a major greenway system from the lake to the Oak Ridges Moraine" (in Deverell, 1994). Some residents formulated a bioregional consciousness of the Moraine that moved beyond its physical boundaries to include surrounding regions. According to one Moraine resident, "the Oak Ridges Moraine is the business of everyone in York Region" (Richmond Hill Council Public Hearing, 2000: no. 73). For another resident, "all citizens of southern Ontario have a stake in the moraine, and benefit from its silent existence" (Garrett, 1999).

The intensity of the expression of place attachment is often reflected in the level of satisfaction or dissatisfaction resulting from environmental changes, particularly when the integrity of places is threatened or destroyed. Attachment to the Moraine was expressed by ominous statements referring to ecological catastrophe (Swainson, 2000b), the "human-caused desiccation of southern Ontario," and the idea that "ignorance is no longer a valid excuse for inaction" (Garrett, 1999). A narrative of loss frequently emerged in testimonies and stories of the Moraine. Newspapers reported a loss of habitat and species, of natural or rural character, of access or enjoyment by future generations, and of a paradise lost to new homes (see Lewis in Swainson, 2001e; Stewart, 2000; Joyner in Small, 2000; Landsberg, 1991). Such tropes of loss have some basis in the deep ecology literature. As Aldo Leopold (1949) eloquently argues, loss produces a sense of disconnection with one's environment – an individual or collective breach of the bond of wholeness with place. Recent work on ecological restoration argues similarly that restoration efforts are sometimes geared towards much more than the restoration of ecosystems; they are also restoring a damaged attachment to place (Higgs, 2003).

The narrative of loss emerging from environmental change is multidimensional. Loss refers to the vanished, but it also applies to what could be lost or what residents fear could be lost if development continues. Recollection of a close or distant past with "unthreatened" and "idyllic" nature renders the potential loss even greater. Memory articulates a relation to both space and time. This relation is expressed by one Moraine resident who wrote: "As a former resident of Richmond Hill and one who grew up there I have many fond memories of the vast tracks [sic] of unspoiled agricultural and forested lands that were once a part of Richmond Hill. It is unfortunate that now the town council is considering allowing the last remaining tracks [sic] of land to become yet more plazas, roads and cookie cutter homes for the benefit of those developers" (Richmond Hill Council Public Hearing, 2000: no. 40).

An environmental activist and resident of Richmond Hill spoke about how she joined the Richmond Hill Naturalists when the organization transformed from a birdwatchers' group in the 1950s to an environmental watchdog committee in the 1990s. This resident moved to a house near Lake Wilcox in 1997 but was soon confronted with unfettered development changes. She recalled: "This was a chance to be in the country and to bring up my children where we would walk from the door and over to the field and the magic forest, as we call it. And we would see coyotes and deer and all sorts of things every time we would walk in there. It was a really nice, healthy place to bring [up] children. After we hooked up the sewers, my children got sick from swimming in the lake [Wilcox]. I haven't been swimming in at least 10 years" (Marsh, 2003).

Although the loss of nature often expresses a loss of control over local environments, the testing of place attachment, alienation, and isolation does not necessarily translate into a feeling of helplessness. On the contrary, loss prompted the residents to often become more vocal in denouncing the forces threatening nature and their attachments to place. They felt that there was no other possible redress for their literal and symbolic loss than environmental conservation and the arrest of development. Residents also correlated emotional attachment to place and ecological commitment with the desire to protect their quality of life. Quality of life, they felt, was often enabled, yet simultaneously threatened, by the hegemonic forces of urban growth. In the case of the Oak Ridges Moraine, residents often connected their assertion of a place attachment with an ecological awakening, ecological knowledge, and a rise of a bioregional consciousness.

Above- and Below-Ground Attachments

Many residents living on the Moraine articulated narratives of attachment to a variety of local ecosystems, with both an "above-ground" (that is, the Moraine as a picturesque haven of green space with rolling hills, wetlands, kettle lakes, and woodlands) and a "below-ground" perspective (that is, the Moraine as source of clean water). Both discourses, integrating a consideration for seen and unseen ecosystems, contain emotional connections to ecosystems, which were forged from familiar imagery, ecosystem science, expressive language, and an emphasis on the irrevocable damage caused by development of "pristine" nature (represented by the richness and uniqueness of local ecosystems) and on hydrogeology (symbolizing and sustaining life).

Residents often took the complex hydrogeology, the Moraine's glacial formation, and its functions and popularized them in mechanistic and/ or functional terms. The Moraine was depicted as having been formed by glaciers, which pushed earth into high ridges. Other imagery stated that "functionally, the moraine constitutes a magnificent water-control system" (Izzard and Leivo, 1990), acting like a "giant sponge, soaking up snow and rain into subterranean reservoirs" (Swainson, 1999). The most popular metaphor for the Moraine was that of the "rain barrel of Southern Ontario" (Bocking, 2002).

Residents understood the impact of development on watersheds as negative. Commenting in 1991, an activist with Save the Ganaraska Again (quoted in Taylor, 1991) stated that the construction of Highway 407 presented a double threat to this watershed: a forecasted population increase and the aggregate extraction required for road construction. Another resident voiced concerns about a road expansion, saying that it "will kill 17 small streams and destroy the delicate underwater rivers and aquifers, which are a source of drinking water" (quoted in Ferenc and Bock, 2000). The same resident expressed particular concern for the sustainability and integrity of the hydrological system when declaring, "You can't dig a new stream; it's not a replenishable resource."

Many residents repeated the tropes of the ecological complexity of their local water system and the impact of urbanization on it that had been articulated by natural scientists. In an opinion piece published in the *Toronto Star*, a Woodbridge resident wrote: "Survival depends upon the unimpaired functioning of our planet's life-support systems. The moraine is a local manifestation of those systems, providing clean water and fresh air. Urbanization of this land will continue the steady, human-caused desiccation of southern Ontario – a disastrous trend that has reduced our urban rivers to shadows of their original selves" (Garrett, 1999).

Similarly, for a resident of Unionville and a member of the Markham Conservation Committee, the Moraine was imagined as "likely the largest environmentally significant land form in North America to be in the path of major urban growth. It is important to understand not only its environmental surface networks but to also understand the role it plays in recharging aquifers and supplying water to its many streams which are so important to the communities abutting Lake Ontario" (Richmond Hill Council Public Hearing, 2000: no. 11). These views were echoed by an environmental activist and resident of Oak Ridges who emphasized that "we are intrinsically connected to our environment and to nature ... We need to preserve this for our own health, not just the flora and fauna. It is so beneficial to us, our drinking water, our quality of life" (quoted in Hudson, 1999).

The Moraine residents' consciousness about water was a crucial element in their position that they were not simply living in a landscape of rolling hills but that (the mostly hidden) hydrogeology of the Moraine was threatened as well. This sentiment led the *Toronto Star*'s columnist David Lewis Stein (2000) to conclude that "the fight to save the Oak Ridges Moraine is about many important issues, of course, but most of all it's about water."

Residents expressed attachment not only to the ecosystems themselves but also to the various animal species that coexist with them on the Moraine. "On my morning walks on different parts of the moraine, I often see deer (four one day last week) or surprise a fox returning from a nocturnal hunt. Waterfowl of every kind, from wood duck to teal, mergansers, green and great blue herons, loons, Canada geese and at least one pair of osprey, can be seen on or about the lake every fall and spring. Muskrats abound, even a beaver visits occasionally" (Harpur, 1992: B7).

Many homeowners living near ravines, woods, and creeks, who had paid premium prices for such proximity, expressed appreciation for the natural world being immediately in and around their homes and gardens, where deer, brush wolves, foxes, and many other small mammals could be sighted (Harpur, 1991). One resident denounced the rapid changes that were scaring wildlife from her "pristine environment" and that were replacing the "neighborhood's slice of serenity" by "rows of townhouses coming up to [her] back door." This particular resident was incensed because "before we moved here, we checked with the planning office and we were told this area wasn't going to change. We were told it would be left as green space" (quoted in McAndrew, 1995).

Many residents expressed a worry about the fate of green spaces and particular species. With the cutting down of forests, they argued, birds lost forest cover, and their breeding populations were at risk. In a letter published in the *Toronto Star*, Cameron Smith (1999) stated that "the more we fragment the landscape of the moraine through development, the more we shrink the deep forest and the more we deny breeding space to the birds." In his view, this was particularly problematic since birds are an indicator of biodiversity.

Amphibians on the Moraine have received particular attention from residents and local biologists. In 1993 Peter Attfield, a local naturalist, lobbied the Town of Oak Ridges to establish a frog-protection zone for the thousands of frogs that cross two roads near a local kettle lake. Attfield nicknamed Oak Ridges "the frog capital of York Region" (quoted in White, 1993). The Town endorsed his proposal by putting up diamond-shaped yellow signs, designating the area an ecological zone, and explaining the frogs' importance in the local marshland ecology.

In 2000 a local biologist unexpectedly found the threatened Jefferson salamander (*ambystoma jeffersoniannum*) in the Jefferson Forest at the headwaters of the Rouge River on the Oak Ridges Moraine. Given the similar names of the salamander and the forest, this observation might not have seemed surprising. However, a previous environmental impact assessment of the $10 million Bayview Avenue extension had established that there were no Jefferson salamanders in the forest. A little historical digging reveals further that the salamander having the same name as the forest is a coincidence: the salamander is named after U.S. president Thomas Jefferson, and the forest after local English immigrant William Thomas Jefferson who settled with his family in the area in 1837 (Jefferson Commemorative Committee, 1980). Yet the salamander was there, and the finding sparked an intense and well-publicized struggle to save it and its forest habitat. A local biologist qualifies it as the most sensitive of all amphibian and reptile species to development impacts, including farming, housing and roads (Helferty, 2004a, 2004b).

The Jefferson salamander was promoted as an iconic symbol of environmental resistance to urban sprawl at the height of the struggle to conserve the Oak Ridges Moraine in the late 1990s. In a front-page colour photograph published in the *Toronto Star*, the salamander is held by environmentalist Glenn De Baeremaeker, then president of Save the Rouge Valley System and currently councillor for the City of Toronto, in front of Osgoode Hall in downtown Toronto; the hall is the home of the Court of Appeal for Ontario, the Supreme Court of Justice, and the Law Society of Upper Canada. The photograph played a central role in the attempt to secure environmental legislation to protect the Oak Ridges Moraine in the face of the planned Bayview Avenue extension and housing subdivisions surrounding it. In spite of its efforts, the Save the Rouge Valley System group conceded defeat after a judicial review endorsed the environmental impact assessment that had earlier approved the extension (Swainson, 2001e). Despite the apparent defeat, the ecological consultants who worked on reducing the impact of the road extension, by using an overpass and amphibian tunnels under the road, have claimed a guarded victory (figure 4.2). Their mitigation efforts received an international award and much praise from a local naturalist club – even though there have not been any sightings of the Jefferson salamander since the overpass and tunnels were built (Gartshore et al., 2005).

Forest ecology also formed the basis of attachment. One newspaper reported that the Moraine woodlands were home to over nine hundred species (Swainson, 1999). The Jefferson Forest alone was identified as being "home to thousands of white spruce, pine, black cherry, elm, red oak, maple and ash trees" and to some "38 species of birds, including eight that are considered rare or uncommon, coyotes, white-tailed deer, yellow-spotted salamanders and red-bellied snakes" (Immen, 1999a). According to Glenn De Baeremaeker, "this is the last large, significant forest we have left in the Greater Toronto Area" (quoted in ibid.). The urgency of the protection of the Jefferson Forest was echoed by others who pointed out that since 1985 York Region had cut down 1.5 million trees (5,995 hectares of forest) to pave the way for more development (Swainson and Mahler, 1999). Residents thus reported witnessing first-hand a wildlife decline, with much more irregular sightings of species such as foxes, pheasants, and deer. They also expressed worries about the combined impacts of humans and development on rare, endangered, threatened, or vulnerable species in Ontario and Canada. As a Moraine resident put it, "when development occurs adjacent to a natural area it's not just the construction, the buildings and roads that can have a negative effect on the natural area. It's the human impact. Humans, with their cars, lawns, dogs and cats can have a long-term negative, cumulative effect" (Richmond Hill Council Public Hearing, 2000: no. 70). Speaking about Caledon, a town whose efforts to protect green space have grown commensurably with the threat of massive rapid growth in neighbouring Brampton and Vaughan, Funston (1996) echoed a similar concern: "Housing developers want to build, build, build and gravel pit operators want to dig, dig, dig but the residents want it all to stop before their beautiful landscape and tranquil lifestyle are ruined."

Figure 4.2: Amphibian tunnels under Bayview Avenue

Built to accommodate the movement of amphibians under the controversial Bayview Avenue extension, the tunnels connect subdivisions rather than wildlife areas in many places. So far, no Jefferson salamanders have been spotted moving through the tunnels. Source: the authors, 2011

Witnessing the destruction of the environment on an everyday basis, residents increasingly painted a scene in which the only way to protect ecosystems and species was to oppose further development on the Moraine. As one resident argued, "the Moraine is an environmentally sensitive area as headwaters for several rivers, provincially significant wetlands, complex habitat for regionally rare birds, beautiful forests, such as the Jefferson Forest, and rare and sensitive kettle lakes and kettle bogs. These must not disappear!" (Richmond Hill Council Public Hearing, 2000: no. 68). Some residents even spoke in defence of nature's "birthright," stating that "we should NOT sell the Oak Ridges Moraine, this 'nature'-endowed 'birthright' of forest, bogs, kettle lakes and the biodiversity that they sustain, to developers or to add to the urban sprawl in our town and region" (ibid.: no. 74). Others used scientific terminology to indicate the threat to ecosystems' integrity and connectivity. In the words of a resident of Richmond Hill, "populations of plants and wild-life in the area's forests and wetlands cannot be sustained if the lands between them are developed. What is needed is more strict protection of the core areas, as well as ecological restoration of wider buffer areas around them and of wider corridors between them" (ibid.: no. 22).

Perhaps the picture of the complexity and the importance of ecological systems was best captured in an opinion letter written by Peter Attfield (2000), a naturalist living in Oak Ridges:

> The Oak Ridges Moraine area of Richmond Hill has the greatest variety of plants and animals in all of the Greater Toronto Area, including many that are rare. It's about wildlife. The Oak Ridges Moraine is a wonderful natural corridor, second only in southern Ontario to the Niagara Escarpment. It's about opportunity. The Oak Ridges Moraine is the crown of the Greater Toronto Area. Its woodlands, wetlands, kettle lakes and headwater streams are the jewel of that crown. It's about greenspaces and human values. For decades, the people of the Greater Toronto Area have been promised but denied a greenbelt. Citizens of Richmond Hill, York Region, Toronto and the Greater Toronto Area are demanding some relief from urban sprawl. They want greenspace more than additional subdivisions. The Moraine presents the last and best chance to create a greenbelt sanctuary to enjoy "nature." And it also provides clean air and a steady supply of clean, clear water.

Attfield's statement summarizes the multiple attachments that many residents felt towards the Moraine's hydrological and geological systems, fauna, flora, and particular ecosystems. Residents also saw nature as fragile, situating it on a localized and bioregional scale of individual and collective responsibilities. Other narratives told by residents were representative of their emotional connections to nature and also allowed nature to be represented, legitimized, and defended in a public discourse. For residents who were educating themselves in ecology, the Moraine was an important part of becoming more involved and concerned for the future.

The new bioregional awareness also produced narratives that fostered different degrees of protecting, sustaining, and restoring local ecosystems and non-human species (McGinnis, 1999). At times, residents referred to a deep ecology philosophy promoting inter-species equity or the equality of life forms. Some people spoke of their responsibility:

"to protect our natural habitat – it is after all our real home as it is to all other living things" (Richmond Hill Council Public Hearing, 2000: no. 82). The desire to leave a healthy and green legacy to their children, and the fear of not being able to do so, was a major concern for many residents. Such sentiment and fear are well captured in the following memo from a Richmond Hill resident to the mayor: "There is no doubt that the health of our children, physically through cleaner air, mentally and emotionally through the peace afforded by nature, and spiritually through the values of respect and concern for our earth and the humanity it holds, will be greatly strengthened by the presence of a green space. Please do not only heed the cries of those whose hearts are only motivated by profit and disregard the cries of our children and us their parents" (Richmond Hill Council Public Hearing, 2000: no. 20).

Many residents linked their personal commitment to material and emotional inheritance with the protection of their environment, as a shared responsibility. In another letter to the Richmond Hill Council, a resident from Aurora argued that "it is the duty of politicians to look after the interests of future generations, and both provincial and local politicians should send a clear message to developers that land ownership does not give the right to develop on environmentally sensitive land" (ibid.: no. 80). In such statements, residents felt that they understood environmental protection and inheritance as directly threatened by urban development.

Many citizens on the Oak Ridges Moraine saw the various aspects of environmental conservation, be they preserving a species habitat, opposing the destruction of a forest or green space, or demanding natural and cultural heritage policies, as different expressions and duties of a newly found ecological consciousness (Dobson, 2003, 2005; Light, 2003; M.J. Smith, 1998). They thus saw their duties as participating in the political process and denouncing elected officials and political actions that were not only detrimental to the natural environment but also abusive of the democratic process. Residents were critical of local politicians who were often perceived as pro-development. A resident of Richmond Hill asked: "What happened to the government by the people for the people? We now have a government for developers by developers" (Richmond Hill Council Public Hearing, 2000: no. 24). Reacting to the planning changes in Richmond Hill that favoured more housing subdivisions, another resident questioned the politicians' accountability by asking, "How can you possibly do this when your public, who voted you in, do not want it to happen" (ibid.: no. 65). Many residents expressed increasing anger and frustration with some of the local politicians' pro-development stance. In a letter to a newspaper, a resident wrote: "I am angry because I cannot understand why the apparent will of the people is being ignored. Elected politicians not listening to their constituents but rather their consultants' reports is a very dangerous thing indeed" (ibid.: no. 52).

Bioregional consciousness and accountability is also well captured in the words of another resident who stated, "The Moraine is a sacred trust and you must listen to the people who have elected you, who are becoming increasingly aware that they don't want this natural resource destroyed" (ibid.: no. 73). This last comment echoes Andrew Light's (2005) view of ecological citizenship as a set of moral and political rights and obligations among humans, as well as between humans and non-humans. The conservation of the Moraine was a very crucial element of political agendas and local elections.

Attachment to and Defence of "Rural Character"

Residents' narratives of emotional attachment to the natural areas of the Oak Ridges Moraine were not, however, the only such narratives that existed. As we have already argued, all landscapes are the manifestations of a variety of emotions, social interests, cultural experiences, economic processes, and environmental and ethical relations (Schein, 1997; Howitt, 2002; Harner, 2001). In this situation, "landscapes are produced and lived in an everyday, practical, very material, and repetitively reaffirming sense" (Duncan and Duncan, 2004: 7). It follows that there is no such thing as the "Moraine" per se, since any landscape is unavoidably invested with a variety of meanings, emotions, and representations.

The concept of rurality is useful in distinguishing between different emotions and place attachments. Rurality suggests that there are different social constructions or visions of what constitutes the rural. We identify three types of ruralities: post-productivism, agri-ruralism, and utilitarianism. Post-productivist rurality corresponds closely to the experience of the residents who live on or in proximity to the Moraine, described above. It emphasizes the aesthetics of the rural as contributing to the quality of life of residents. This aesthetic discourse is rooted in the naturalistic, artistic, or recreational values in which nature is held as nurturing and enriching the experiences of life. Self-fulfilment, enjoyment, and remedy to the alienation of the urban experience are the *leitmotifs* for the conservation of the countryside and the improvement of rural landscape qualities. Nature is represented as a relative wilderness that is understood as unspoilt by human development and therefore associated with being a safer, healthier, happier environment than urban areas. The language used to protect place is laden with natural science and ecological words and concepts. The words and practices of the episteme and epistemic community that we outlined in chapter 3 are effectively embraced and manipulated by the residents. The Moraine is typically an object of desire to former urban and suburban residents who have left the metropolitan region for distant small towns and villages where they find a quiet haven, a refuge from modernity. This sense of "existential" or "ontological" security (Giddens, 1991) is directly attributed to the "proximity of nature" and creates the desire to live in it (Murdoch, 2001; Halfacree, 1995; Cloke, 1996).

The agri-ruralism discourse of rurality emphasizes the social dimension of rurality (Frouws, 1998). In combining the terms *agrarianism* and *ruralism*, this discourse denotes the crucial importance of agriculture as the interface between people and the environment and identifies farmers as the stewards of the land and its natural resources. The preservation of natural and environmental qualities is said to be realized through different styles of family farming offering "multi-functional agriculture that meets the social demands for items ranging from healthy food and pure drinking water to attractive landscapes and country recreation" (ibid.: 58).

Finally, the utilitarianism discourse conceives of rural areas as underdeveloped. This discourse seeks to maximize the countryside's economic advantages, to create employment and opportunity for investments, and to generate income. The countryside is thus seen as integrated in the dynamics of "modern markets for housing, recreation, food specialties, high-tech agriculture, attractive business parks and so on" (ibid.: 60). Rural areas and landscape amenities simply become commodities offered on the market – an object of individual and collective competitions for space to live, work, recreate, and travel (figure 4.3).

While these three ruralities or rural discourses are structured along different ideologies, social relations, interests, sciences, and political choices, aspects of one discourse may overlap or come to dominate those of other discourses. There are social, economic, and cultural dimensions attached to all of them even though each one emphasizes a particular dimension. Rural and ruralized experiences are far from homogeneous (Pratt, 1996; Cloke, 1996). There is a continuous transformation of the socio-spatial composition of rural areas that is associated

Figure 4.3: Farmland as commodity

Farmers typically treat land as a commodity, especially at the time of retirement. Former pasture lands that have nurtured cows are now sown with utility
lines and yield suburban homes. Source: the authors, 2003

with an increasing influence of urban and non-agricultural activities. A
shift from agricultural and utilitarian to post-productivist ruralities has
been referred to as a production-oriented or a rural-to-post-rural transition (Halfacree and Boyle, 1998; Murdoch and Pratt, 1997). The term
rurality is, therefore, a contested concept referring to different ideas and
meanings of the rural. Yet, the term *rurality* is useful in providing context for the Oak Ridges Moraine.

Preservation raises issues about the perceived compatibility or in-
compatibility of rural land use, the desire of residents to maintain the
quality of landscape from any type of development, and the reaffir-
mation of landscape identity by one particular group over others. In
the process of reaffirming the characteristics and boundaries of one
group's identity, the identities of other groups are set apart. While everybody's place attachment is valid, some groups more than others

have the means to advance their interests in the defence of their desired and desirable landscapes. For many residents of the Moraine, rural character has come to mean the protection of open spaces rather than of farmlands specifically. The post-productivist discourse, therefore, as we have noted in previous sections, dominates other forms of ruralities on the increasingly urbanized Moraine.

The Farmed Moraine

In the last twenty-five years a constant decline in the rate of loss of farmlands and farms indicates that the utilitarian and recreational rural discourses are literally encroaching on traditional agri-ruralism. From 1976 to 1996 the Greater Toronto Area lost 60,000 hectares (or 16.5 per cent) of productive farmlands to development. An additional 20,125 hectares (7 per cent) was lost between 1996 and 2001 (Walton and Hunter Planning Associates et al., 1999; Planscape, 2003). From 1976 to 1996, the number of farms declined by 16.5 per cent, and the percentage of total farmland rented remained constant since the late 1970s at 47 per cent (Walton and Hunter Planning Associates et al., 1999). Farmlands continued to decline in the Greater Toronto Area at a faster rate than in any other part of the province (ibid.). From 1976 to 1996 the largest loss of farmlands took place in York Region (36 per cent), followed closely by Peel Region (35 per cent); Durham Region registered the smallest lost rate (25 per cent) (Walton and Hunter Planning Associates et al., 1999). The decline continued from 1996 to 2001, however, at a much slower rate. During this period the largest loss of farmlands occurred in Peel Region (13 per cent), followed by York Region (9 per cent) and Durham Region (2 per cent) (Planscape, 2003). The loss of farmlands represents a major threat not only to agriculture but also to farming activities and farmers' livelihoods.

Agriculture sits at the interface between people and the environment in the Greater Toronto Area; it also sits at the interface between the rural and the urban. Since the 1950s, agriculture in the Greater Toronto Area has been continually squeezed out, and farmers have therefore had to adapt in order to meet global and local market demands. As some of the most productive farmlands (classes 1, 2, and 3) in Canada are permanently lost to residential and commercial subdivision lots, farming in the urban shadow becomes increasingly challenging (Walker, 2000). Proximity to the large markets of Toronto has always benefited local agriculture (enabling diversification of crops and innovation in farming activities), but affluent exurbanites relocating in the urban-rural fringe in search of a rural lifestyle have displaced farming services and have interfered with farming operations and practices (by complaining about traffic, smells, or noise) (figure 4.4). Farmers and suburbanites and exurbanites have a very different conception of the rural and the rural character.

Farmers in the Toronto metropolitan region have to contend with the escalating speculative land value of rural areas under development pressures. In 1996 almost half (47 per cent) of all farmlands in the Greater Toronto Area were rented (for cash crop farming) from speculators, governments, non-farmers, retired farmers, and families (Walton and Hunter Planning Associates et al., 1999: 3.9). For example, in Richmond Hill, a municipality dissected by the Yonge Street corridor, a farmer is reported to have worked 1,600 hectares but owned only about 40 hect-ares, which had been in his family for 195 years (Stein, 2001). The uncer-tainty and unsustainability of tenant farming, directly created by the inflationary value of land caused by housing development, offer very few alternatives. Unable to afford land and unable to keep farming (be-cause of constant borrowing against assets in order to meet production costs), some farmers have made substantial profits by selling their farms to land-hungry developers. However, with recent provincial legislation to protect agricultural lands from development, farmers lost the oppor-tunity to sell their farms at such profits. At one point in time, the sale of developable land reached $625,000 per hectare, compared to agri-cultural land at $25,000 (Galloway, 2004). For farmers, there is a con-tradiction between land protection and farming. Land protection strips farmers of their retirement income, frustrating, angering, and putting them at odds with environmental conservation. In the words of a farmer living in Mississauga, "we're the first environmentalists and we want to preserve farmland but we feel that, if it's for the benefit of society as a whole, society as a whole should pay" (quoted in Galloway, 2004).

As urbanites move into the countryside, their post-productivist val-ues of rurality affect agriculture and transform the countryside. Exur-banites generally differentiate themselves from farmers "in terms of their affluence and of their close association with work opportunities in the city" (Walker, 2000: 109). For exurbanites, the countryside is a de-sirable amenity grounded in the coupled values of romantic ruralism and anti-urbanism. In the minds of many suburbanites and exurban-ites, rural living comes to signify living in the countryside rather than living from the land.

Figure 4.4: Change in zoning from agriculture to commercial or recreation

In recent years signs announcing an application for a change of land use zoning have become pervasive in some areas of the Moraine. This particular sign in Richmond Hill announces a change of zoning from agriculture to a golf practice facility. Source: the authors, 2004

Exurbanites leave the city in search of the "ideal countryside" based on an Anglo-American countryside idea, hoping to become more closely connected to nature (Bunce, 1994). These newcomers often make the most confident claims to nature and rural lifestyles. They often have the financial means and professional connections to create and protect their idealized rural landscapes. Their relocation in the rural-exurban fringe of the metropolitan area expands the urban interface or the urban commuting field. Such a view corresponds to a post-productivist discourse of rurality that is becoming increasingly dominant on the Oak Ridges Moraine (Williams and Stewart, 1998).

Our study shows that the Oak Ridges Moraine is replete with examples of the post-productivist discourse displacing and colouring other rural discourses. One resident of Richmond Hill (Richmond Hill

Council Public Hearing, 2000: no. 60) expressed it as follows: "A walk through the Moraine provides an escape from the hustle of everyday life as it has miles of walking, hiking and bicycling trails. The area is quite diverse as one moment you are on a dense path through the forest and in the next moment you are in the open surrounded by a hilly terrain. This area is private and allows you to think by yourself or hike with your dog without worrying about traffic. In a word, it's freedom." Although this resident referred to the utilitarian discourse of recreational amenity, the post-productivist discourse is clearly emphasized in words such as *private, think by yourself,* and *freedom*. A mix of the utilitarian and post-productivist discourse of rurality is most frequently captured in the reactions and emotional attachments of residents to the Moraine environment. Yet, paradoxically, residents and visitors to the Moraine emphasized the threat to the agri-"rural character" of the Moraine that they saw as essential to preserve.

Rural character can be understood as a commodity, destroyed by development but reconstituted in the building of amenities. On the Moraine many people spoke of the rural character in such terms, as an emotional tie to "healthy living" and "quality of life." This rural character is based on a romantic ideology of pastoralism and agrarianism, which, with its anti-urbanism and anti-modernism connotations, assumes that protection must shield the countryside from the perceived negative impacts of the city. Yet exurban values shape the agricultural in many ways. The deep roots of the transition from an agri-ruralist to a post-productivist discourse are vividly described in the following "adventure" organized in Durham Region by the Save the Ganaraska Again organization as a fund raiser "to pay off a huge legal bill they rang up fighting to preserve the community" against forestry, aggregate mining, and rural subdivision development: "For just $10, people were invited in August to visit 68 different farms and gardens in the rolling hills of the Ganaraska area. The farming operations range from dairy to goat to trout. Many local artists demonstrated traditional rural crafts, gardeners shared their secrets and equestrians explained how to train horses. And there was plenty of food, fun and old-fashioned hospitality" (Leahy, 1995). Such fund-raisers based on ecotourism or agritourism and their associated spin-off benefits (seminars and workshops) have changed "the way others look at the area." According to a member of Save the Ganaraska Again, "it is not just vacant farmland" (McCrea quoted in ibid.). This is just one of the many cases where agriculture has been transformed into "agritainment" for the urban and suburban visitors interested in fresh produce, pick-your-own activities, and other family-oriented rural attractions.

In many cases newcomers become more passionate defenders of the rural character of the landscape and green spaces than they are of agriculture and agricultural enterprises. As Bourne et al. (2003: 262) argue, the practices of modern agriculture often conflict with ecological conservation even though both agriculture and green space make up the open space character of the countryside. Both the so-called rural and natural landscapes have been appropriated by the amenity agenda. When commenting on the expansion of a road and on the loss of farmlands, one resident showed a seemingly practical and a philosophical understanding of farming in stating, "I can't imagine anything worse for the countryside" and adding, "We have to learn that our farmland is only borrowed and we can't destroy it" (quoted in Taylor, 1991).

Yet the pleasurable and recreational aspect is indelibly stamped on the farming community. For many residents the appeal of the rolling hills of the Moraine had to do less with agri-rurality than with a scenic backdrop for living. One resident felt that rural character was associated with recreation rather than with production since "it was like moving into a cottage area for us" (quoted in O'Reilly, 1999). Another resident pleaded, "Please don't open the door to continued urbanization of the moraine, but rather, strengthen the present rural designation with strong environmental policies that will sustain this landform predominantly as a natural heritage area" (Richmond Hill Council Public Hearing, 2000: no. 81). Agriculture is imagined as serving the amenity and recreational aspirations of exurban residents and tourist visitors rather than serving the traditional family and/or industrial farm. Exurbanites are thus willing to defend their view of rural character even if it might present some tensions with the more traditional rurality experienced by local farmers (Walker, 2000). In contrast, farmers decry the assumption that their farmlands are to be maintained and open to urban visitors for hikes with their dogs on weekends and the resultant destruction of crops. Indeed, many farmers have rallied together in a landowners' rights movement that is protesting government regulations and interventions generally, be they about headwater protection, greenbelt legislation, or expropriations for highway constructions (figure 4.5).

The Moraine of "Others"

The infringement of development threatens the sense of distinctiveness and uniqueness of the Moraine (McElhinny, 2006). Suburbanites and

Figure 4.5: The landowners' rights movement

Landowners, including farmers and other rural residents, are in the forefront of protesting the *Oak Ridges Moraine Conservation Plan* and other provincial legislation that infringes on the use of their lands. Source: the authors, 2011

exurbanites living in the countryside defend the need to curb sprawl in order to protect natural resources and areas of the Moraine. They are alarmed by the rapid transformations of the countryside and the dramatic demographic projections (almost four million in the next twenty-five years in southern Ontario). They also often associate rurality and ruralism with a nostalgic, simpler, "natural" social order of re-settlers of British descent, in contrast with the large immigration characterizing the Toronto region. However, many municipalities in York (for example, Markham, Vaughan, and Richmond Hill) and Peel Region (for example, Mississauga and Brampton) have now joined Toronto in having about half or slightly more than half of their populations being made up of immigrants (Statistics Canada, 2006). Immigration is thus transforming the Greater Toronto Area in terms of diversification of origins (predominantly Asia) and settlement. As a result of Canadian immigration policy's favouring the highly educated and the highly skilled, and the existence of social (immigrant) networks, newcomers are increasingly settling directly in the suburbs of Toronto. Thus, in addition to the tensions between urban and rural visions of the countryside, immigration may reveal another set of tensions between known and unknown cultures (and religions). This tension occurs in spite of the ideals of Canadian multiculturalism, which do not always prevail when rurality is threatened by different aesthetics.

One case of competing rural attachment on the Moraine is manifested in the conflict between a Laotian community and the Albion Caledon Citizens Trust in the construction of a Buddhist temple in Caledon. The latter organization opposed the construction on the basis that the temple was deemed not compatible with rural land use. In 1997 a Buddhist organization, the Wat Lao Veluwanaram (boasting 400 members) purchased a 29-hectare farm (for $385,000) in Caledon, located on the Niagara Escarpment at a short distance from the Oak Ridges Moraine, with the intention of building a temple for their community (Keung, 2001; Wat Lao Veluwanaram of Ontario, 2008). The Niagara Escarpment Commission approved the Wat Lao application, and so did the Region of Peel and the Town of Caledon. However, a group of fifty local residents, many with properties on the Moraine, formed the Albion Caledon Citizens Trust and appealed the decision to the OMB. They were concerned about the proposed size of the temple and the type of events it would harbour, as well as the excessive noise and traffic that would be generated. They also decried the environmental impacts of the temple and its visual interference on the rural character of Caledon landscapes (Finkler, 2001).

As a result of these interventions, issues of site capacity, scheduling of activities, noise and traffic restrictions, and colours and materials of the temple were added to the development conditions. Environmental impact issues were not, however, considered because all authorities agreed that the Wat Lao development complied with all environmental regulations. Yet, the Albion Caledon Citizens Trust continued to fight the temple, "question[ing] the authenticity of the Lao Buddhist group; the erosion of the existing rural culture; and the distinction between cultural and religious gatherings" (McLellan and White, 2005: 244). Representing the Trust, development lawyer Jane Pepino argued that noise and 200–300 people "doesn't seem to be compatible with the land use of a rural area" and that the proposed temple was to be located in an environmentally sensitive area designated by the conservation authorities, the Town of Caledon, and the Region of Peel (quoted in

Keung, 2000). She emphasized, "I cannot name you a site that has the same collision of environmental sensitivity" (quoted in Keung, 2000).

Finkler (2001) notes that in their letters of appeal to the Niagara Escarpment Commission, residents primarily questioned the fragility of the Oak Ridges Moraine headwaters area for the Humber River and the monitoring capacity of the commission. They also argued that wetlands and wildlife habitats, as well as water supply, would be threatened by the temple development. Residents returned to their arguments of noise and traffic and questioned the validity or the absence of specific assessments in the application. They also contended that the noise generated by the Buddhists would prevent them from enjoying their own lifestyle, that debris on temple land would ruin their views, and that directional and No Parking signs would spoil the rural countryside's aesthetics. Residents also emphasized the fact that the members of the temple did not live in Caledon but were drawn from across the Greater Toronto Area and that the temple would not serve the immediate community (ibid.). A resident suggested that the Laotians' difference and different language made local people nervous. Not only did the claims of residents show their attachments to place, but they also demonstrated a superior social position to other and future populations of the Moraine (McElhinny, 2006). As McLellan and White suggest (2005: 242), "the establishment of Wat Lao Veluwanaram not only reflects the struggles of a refugee community to recreate a minority religious tradition, but also the concerns of the residents who opposed the temple and the ineffectiveness of newspapers, town staff, and government policy to enhance the dialogue between the two communities. In this particular situation, multiculturalism was not a portal to relational engagement; rather, environmental concerns masked underlying anti-multicultural agendas."

Hoping to solve the conflict, the Albion Caledon Citizens Trust eventually offered the Laotian group $400,000 for the land in the hopes of giving it to a public conservation agency (Keung, 2000). However, the Laotian group was by now emotionally and financially tied to the site. In 2001, Wat Lao Veluwanaram was given permission to construct the temple provided it met thirty-one extra conditions, ranging from the prohibition of more than three vehicles in the visitor parking lot and the storage of buses on the property, to the required planting of a cedar hedge in order to minimize the visibility of the temple from the roadway (McLellan and White, 2005). The Wat Lao Veluwanaram temple was built in 2004 despite all the issues of cultural and ecological sensitivity raised over a period of five years (figure 4.6). The Buddhists

Figure 4.6: Wat Lao Veluwanaram of Ontario in the Town of Caledon

The Oak Ridges Moraine largely constitutes a preserve for white residents of British origin. A couple of Buddhist retreats in proximity to the Moraine caused vocal protests by nearby residents. Source: the authors, 2011

simply stated, "All we want is a peaceful environment for our religious worship. We want to be a good neighbor. We are not here to create troubles" (quoted in ibid.).

A councillor for the Town of Caledon countered by saying that their town was a refuge and that people moved there specifically to get away from development, referring particularly to the Wat Lao temple, and therefore did not want any kind of changes to their environment. Yet Mary Wiens (2001) noted that with its 464.5 square metres the temple was in fact smaller than some of the houses in the area. It appeared "that classism and ethnocentrism play at least a part in the vehement opposition to the Buddhist development" (Finkler, 2001: 13). The Wat Lao temple was not the only one to experience a difficult insertion into the social and environmental fabric of Caledon. In 1988, Soka Gakkai International (SGI), a Buddhist group following the teachings of Nichiren monks, bought 54.2 hectares in Caledon and faced similar opposition before SGI-Canada's Caledon Centre for Culture and Education opened its doors in 1996.

For exurban residents, farmers, or Buddhist worshippers speaking about rural character on the Moraine, what is at stake is not only open spaces, ecologically sensitive areas, plant and wildlife species, and agricultural lands but also the presence of all natural and cultural elements in familiar and naturalized landscapes. Rural landscapes are invested with moral and ethical values that translate desires to protect nature, local history, new futures, and ways of life – and thus the attachment and appreciation of landscapes affirms old and new moral and ethical values.

In the case of the Wat Lao temple, Emmanuel Levinas' differentiation of otherness as "the other-that-is-like-me, and the entirely other," might be more appropriate in capturing the cultural differences between the Laotian Buddhists and the local residents (quoted in Howitt, 2002). This tension shows that landscapes are far from neutral; they are "produced, lived, and represented space constructed out of struggle, compromises and temporarily settled relations of competing and cooperating social actors" (Mitchell, 1994: 10). While the defence of the rural character of the Moraine may show a deep attachment to place and to the ecologies of place, it is also a process that is open to interpretation and contestation along the lines of class, race, and culture.

Conclusion

During the battles over the Oak Ridges Moraine, residents presented themselves as stewards by referencing first-hand the changes over time in the fields, hills, valleys, lakes, rivers, and forests where they lived. They insisted that they had an emotional below- and above-ground attachment to the Moraine ecosystems that extended beyond self-interest and the desire to preserve their quality of life. They used familiar imagery or everyday experiences to elucidate complex ecological processes and to communicate their attachments and desires to protect the environment. They produced or reproduced discourses of urgency, fragility, and uniqueness that legitimized such desires – often understanding *home* and *nature* as metonyms. They challenged development by using the language and concepts derived from ecosystems and watershed planning, once reserved to professionals and experts.

Residents' expression of an attachment to and defence of place was made more evident in relation to the conservation of the Moraine's rural character. The attachment to "rural character" and utilitarian and agri-ruralist traditions was typically subsumed and subordinated to an exurban and post-productivist discourse. In their desires to protect the remaining "pristine" nature, residents clung to the idea of an "unspoilt" rurality not exposed to the tensions between natural settings and rural activities. The so-called rural character was not so much rural as it was ruralized. Residents' defence of the rural character of the Moraine showed, however, the duplicitous nature of environmental conservation. A profound attachment to streams, forests, and vistas was an unnamed defence of place and a politics of exclusion of newcomers. A closer look at the ecological discourse can thus show a self-legitimizing "greening" and unequal distribution of environmental goods. From this perspective, ecological concerns may be expressed as an unreciprocated ethic of protection towards non-human species while leaving the social privileges of environmental conservation unexplored.

Chapter Five

Taking a Stand: Preserving Place and Nature on the Moraine

What this is all about is getting an anti-urban sprawl policy in place from the provincial government ... The moraine is the springboard. If we can't stop urban sprawl here, we won't ever be able to stop it.

(Crandall, quoted in McAndrew, 2000: 1)

When one thousand enraged citizens showed up for an evening city council meeting on 12 January 2000 in the town of Richmond Hill, 25 kilometres north of Toronto, it made front-page headlines in Toronto's major daily newspapers (Swainson, 2000a). Citizens demanded a stop to the rezoning proposals that would convert 2,800 hectares of agricultural lands and green space on the Oak Ridges Moraine into 17,000 new housing units. "Save, Don't Pave, the Oak Ridges Moraine" became the rallying cry for what the media described as a "landmark battle" between Richmond Hill Council, homeowner groups, and environmentalists (figure 5.1). The flooding of a local council meeting with homeowners who challenged further development was noteworthy because it occurred in a fast-growing suburban community that still had rural remnants – a community in which protest politics and resistance to local authorities were virtually unknown. Homeowner groups formed in response to direct threats to local kettle lakes and forests from sprawl development, new roads, golf courses, and related urban amenities. Environmental groups joined homeowners in their protests. They included Earthroots, best known for its direct action campaigns to stop clearcuts in Temagami; Save the Rouge Valley System, a group focused on the creation of a national park on the eastern edge of the Greater Toronto Area; and the Canadian Environmental Defence Fund

Figure 5.1: Protests at Richmond Hill

Suburban municipal councils are rarely the site of public protests by home-owners.The support by municipal councillors and planners in Richmond Hill for development incited local residents to organize opposition. In this scene from a public meeting of Richmond Hill Council, residents protested the building of housing subdivisions in the township. These actions and protests became a flashpoint for citizen mobilization across the Moraine and played a prominent role in triggering the Oak Ridges Moraine Conservation legislation. Source: *Toronto Star*, 13 January 2001: A1; Toronto Star and GetStock.com

(Environmental Defence Canada since 2002), a national legal defence organization. Local groups allied themselves with Save the Oak Ridges Moraine, which had formed a pan-Moraine coalition that included rural, homeowner, stewardship, and environmental groups.

This chapter examines the convergence of homeowners, environmental organizations, and rural activists that was only the latest manifestation of a long line of struggles on the Oak Ridges Moraine over the spread of urbanization, particularly the uses of land and participation in environmental and land use policy. Ongoing contention included rural challenges to resource extraction, tree cutting, and loss of farmland, as well as exurban mobilizations to contest the despoliation of sensitive natural areas, urban development, and the extension of urban sprawl. These movements brought together urban, exurban, and rural interests that focused on preserving specific features of a landscape at a regional scale, rather than fighting battles site by site. They accomplished this alliance by mobilizing around identification with the Moraine as an idea and a place and by gaining wider public support that engaged not only people with direct interests in the Moraine but also people throughout the region, including Toronto, and beyond. Struggles over the Moraine placed in bold relief the contestations over the constructions of nature and growth in the region and highlighted environmental claims over land use change and sprawl. As local battles to preserve existing land uses and natural features proved increasingly futile, wider political campaigns were organized to secure provincial legislation to protect the Moraine.

In this chapter we focus on the way in which a range of actors formed alliances, seized opportunities, and developed a repertoire of campaigning strategies. We analyse the way they framed and told changing stories about the Moraine and urban development on the growing edge of Toronto and engaged multiple publics in demanding change. We examine the manner in which the opponents to development of the Moraine emphasized the role of ecological processes in the production of suburban and exurban space. We document the ways in which they used planning to challenge a land use planning system that promotes growth, sprawl, and the destruction of nature. We explore the means by which environmental movement politics engaged in both protest and conventional political actions, and by which social movement groups developed a dynamic relationship with the state, particularly the provincial government to gain an influential role in land use and environmental policymaking in the exurban region north of Toronto.

A Convergence of Movements, a Plurality of Environmentalisms

Battles over land use and environmental policy on the Moraine gained substantial media and public attention from the late 1980s until the passage by the provincial government of the *Oak Ridges Moraine Conservation Act* in 2001. While these campaigns received a great deal of attention in Ontario, they are not unique to Ontario. Environmentalist challenges have become common in campaigns against development in rapidly urbanizing areas of the United States and Canada. In the United States, starting in the late 1950s and into the 1960s and 1970s,

Adam Rome argues that the rise and timing of environmentalism was rooted in opposition to suburban development during the period that suburban sprawl was identified as a critical issue threatening watersheds and the ecological balance (Rome, 2001; Hays, 1987). Rome describes the mobilization of environmentalism to challenge development as the "urbanization of conservation," when ecological ideas began to play a part in the critiques of suburban development and in calls for the preservation of open space to protect an ecological balance (2001: 9). Environmentalists and homeowners have often worked together. For instance, in the San Francisco Bay area of California, as Richard Walker (2007) documents, every building cycle generated a new outburst of growth-control activism that triggered local campaigns to control sprawl through land conservation measures. Attempts to manage sprawl and to conserve nature have also spawned countermovements of defenders of private property rights, particularly in the United States (McCarthy, 1998; Flint, 2006) but also in parts of the Toronto region; the Ontario Landowners Association has been active in eastern parts of the Oak Ridges Moraine.

Rural movements to preserve a way of life have also been on the upswing. As rural areas and small towns have been engulfed by developments for second homes or urban in-migrants (Walker, 2003; Duncan and Duncan, 2004), resistance to further development has often been framed by opponents as protecting the environment and defending the rural way of life (Woods, 2003a, 2003b). Writing primarily about the United Kingdom, Michael Woods notes that since the late 1980s there has been an upscaling and integration of rural protests. In contestations over the spread of urbanization, new alliances have been formed among homeowners and environmental and conservation movements around issues that are seen to threaten the rural lifestyle, such as road building, traffic, noise, pollution, and wind farms. Woods (2003b: 309) argues that "in each case a central motivating force is either the defence of the 'rural' (or the 'rural economy,' 'rural landscape' or 'rural way of life') against external threat, or conflict over the meaning, use and regulation of rural space."

Environmental movements have turned their attention and their resources to locality-based struggles that, on the face of it, seem to be focused more on urban and housing issues than on conventionally framed environmental concerns such as climate change, air quality, forests, or water. Environmental activism takes diverse forms and operates on a range of scales. As outlined by Manuel Castells's (1997) typology of environmental movements, some environmental groups focus broadly on "saving the planet" while others emphasize nature conservation on various scales. Stewardship groups often focus on the defence of nature in particular places, while public interest groups bring together diverse stakeholders and support legal challenges or provide expertise to local groups and link them to other organizations. Table 5.1 shows how this typology is reflected in the range of environmental groups and organizations that became involved in the campaigns to preserve the Oak Ridges Moraine.

Campaigns to save the Moraine brought together a spectrum of environmental groups operating on various scales, including prominent nature conservation groups comprising local and provincial naturalist groups, land trusts, and conservation authorities. Global save-the-planet environmental organizations, national representatives of international organizations, and national and international public interest groups specializing in legal challenges or in wider policy issues also spoke for the Moraine, though less frequently and in different voices across time. An organization like Earthroots presented itself as engaged in more radical restoration initiatives, while public interest and advocacy groups, such as Environmental Defence Canada, lent their legal expertise to the Moraine campaigns.

Most prominent and numerically dominant were the homeowners associations and a large array of stewardship organizations that tended to focus on the defence of their own space in trying to protect specific rivers, watersheds, kettle lakes, and river valleys from development. The emphasis on defence of own space is rooted in local identities and local democracy issues. Groups often demanded that local government and the province regulate development by using state regulatory powers through the planning system. Castells (1997) notes that grassroots environmental, locality-based, stewardship groups that are focused on the protection of natural features, such as wetlands or wildlife habitats, are one of the fastest-growing types of environmental activism. Labelling this phenomenon an "environmental localism" that often challenges technical and economic interests on behalf of actual use by actual people, Castells notes that these movements assert "control over space, the assertion of place as a source of meaning, and the emphasis on local government" (ibid.: 124).

The Moraine campaigns also attracted the support and advocacy of special-purpose bodies that included state and privately funded organizations with government-appointed representatives from a range of

Table 5.1 Emphasis of the environmental organizations engaged in Moraine campaigns

Types of environmental preservation (based on Castells, 1997)	Environmental organizations involved in Moraine campaigns (partial list)
Nature conservation	Conservation Authorities Moraine Coalition
	Durham Land Stewardship Council
	Durham Region Field Naturalists
	Federation of Ontario Naturalists
	Nature Conservancy of Canada
	Oak Ridges Moraine Foundation
	Oak Ridges Moraine Land Trust
	Oak Ridges Trail Association
	Ontario Land Trust Alliance
	Pickering Naturalists
	Public Spaces
	Richmond Hill Naturalists
	Rouge Valley Naturalists
	Sierra Club – Peel Region
	Sierra Club – Toronto Chapter
	Toronto and Region Conservation Authority
	Wildlands League
Defence of own space	Ajax Citizens for the Environment
	Caledon Coalition of Concerned Citizens
	Caledon Countryside Alliance
	Citizens' Alliance of Uxbridge
	Citizens for Carruthers Creek
	Concerned Citizens of King Township
	Credit River Alliance
	Don Watershed Council
	Durham Environmental Network
	East Rouge Greenway Association
	Friends of the Rouge Watershed
	Jefferson Forest Residents Association
	Kettle Lakes Coalition
	King City Preserve the Village
	King Environmental Group
	Peel Environmental Network
	Protect the Ridges
	Rouge-Duffins Green Space Coalition
	Save the Ganaraska Again (SAGA)
	Save the Oak Ridges Moraine (STORM)
	Save the Rouge Valley System (SRVS)
	Uxbridge Watershed Committee
Radical restoration	Earthroots
	Niagara Escarpment, Oak Ridges Moraine, Algonquin to Adirondack Heritage Project (NOAH)/A2A

(continued)

Table 5.1 (*continued*)

Types of environmental preservation (based on Castells, 1997)	Environmental organizations involved in Moraine campaigns (partial list)
"Save the planet"	Nature Conservancy Sierra Club World Wildlife Fund
Public interest and advocacy	Canadian Environmental Law Association Environmental Defence Canada Great Lakes Innovation Committee (GLIC) Great Lakes United Sierra Legal Defence Fund

Source: the authors, 2004

interest groups, including environmental groups, state representatives, development agents, and resources users. At first glance, this convergence of advocacy groups and movements seems to bring together unlikely allies: homeowners and environmentalists; defence-of-place advocates and nature conservation movements operating on different scales; rural residents; and urbanites. However, these new networks follow the patterns seen in other places. Alliances were not forged in a moment; connections developed over decades as battles challenging development were fought in specific places across the Moraine. The new element was the convergence of separate Moraine campaigns into a region-wide movement that engaged a diverse range of political actors and strategies.

Phases of Contention on the Oak Ridges Moraine

On the Oak Ridges Moraine the relative importance of citizen activism has changed over time, with some groups dominant in the early phases, others in mid-term, and still others more recently. The political opportunities and strategic frames used by groups in promoting their causes have also changed in time and space. Social movements do not exist or take action independently of timing and context. In explaining the *when* of social movement formation and activism (why now and not other times?), the concept of political opportunity structure addresses the opening up of access to power, the shifting alignments, the availability of influential allies, and the ways in which "the policy and institutional environment channels collective action around particular issues and with [specific] consequences" (Tarrow, 1996: 42).

Collective action frames are sets of beliefs and meanings that both inspire and legitimate social movement campaigns (Snow and Benford, 1992), organize discourse, and direct action (Tarrow, 1998). Throughout the Moraine struggles, the focus on land use change, the advocacy of large ecosystem plans, the appeal to protect endangered species and habitats, and sometimes the bioregionally-based conceptions of nature (Gilbert, Sandberg, and Wekerle, 2009) have been part of the framing of issues and the discursive strategies of most groups and have also filtered in and out of media coverage and public discourse. Various and shifting conceptions of the Moraine have a history that expresses itself in many different ways, both as ideas in lobby and policy statements and as material practices and interventions on the ground.

We identify three periods of citizen engagement in the Oak Ridges Moraine campaigns. The first phase involved contention over relatively isolated land use issues across the Moraine, where residents and activists acquired and used the tools of planning to fight development proposals. A second phase was characterized by the creation of a broad-based coalition across the Moraine that appealed to wider nature and ecological concerns, with the goal of putting into place a broader set of land use restrictions on the Moraine. Finally, there was a period during which the combined efforts of the state, the private sector, residents, and environmentalist interests sought to protect the Moraine as a significant landform in the Greater Toronto Area through provincial legislation. We contend that these three phases in the cycle of contention over the land uses allowed on the Moraine contain both remarkable change and compromise. Over several decades, environmental and resident groups resorted to different forms of activism and strategies. While seemingly acting independently of the state and forcing the provincial government's hands, in fact, citizen groups operated within a set legal and planning framework that had wide-ranging impacts both on the Moraine and in the wider region.

Early Beginnings: Land-Based Activism on the Oak Ridges Moraine, 1980s–1998

In the 1980s, development proposals to change land uses at diverse sites on the Moraine, and associated required public consultation exercises

and government reports, opened up political opportunities for organized challenges to development. In 1989 the Liberal provincial government (1987–90) established a formal process of citizen consultation,
commissioned scientific and planning reports, and proposed an ecosystem approach to planning for the Moraine as a whole. The New Democratic Party government (1990–95) that followed continued these efforts
with a series of reports, investigations, and hearings on the protection
of the Moraine. These developments and discussions stopped abruptly
when, in 1995, a Conservative provincial government was elected that
immediately set about relaxing the planning and environmental controls. Yet there was not only change but continuity when the Conservatives took over the reins of power.

It was in this context of promises and disappointments that several
distinct local struggles started on the Oak Ridges Moraine. The Save
the Oak Ridges Moraine Coalition was formed in 1989. In attendance at
the first meeting were members from the Concerned Citizens of King
Township, Save the Oak Ridges Moraine Peterborough, Save the Rouge
Valley System, Save the Ganaraska Again, the Gormley Ratepayers, the
Lake Wilcox Ratepayers, the Musselman's Lake Ratepayers, some residents from the Town of Aurora, and a member of the Town of Caledon
Municipal Council (Alexander, 1994: 50). The coalition eventually comprised twenty-five member groups from across the Moraine and was
affiliated with many other groups off and on the Moraine. In its early
stage, however, the organization was more of a loosely connected coalition where smaller, localized struggles mattered most (as illustrated by
the place-based names associated with many member organizations),
while at the same time these groups appealed to the larger project of
the conservation of the Oak Ridges Moraine. On the whole, they resembled the defence-of-place environmentalism identified by Castells
(1997). Activists suggested that, prior to 1999, people initially got involved in the Moraine battles to protect their own backyard. A variety
of rural and environmental battles were fought at the time, including
opposition to the development of golf courses and retirement communities, huge commercial water takings, paper sludge applications, bio-
solid applications, garbage dumps, aggregate pits, and expansions of
the urban settlement areas.

A type of land-based activism guided the opposition and struggles
against development proposals. The common strategy was to acquire
the expertise and knowledge of the planning system that guided land
use. As we noted in chapter 3, one of the founding members of Save the

Oak Ridges Moraine Coalition refers to its formation and evolution as a process of "planning as learning" where the members learned about the institutional structure, function, and politics of the planning system in order to fight specific development projects (Alexander, 1994). Debbe Crandall, Executive Director of Save the Oak Ridges Moraine Coalition (2004), claimed that she never saw herself as an environmental activist but as a place- or land-based activist, using the tools of planning to pursue her goals. Setting herself apart from the nature conservation movement in Ontario, Crandall (ibid.) explains the way in which land use and planning issues gradually evolved into land-based activism:

> The early days of STORM were spent learning about planning and also in helping other groups develop the capacity. STORM was, in our neck of the woods, the leader in making this thing called land use planning activism. Up to that point, Pollution Probe was quite active about point source contamination, whether it was air or water. And there were groups like the Federation of Ontario Naturalists and the naturalist clubs that were looking at conservation issues ... But I don't think when we were in the climate of 1989–90, that there were these things called land-use planning activists ... I coined it for me because I didn't want to call myself an environmentalist because that doesn't speak about what we do. Our area of influence is when ... land use changes from one to another – that's the point the big change takes place.

The Federation of Ontario Naturalists also became engaged in planning issues to challenge sprawl and to further the idea of planning for complete ecosystems rather than focusing on development applications for each parcel of land. According to Ric Symmes (2007), former director of the federation:

> Linda Pim [a staff member] and others were seeing that nature could not be effectively protected in tiny islands. There had to be a larger solution. Also, at the OMB, 70% of all natural heritage cases were decided in favour of the developers ... so nature almost always lost on individual cases. There needed to be a new set of policies. In fact, the government of the day needed to be persuaded to re-engage in land use policy. The provincial natural heritage groups could see the need for a protection system on an ecosystem basis, and sprawl was clearly a cause of habitat fragmentation, excessive road building, forest cutting, etc. So we had to fight sprawl and planning that supported or allowed this result.

Across the Moraine local groups in defence of own place found that they were coming up against the walls of the planning system and its role in maintaining undesirable (or in changing desirable) land use patterns on the Moraine. Debbe Crandall (2004) outlines the connections that started to be made in the late 1980s and early 1990s: "We started to see a lot of changes on the south slopes of the Moraine. That is how a lot of people were mobilized at the very beginning ... In looking to educating themselves about what an Official Plan was ... a number of people ... realized that ... they didn't even know what planning meant back then. People weren't conversant in the language of planning."

In the Town of Caledon residents' actions were triggered by an attempt of the local council to transform a no-development zone into a development zone. Crandall (ibid.) recounts: "Local Council ... decided to turn this land into land re-designated from agricultural to urban ... I was asked to be the spokesperson for all the local groups, unincorporated, just a bunch of people who sat in people's kitchens and living rooms planning this out. We went to make a delegation to a public meeting." Afterwards Crandall was invited to meet the mayor and the planning department. In the end, Caledon Council bought into the "no development" condition, and the area became part of the so-called Palgrave Estates development where large lots measuring 0.8 hectares (two acres) or more are attuned to the capacity of the local soils to accommodate the effluence of septic tanks (Crandall, 2004).

Save the Ganaraska Again (SAGA) was another rural group that formed in 1988 and incorporated in 1989. Rural residents were concerned about what they viewed as bad planning in a very small, sensitive area in the headwaters of the Ganaraska River, far from any other settlement. This area had been deforested through insensitive agricultural practices and by the 1940s was a desert of sand dunes and a flooding river. Save the Ganaraska Again formed in reaction to over 405 hectares being landbanked by developers who wanted to avoid any future conservation measures. With almost no environmental data against which to measure or predict what this change could mean, and concerned about the lack of planning controls, Save the Ganaraska Again wanted to participate in the land use planning process. However, after Save the Ganaraska Again found that environmental considerations were lacking in the *Ontario Planning Act* of 1983, it applied for designation of the headwaters area under the *Environmental Assessment Act*. Instead of granting a designation, the Environmental Assessment Advisory Committee held a hearing on the planning and approvals process in the Ganaraska headwaters area. Their report was damning of the planning process in Ontario, was widely circulated for comment, received unprecedented public support for its recommendations, and influenced subsequent thinking in environmental management in the province.

In 1994 Save the Ganaraska Again's 334 members were drawn from two large groups in Durham Region and Northumberland County. One member describes the way in which the organization had had "successful input into the reviews of the Durham regional official plan and the municipality of Clarington official plan. We've twice fought development applications at the OMB, one of which was a test of the Oak Ridges Moraine implementation guidelines. When it comes to planning, we've been there, done that" (Guselle, 1996).

King City Preserve the Village was started in 1994 to challenge a pro-growth planning process and preserve the heritage and environment of the rural community, which is entirely on the Moraine. They engaged in planning exercises, hired their own planner, and participated in hearings. Jane Underhill (2005), founder of the organization and municipal councillor, noted: "We are the last rural town in the Greater Toronto Area ... There were smaller losses and bigger losses: frogs, turtles, habitats. When we destroy their habitat we destroy our own through the juggernaut of sprawl. Citizens are environmental stewards in the Greater Toronto bioregion. We fight environmental degradation and the compromise of the quality of life. We are the living witness to the ongoing threats to the environment from suburban sprawl."

King Environmental Groups was formed to challenge a community plan that included infrastructure to increase by 140 per cent the population of the King City headwaters community. Out of a population of five thousand, seven hundred residents joined the group to preserve the heritage and the environment of the rural community. Opposition focused on proposals to connect King City to the York-Durham sewer system, dubbed the "Big Pipe," which would replace household septic systems with a massive sewer pipe system to carry sewage to a central treatment plant in the Town of Pickering on Lake Ontario. Installing sewers would open up large swathes of land to housing and commercial development. The extension of the Big Pipe to King City and other places on the Oak Ridges Moraine, including the City of Markham, has created flashpoints in the struggle to conserve the Moraine (McMahon, 2003; Macaraig and Sandberg, 2009). These struggles have helped to educate and teach environmentalists about both local and wider struggles, though in the end they failed to stop the extension. (We will return to some of the reasons behind these failures in chapter 6.)

Another prominent protest occurred in the City of Vaughan over the continued existence of the massive Keele Valley landfill site that had been established in 1983 on the Oak Ridges Moraine and received a significant proportion of the Greater Toronto Area's garbage (Eyles et al., 1992). The protest against the dump site is illustrative of some of the continuities in environmental policy despite changes in the party affiliation of various provincial governments. In the 1990 provincial election all political parties made allusions to the pending closure of the landfill site. In contrast to other conservation measures related to the Oak Ridges Moraine, which were considered progressive, the New Democratic Party government, once in power, presented emergency plans to expand the Keele Valley site.

Vaughan Committee of Associations to Restore Environmental Safety (CARES), claiming to represent all of Vaughan's 100,000 residents, made appeals for both the protection of the Moraine and their more immediate concerns for the closure of the landfill site (Dexter, 1989). CARES and its supporters were able to point their fingers at the City of Toronto and challenged Toronto's often superior environmental stance towards the surrounding municipalities. Yet the provincial government insisted that the sheer amount of garbage generated necessitated extension of the life of the landfill. In order to cope with the garbage problem, the New Democratic Party government appointed the Interim Waste Authority to oversee the process of siting and building landfill sites for each of the five regional municipalities of the Greater Toronto Area. This effort proved widely unpopular. Although all sites identified by the Authority were off the Moraine, four were very close "to the 1988 boundaries of the Moraine, an almost sacred upland" (Walker, 1995: 25). As Walker has shown, the Interim Waste Authority contributed greatly to the unpopularity of the New Democratic Party government and to its defeat in the 1995 election.

The late 1990s was a period of transition. Local land use conflicts were fought on a number of issues in a variety of places, not all of them covered here. Save the Oak Ridges Moraine Coalition was increasingly taking on the role as a coordinating group for opposition to development across the Moraine, a role that was catalysed by the gutting of environmental regulations and planning controls under the Conservative government of Mike Harris. Crandall (2004) points to the contradictions that set the stage for heightened land use activism and the passing of Oak Ridges Moraine legislation in 2001. Premier Mike Harris, she said half-jokingly, "was very good for the environmental movement because, while he stripped people of financial resources, he is partly responsible for this phenomenal network that actually exists. Because it was a common enemy, we knew who the enemy was and that was Mike Harris and his government. And so we developed a whole bunch of different skills – fundraising, networking." The Harris government's aggressive retrenchment of planning controls and its cutbacks in public spending in the beginning years of its mandate heightened and invigorated the struggle over the Oak Ridges Moraine by creating an environment of confrontation over urban growth that brought together new allies.

Confrontation and Consolidation: Unlikely Allies in Richmond Hill, 1998–2002

Certain events can be pivotal, providing dynamic opportunities that either propel or permit social movements to forge novel and innovative political strategies and plans in an environment of state change (Tarrow, 1996: 41). As a result of the Progressive Conservative government's relaxation of planning controls in 1995, municipalities were flooded with development applications to build tens of thousands of new homes, as well as golf courses and other projects on greenfield sites across the Moraine, including towns such as Caledon, King City, Richmond Hill, and Vaughan. Resident associations and smaller rural and environmentalist groups were prompted to act collectively rather than individually to lead a number of campaigns to "save and not pave" the Moraine. Larger environmentalist groups, many of them located in Toronto and having a regional and national mandate, were also concerned about wider environmental impacts. Besides supporting local struggles to preserve nature on the Moraine, they also saw opportunities to gain media attention and public support to grow their organizations and fund-raising base by becoming active in the Moraine campaigns.

Groups across the Moraine were mobilized by a political scandal in October 1999 when Steve Gilchrist, Minister for Municipal Affairs and Housing, was removed from his Cabinet position and replaced with Tony Clement. Gilchrist had suggested that development might be curtailed and was accused by developers of inappropriate behaviour with respect to some development applications on the Moraine (Edey, Seasons, and Whitelaw, 2006). The attendant debates in the legislature and the media presented activists with an opportunity to reframe development on the Moraine in environmental terms (ibid.) and to challenge planning as usual.

By far the most widely publicized examples of naturalist and ratepayer groups on the Moraine turning their attention to planning and development issues occurred in the town of Richmond Hill, a town along the Yonge Street corridor that is located at the middle and narrowest point of the Moraine (Wekerle, 2001; Gilbert, Wekerle, and Sandberg, 2005; Hanna and Webber, 2010; Edey, Seasons, and Whitelaw, 2006; Wekerle, Sandberg, and Gilbert 2009a; Abbruzzese and Wekerle, 2011). Gormley residents were fighting a local recycling outfit that was giving off odours, and Lake Wilcox and Jefferson Forest residents were protesting a series of official plan amendments to allow residential development in sensitive natural areas. Along with the proposed subdivision expansions in Richmond Hill, the provincial Ministry of Environment and Energy and York Region approved the construction of the Bayview Avenue extension through the Moraine to allow improved connectivity for past and future subdivision residents in the northern parts of the town.

The events in Richmond Hill, though initially similar to other struggles in defence of place, became pivotal in focusing activists' campaigns and the public's attention. Challenges to development proposals in Richmond Hill triggered a qualitative change in campaigns for the protection of the Moraine, as well as coming to characterize and shape the conservation agenda of the whole Oak Ridges Moraine for the future. Instead of fighting these battles site by site, the Moraine activists crafted a Moraine-wide and regional campaign that sought to instil concerns for the fate of the whole Moraine, not just its parts, and to engage the commitment of activists from across the Moraine and from Toronto. Their success in developing a Moraine identity across a 160 kilometre wide geological feature put the Moraine and resistance to its development on the political map (Wekerle, Sandberg, and Gilbert 2009b; Wekerle and Abbruzzese, 2009).

Activists used a range of strategies and tactics, including direct action, judicial challenges, and more conventional lobbying (see table 5.2 for a summary of strategies in the Moraine campaigns). The cumulative impact of the almost-daily protest activity drew the media's and the public's attention. On 15 November 1999, environmental groups arranged a "funeral for the Moraine" to publicize the cutting of the Jefferson Forest to make way for a road extension, and twelve people,

Table 5.2 Social movement strategies to save the Oak Ridges Moraine

Social movement strategies	Actions or organizations (partial list)
Utilize changing political opportunity structure	• Walkerton water crisis • Conservation biologist Reed Noss is sponsored by Save the Rouge Valley System to give expert testimony at OMB hearing • Oak Ridges Moraine Advisory Panel holds public consultation and stakeholder meetings
Engage in "war of words"	• Public consultations on development proposals • Appeals to the OMB • Save the Oak Ridges Moraine Coalition and Save the Rouge Valley System hire scientists and planners • 450 scientists sign petition to save Oak Ridges Moraine • Communication strategies include flyers in Greater Toronto Area newspapers; press releases; ongoing media coverage; websites; and LISTSERVS
Form political alliances	• Ally with progressive municipal politicians across region • City of Toronto Oak Ridges Moraine Committee allocates $1.6 million to OMB fight • City of Toronto Council Subcommittee on the Oak Ridges Moraine, Federation of Ontario Naturalists, and Save the Oak Ridges Moraine Coalition submit Environmental Bill of Rights challenge • Provincial Liberal and New Democratic environment critics focus on Moraine • Provincial New Democratic Party and Liberal Party governments are in power • Metro Toronto and Region Conservation Authority takes position on preserving the Moraine
Institutionalize change	• *Oak Ridges Moraine Protection Act*, 2001 (Bill 55), freezes development for six months • Federal government donates land for Rouge Valley Park • Appointments are made to Oak Ridges Moraine Advisory Committee • Bill 22, *Oak Ridges Moraine Conservation Act and Plan*, is introduced • Land is swapped for Seaton lands • Municipal official plans must comply with Oak Ridges Moraine Conservation Plan • Oak Ridges Moraine Legacy Trust and Foundation are created

(continued)

Table 5.2 (*continued*)

Social movement strategies	Actions or organizations (partial list)
Mobilize civil society	• Save the Oak Ridges Moraine Coalition • Save the Rouge Valley System • King Environmental Groups • Federation of Ontario Naturalists • Environmental Defence Canada • Sierra Club • World Wildlife Fund • Nature Conservancy
Engage in oppositional politics	• Blockades are set up to prevent bulldozing trees for Bayview Avenue extension • 1,600 citizens protest at Richmond Hill Council meeting • Protests are made at Ontario legislature • The presentation centre for the new housing that Liberals promised to stop is picketed

Source: the authors, 2004

including local homeowners, were arrested for blockading the bull-dozing of trees in the forest. On 19 November, the OMB started a pre-hearing to consider challenges to the proposals to build two thousand houses around Bond Lake and two thousand around Phillips Lake, both being kettle lakes in Richmond Hill. The Ministry of Natural Resources had identified these lakes as areas with dozens of rare plant and animal species that could be degraded by fertilizers, pesticides, and pollutants from housing developments (Immen, 1999b). The Jefferson Forest Residents Association affiliated with Save the Rouge Valley System, an organization that was not on the Moraine and was focused on preserving the Rouge River as a national park, to gain legal standing at the OMB hearing to examine witnesses and bring in experts for testimony (McMahon, 2000). They were represented by Canadian Environmental Defence Fund, a national organization that provides legal assistance to residents and environmental organizations in high-profile and potentially precedent-setting cases.

On 8 December 1999 the City of Toronto (which had signalled its concern over watershed planning) heard that its bid for standing at the OMB hearing had been rejected on the grounds that it was not located on the Moraine. The City found another way to intervene in the decisions affecting its water supply by allocating $1.6 million to Save the

Rouge Valley System and the Toronto and Region Conservation Authority to oppose housing developments on the Moraine in the towns of Richmond Hill and Uxbridge at the OMB hearing (Rusk, 2000). This funding from the City of Toronto provided the resources for environmental groups to challenge developers with deep pockets, their own local politicians, and the provincial government.

By 1 February 2000 the OMB had before it at least thirty appeals of development plans for more than two thousand new homes on the Oak Ridges Moraine (Immen, 2000a). Of these the applications that generated the most outrage, and therefore the greatest opportunities for environmental activism and media attention, pertained to the Town of Richmond Hill. In the face of the planned Bayview Avenue extension and proposed housing developments a group of environmental and resident groups pooled their efforts. Save the Rouge Valley System, Richmond Hill Naturalists (a local branch of Federation of Ontario Naturalists), Save the Oak Ridges Moraine Coalition, and others organized jointly to call for the protection of what they labelled the narrowest part of the Moraine, a two-kilometre-wide strip in Richmond Hill, represented as the "pinch point" that could split the Moraine in two unconnected parts, thereby threatening the connectivity of the green corridors (as seen in figure 3.3).

As citizens' protests escalated, the developers that had applied to rezone and develop sites on the Moraine became concerned that Richmond Hill Council would delay or stop development. They appealed directly to the OMB when York Region proposed a reduction in the eleven thousand houses proposed to be built on properties east and west of Yonge Street in Richmond Hill (Mallan, 2004). Consequently, the organizing and media campaigns intensified in Richmond Hill, gaining daily coverage in Toronto and regional newspapers in the first months of 2000. The Moraine campaign was also taken directly to ex-urban residents as volunteers delivered sixty-five thousand flyers door to door in the town of Richmond Hill to publicize a 12 January council meeting, which attracted one thousand concerned residents.

Despite the intense show of opposition, Richmond Hill Council voted to move forward with the rezoning plans to approve development on the Moraine. The environmental campaigns were then redoubled. Save the Rouge Valley System organized a "Wilderness, Not Wood Chips, Project," a massive drop of twenty thousand small wood-chip bags to individual homeowners (from the remains of trees cut for the Bayview Avenue extension), including drops to the offices of Richmond Hill councillors. These actions culminated in another council meeting, on 23 February. In a meeting held in a large hotel ballroom sixteen hundred people demanded that council reject the official plan amendment and reverse its decision to build seventeen thousand new homes on the Moraine. Richmond Hill Council responded by voting to suspend its plans to urbanize the Moraine and asked the provincial government to step in and pass legislation to regulate land use on the Moraine.

Activists also tried to utilize existing provincial legislation to challenge development. On 24 March the City of Toronto, the Federation of Ontario Naturalists, and Save the Oak Ridges Moraine Coalition, funded by the Sierra Legal Defence Fund, used the provincial *Environmental Bill of Rights* to challenge existing provincial land use planning laws and policies in order to protect the Moraine. This strategy was unsuccessful. About six hundred people made submissions to the Environmental Registry, of which only sixty were considered relevant to the terms of reference.

On 29 May the formal OMB hearing commenced to consider the developer proposals to build housing around the two kettle lakes in Richmond Hill. The months of testimony by developers' experts and the responses to these positions by environmental groups were covered on an almost daily basis by the major newspapers and other media in Toronto and the region. Environmental groups eagerly awaited their turn to call witnesses. Their first witness was Reed Noss, an internationally known conservation biologist and deep ecologist based in the United States. Noss explained his view that the Oak Ridges Moraine represented the best opportunity to maintain and enhance a life supporting continentally significant system of natural and agricultural areas within the Lower Great Lakes Region. In soliciting Noss, the environmentalists felt that they capitalized on the words of a respected scientist and visionary who inspired local environmentalists and who would likely impress the media and hearing officers at the OMB. However, his testimony was discredited when cross-examination revealed that he had not read some relevant documents. Noss had been closely involved in planning larger ecosystems to preserve the Florida panther. He urged Moraine activists to think beyond the Moraine to consider an even larger scheme to create a green corridor that would connect Algonquin Park to the Appalachian National Scenic Trail, thereby transcending national borders.

The opportunity to call more witnesses on behalf of the environmentalist challengers was denied when the Minister of Municipal Affairs and Housing, Tony Clement, summarily cut off the hearing after the environmentalists had called Noss. On 17 May 2001 the provincial Tory government passed the *Oak Ridges Moraine Protection Act* (Bill 55), temporarily freezing all development on the Moraine for six months while allegedly pursuing a long-term solution.

Place-based movements are easily dismissed as self-interested. However, the protracted and multifaceted Moraine campaigns reveal a more complex dynamic, as ecological concerns intermingled with defence-of-own-place initiatives. Defensive politics based on "not in my backyard" are portrayed as oriented to the protection of economic, cultural, and property assets that maintain class and/or race privilege and utilize the power of the state to exclude unwanted development (Pulido, 1996, 2000; Murdoch and Day, 1998; Purcell, 2001). However, in the dismissal of "most attempts to preserve local autonomy, even for sound ecological reasons, as a conservative defense of positional goods by small special interests" (Luke, 2002: 301), little credence is given to the legitimate claims and concerns of people whose lives and histories have been intermeshed with particular places and landscapes. As Timothy Luke (2002: 301) notes, "these essentially populist expressions of ecological concern also mobilize special claims on behalf of the people living in specific bioregions or at particular sites, because they allegedly possess greater awareness, care, or wisdom about what should be done in these environments to safeguard their ecological integrity."

Environmental Organizations Weigh In

Environmental organizations weighed in as important actors on the Moraine, not just in their own right but also owing to the connections they made with rural organizations and homeowners associations. As table 5.2 illustrates, environmental organizations engaged in a range of strategies. They focused both on the negative impacts of sprawl on the quality of life for humans, and on the destruction of ecosystems. The organizations included a wide range of environmental groups that sought influential allies, from environmental critics in the provincial legislature to councillors in the City of Toronto to politically well-connected and affluent local exurban residents, including former provincial premiers living on or near the Moraine. They drew upon scientific knowledge from regional quasi-autonomous agencies such as the conservation authorities and from sympathetic scientists. By becoming active participants in the policy process, activists sought to institutionalize change, pressuring for the passage of legislation; through participation in various land trusts, they assisted in its implementation.

Residents relied on the expertise of environmental groups like Save the Rouge Valley System, the Federation of Ontario Naturalists, Environmental Defence Canada, and Earthroots to give them information about the scientific arguments for preserving the Moraine, to provide access to previous research, and to advise them on how to interpret the claims of developers and local town planners regarding the potential impacts of development (see Bocking, 2005, for an in-depth analysis of the uses of natural science). They also learned new organizing tactics. One Moraine activist (Marsh 2003) outlines the way in which environmental groups filled an information vacuum left by three levels of government:

> The environmental groups provided information on what is the Moraine and why it is important but also the organization and the structure, and also getting the information out. Without the environmental groups, I don't think we would have gotten involved much because there was no other information coming from anywhere else. It wasn't the Town, and it wasn't the Province or the Region. That credit would have to go to the environmental groups. Save the Rouge, primarily. They were the most vocal … Save the Rouge was sophisticated enough to put their information out to appeal to regular people like us … Save the Rouge [brought] that political bent and [made] it more consumer friendly … There have been other groups that have been active in saving the Moraine forever, who perhaps wouldn't have gotten to us.

Save the Rouge Valley System, although initially a local organization, became a regional player when it gained "standing" at the 2000 OMB hearing related to the development plans in Richmond Hill. The organization was led by Glenn De Baeremaeker, a flamboyant man who had had municipal political experience (as staff to a councillor) and who garnered media attention. He was able to involve the City of Toronto, which began to view the headwaters as the source of its water, too.

Earthroots, founded in 1986 with a mandate to protect the old-growth pine forests in Temagami, translated its experience of delivering a grassroots campaign into work on the Moraine campaigns. As an organization, it focused largely on provincial policy, expanding its mandate in 1991 to other issues, including the protection of wilderness close to urban areas and of wolves in Ontario. Lea Ann Mallett, the director of wilderness conservation campaigns at Earthroots from 1995 to 2000, started and led an Oak Ridges Moraine campaign from 1998 to 2000; thereafter, it was coordinated by Josh Matlow. In 2000, Earthroots was approached by the Jefferson Forest Residents Association for assistance with their protest of Bayview Avenue's extension through the Jefferson Forest. Josh Matlow (2005) remembers it this way: "So they [the residents' association] asked us to come and help with our expertise with respect to peaceful civil disobedience, blockades if need be, government lobbying, methods to get media on a subject. They were a kitchen table organization that knew… what we did and wanted support … We went and supported them and while we supported them we realized [that] this is a huge campaign [and] that we really needed to put our resources in. And then we started working with groups like Save the Rouge, STORM and the Federation of Ontario Naturalists."

For Earthroots, working on the Moraine campaign was also a strategic decision as it attracted new members and gained the support of its approximately four thousand existing members. Matlow (ibid.) adds: "We gained new members … because people in Toronto wanted to see their backyard protected. As a group based in downtown Toronto, working on northern old growth forest issues, we needed to be able to garner Toronto media attention to be able to just build our profile and also work on issues that people in the city care about. So, without a doubt, supporting the Oak Ridges Moraine campaign helped us raise funds that we could spend on all of our campaigns. But at the end of the day, while it was strategic, it also was altruistic in nature as well. We just realized that this was a big issue and we needed to be part of it as an environmental organization."

Another prominent environmental organization was the Federation of Ontario Naturalists (now Ontario Nature) with a membership of thirty thousand across the province. Formed in the 1930s, it is one of the oldest nature protection organizations in Ontario and maintains local branches in many communities. In 2005 the organization was particularly focused on urban sprawl, explicitly taking on planning in its publication *A Smart Future for Ontario*, which was an analysis of urban sprawl and a manual on "how to create greenways and prevent urban sprawl in your communities" (Pim and Ornoy, 2002). The Federation of Ontario Naturalists' strategy focused on the "larger picture." According to former executive director Ric Symmes (2007), the federation concluded that environmental groups needed to move beyond advocacy to engage the Province of Ontario in passing legislation. As Symmes explained, the Federation of Ontario Naturalists' five local clubs on the Moraine were losing on a piecemeal basis, and they called for the federation to justify its existence by developing a regional focus.

> At FON [Federation of Ontario Naturalists] we were convinced that an ecosystem approach was needed to be effective for the natural values. Also, the OMB fights and "hot spots" consumed too much time and money for FON to participate effectively ... a larger picture approach was more suited to our strengths and was far more effective in terms of results for efforts expended ... Environmentalists have often had only pyrrhic victories, e.g. Temagami. It consumes energy and resources with limited results. It is really important that groups protecting natural heritage have strategic tools.
>
> We were going for the structure – to get it in place. Some things could be done by volunteers. Others required legislation. To stop the development industry, we needed an Act and a Plan. We were influenced by the Niagara Escarpment Plan. We wanted a bottom-up plan. We didn't want a technical and top-down driven Plan. It was an opportunity for bottom-up support. The municipalities were concerned with development. If we get everything embedded in the Official Plan, there is a better chance for local plans. This is a key element of the structure.
>
> Small groups struggled with poor tools. We wanted to set an atmosphere that was more effective and provide better policy support – a larger scale thing that was more strategic, not a watershed protected through advocacy, a more comprehensive approach. When the political stars aligned, there was an opportunity on the Moraine after the years of futile efforts and false starts.

Protecting the Moraine drew environmental organizations beyond the Moraine for strategic reasons but also because a piecemeal approach to protecting environmental hot spots was not working. A networked campaign that focused on nature conservation on a larger scale and addressed regional land use policy seemed like a more promising approach. Throughout the lengthy Moraine campaigns, social movement groups mobilizing on the Moraine engaged in a range of strategies. Use of the media and communication strategies was essential in gaining public support. Some groups, such as Earthroots and Save the Rouge Valley System, engaged in oppositional politics that were critical and confrontational and could be relied upon to gain public attention when negotiations with the Province stalled. Others, including Save the Oak Ridges Moraine Coalition and the Federation of Ontario Naturalists, focused on institutionalizing change through negotiating a new policy process and legislation, including participating in interest-based negotiations organized by the Province. Shifting political alignments within the provincial government, and alliances with other levels of government across the region, including the City of Toronto and with the conservation authorities, which created a coalition of authorities with interests in the Moraine, were essential in building support and momentum for change.

Framing the Moraine

The Oak Ridges Moraine became more than an object of conservation. It was invoked to strategically capture the attention of the media, the public, politicians, donors, and potential members. These efforts in framing the Moraine were both a by-product of and produced by the disparate emotional sentiments expressed by residents. Over the course of the intense environmental mobilization from 1998 to 2002, the movements to "save the Moraine" gained visibility, gathered momentum, and changed the way that the public saw the Moraine. They accomplished this transformation by connecting multiple frames into a broader structure of concepts and policies based on ecosystem planning and bioregionalism.

The entry of the larger professional environmental organizations resulted in a more organized, strategic, and complex framing of the Moraine. In an early strategy meeting of the Greater Toronto Area Moraine Committee on 30 November 2000, a group of environmental organizations agreed to strategically focus on multiple frames that included water, transportation, agriculture, infrastructure, planning and sprawl, and political accountability in geographically identified battles. They debated whether the emphasis should be on regional or on technical interests; whether priority should be given to influencing the politicians or influencing the public; and who would put pressure on the politicians. The decision was made to construct an environmental framing that drew on multiple issues and discourses, thereby aiming for continuous media coverage in multiple newspaper articles with changing focuses (Martin, 2004).

Over time, several frames converged. The protection of endangered species, forests, and headwaters became the focus of campaigns by conservation groups with a large membership base, such as the Federation of Ontario Naturalists, and of smaller naturalist groups, but it was also frequently a theme in public presentations by homeowners' associations and rural groups. While resident associations still voiced concerns for protecting their own amenities and quality of life (and implicitly their property values), their public presentations now also raised concerns about the disappearance of aquifers, forest lands, and green space. Through connections with environmental organizations, homeowners' language also began to borrow from the more science-based language of ecosystems and watershed planning.

An initial choice was made to frame the Oak Ridges Moraine in terms of sprawl and the planning changes needed to combat sprawl (Immen, 2000b; Gillespie, 2003a, 2003b). This framing built upon and fed into the ongoing debates in the province on the negative impacts of sprawl and the need for smart growth (Filion, 2003, 2007). The Ontario government under Mike Harris had established Smart Growth panels in different parts of the province, a Central Ontario panel being chaired by Hazel McCallion, the mayor of Mississauga. A Smart Growth secretariat was also established within the provincial bureaucracy. Sprawl and smart growth alternatives were brought to the public's attention by both the *Toronto Star* and the *Globe and Mail*, which published two series on the impacts of sprawl and smart growth best practices elsewhere. According to Debbe Crandall (2003) of Save the Oak Ridges Moraine Coalition, "the Oak Ridges Moraine dispute focused on environmental issues. The selling point was 'urban sprawl.' This concept got people's attention. 'We don't know what will happen if this area is paved.'" Combining the environment and sprawl into one campaign provided a wider base of support by avoiding the charge of "not-in-my-backyard"-ism often levelled at suburban homeowners' associations and by engaging the resources of Toronto-based environmental groups and the City of Toronto itself – organizations that were more concerned with environmental issues than with sprawl.

Water was adopted as an increasingly important frame that linked watersheds, aquifers, and users of water. Both Save the Oak Ridges Moraine Coalition and Save the Rouge Valley System hired scientists to do studies of the impact of development on the Moraine's water resources. Framing the Moraine as the "rain barrel" of the region, environmental groups formulated intensive media campaigns about the aquifers of the Moraine that provided drinking water for 250,000 people and the threats posed by Moraine development applications to the aquifer recharge and the headwaters of major river systems. In an early flyer developed by Earthroots the Moraine was portrayed as a rain barrel (figure 5.2). In the flyer there was a link with the downtown core of Toronto through a background image of the SkyDome (now known as the Rogers Centre) and the CN Tower. In flyers produced by some environmental organizations, questions were raised about who gets the water and how the precious water should be shared. A four-page, full-colour flyer, produced by Save the Oak Ridges Moraine Coalition and the Federation of Ontario Naturalists in 2000, had the heading "The Moraine: Water under Threat" and conjured up the image of the Moraine as "a huge sponge," "a public rain barrel that provides fresh, clean water not only to the rivers but also to wells that supply water to over a quarter of a million people ... Even with expensive technology, developers can't replicate what the Moraine does for free – control storm water runoff and steadily replenish underground aquifers."

A flyer produced by Save the Rouge Valley System in early 2000 combined an emotional appeal that linked the needs of children and future generations (through a picture of a young child wading in a stream) for clean water, and calls for political action at the OMB hearing on developers' proposals to build housing on the Moraine in Richmond Hill:

> Stand up for clean water! Stop the destruction of the Oak Ridges Moraine. Children depend on us for so many things, but one of the most important is water. Right now, the future of this precious resource – and the future of our children – is being decided in a small room filled with lawyers at a place called the Ontario Municipal Board. Most of these lawyers are there, not to represent children, but to speak for developers – developers who want to pave over a crucial section of the Oak Ridges Moraine, located in Richmond Hill. At stake are more than a hundred fragile wetlands, huge underground aquifers, pristine lakes and sensitive headwater streams that feed our rivers. Save the Rouge is at this hearing fighting for future generations, but we can't do it alone. We need your help. For the first time in history, we want thousands of citizens to show up at an OMB hearing and do something very simple: speak for the children. (Save the Rouge Valley System, 2000)

Environmental groups seized the political moment when the news of contaminated drinking water in the town of Walkerton, Ontario, became public on 23 May 2000. This event, in which a bacterial outbreak in contaminated groundwater killed seven people and made another 2,300 ill (Ali, 2004; Prudham, 2004; Oziewicz, 2000), focused the public's

Figure 5.2: The rain barrel of southern Ontario

**Over 100 community groups
and 450 scientists agree...**

The Rain
Barrel of
Southern
Ontario

**SAVE THE
OAK RIDGES MORAINE!**

The Oak Ridges Moraine acts like a rain barrel by collecting
precipitation, storing it in huge aquifers, and feeding the rivers
and streams which provide clean drinking water to millions of
people in the GTA.

Call Premier Mike Harris at 325-1941 to tell him you want this
irreplaceable area protected for its water, wildlife habitat and
natural beauty.

For more information contact **EARTHROOTS** *599-0152 / info@earthroots.org*

"The rain barrel of southern Ontario" constituted a common metaphor in the
defence of the Moraine. In the cartoon the Moraine's significance is symbol-
ized by the size of the barrel in comparison to the city of Toronto. The text
of the cartoon does not mention the fact that most residents of the Greater
Toronto Area rely on lake water for residential and drinking purposes. Source:
Earthroots, 2001

attention on water quality, groundwater, and human health issues. Although Walkerton is not on the Moraine, the scandal drew attention to the Conservative government's downsizing and privatization of environmental monitoring. Moraine activists used the Walkerton tragedy as a wedge issue to attract public and media attention.

While water remained an important theme in the Moraine campaigns, over time a dominant frame became that of ecosystem planning and bioregionalism, with a focus on natural connections, corridors, and watershed protection (Gilbert, Sandberg, and Wekerle, 2009). This was most clearly articulated by groups such as Save the Oak Ridges Moraine, Save the Rouge Valley System, the Federation of Ontario Naturalists, and Earthroots and various place-based stewardship groups. Many of the campaigns by environmental organizations relied on ecocentric narratives that enlarged the boundaries of the community to include water, plants, and animals. The underlying premise is that humans are part of nature, and the environment has an independent value and a right to life. In a full-colour flyer produced by Save the Rouge Valley System and distributed as an insert in the Saturday edition of the *Toronto Star* to almost half a million households in the region, a picture of a helpless fawn is the dominant image of nature preservation on the Moraine (figure 5.3).

The caption reads: "Homeless. Just like you, this baby fawn needs a place to live. Yet very soon, thousands of animals, birds and amphibians will be driven from the only home they've ever known – the Oak Ridges Moraine. As the bulldozers move to make way for houses, factories and gravel pits, these defenseless creatures will literally run, fly or crawl for their lives." This image suggests the interconnection of the fate of human and non-human natures and plays upon readers' identification with baby animals, perhaps through remembrance of childhood exposure to Walt Disney's *Bambi* film.

Running through the newspaper coverage of environmental devastation on the Moraine were themes of the habitat destruction of specific amphibians and animals, preservation of natural heritage for future generations, the security of water quality, and the security of food. An illustration by Barry King (figure 5.4) shows the bulldozer, representing urban sprawl, that threatens sensitive nature and species. The strategic use of emotionally charged images both in environmental publications and in newspapers communicated a powerful subtext of environmental loss and the devastation of the land wrought by urban development.

Figure 5.3: Homeless fawn

J ust like you, this baby fawn needs a place to live. Yet very soon, thousands of animals, birds and amphibians will be driven from the only home they've ever known — the Oak Ridges Moraine. As the bulldozers move in to make way for houses, factories and gravel pits, these defenceless creatures will literally run, fly or crawl for their lives. And then they'll begin a desperate search for a new place to live. At best, some will crowd into habitat that is already occupied by other wildlife. Many will simply die.

Stop the destruction of the Oak Ridges Moraine.

Change the course of history by urging Premier Mike Harris to permanently protect the moraine.

"One last heave, one last massive show of public concern is needed now to preserve the Oak Ridges Moraine."
– David Lewis Stein
Columnist, *Toronto Star*

www.savetherougevalley.com

Call Save the Rouge Valley at (416) 282-9983

In this advertisement, created by Save the Rouge Valley System, which appeared in a weekend edition of the *Toronto* Star that was distributed to more than half a million readers, the homeless fawn is used as a symbol of fighting urban sprawl. Readers are encouraged to link their attachment to home with the fawn's loss of habitat. The ad appeals to "bambi-ism," the common benign and protective sentiment towards deer that is held by urban residents. An alternative view held by wildlife biologists is that the white-tailed deer population on the Oak Ridges Moraine is so healthy that it threatens the forest ecosystems. Many residents consider the deer to be pests that ruin their prized gardens. Source: Ramona Wall and Save the Rouge Valley System, ca. 2001

Figure 5.4: "Save, Don't Pave, the Oak Ridges Moraine"

"Save, Don't Pave, the Oak Ridges Moraine" was a common slogan employed by residents on the Oak Ridges Moraine when they faced the media, courts, and politicians. The bulldozer represents the villain urban sprawl in whose path wildlife and trees are destroyed. Barry King's cartoons have been prominent in the Oak Ridges Moraine battles. His most recent contributions appeared in 2011 when he provided the Oak Ridges Moraine Foundation with five cartoons illustrating various aspects of the urgency to continue the protection of the Moraine. King has personally been involved in a conservation battle concerning a tallgrass prairie and savannah adjacent to his home on the Moraine in Northumberland County. Source: Barry King, Office of Liberal MLA Michael Colle, and Save the Oak Ridges Moraine Coalition, 2001

Environmental organizations also framed and controlled their own media stories through websites and electronic mailing lists that made available images, flyers, and position papers, and by sending out urgent notices of public meetings and protest events. The funding from the City of Toronto in the spring of 2001 allowed the Federation of Ontario Naturalists to run radio advertisements aimed at a wider public. Environmentalists' control of media framing was demonstrated in the way that the stories managed to stay focused on the issues as activists defined them and avoided the more conventional media typecasting of social movements as groups of violent and out of control anti-government protesters. For example, Earthroots chose to illustrate a protest in front of the Ontario legislature with the Raging Grannies (figure 5.5).

A novel tactic was the protest at the opening of a presentation centre for a new suburban housing development, McLeod's Landing, one of the grandparented developments on the Moraine. Although this protest might be construed as challenging home ownership rights, the *Toronto Star* chose a benign photograph of young children hoisting protest signs, ironically juxtaposed to the Grand Opening sign, to accompany its article (figure 5.6). The choice by social movements to utilize multiple and convergent frames and the complicity of mass media reportage pulled together such a diverse group of activists, including state agencies from various levels of government (for example, supportive local governments and conservation authorities), that the resistance to development on the Moraine could be neither easily ignored nor dismissed as self- interest or the work of special interest groups.

Rural and environmental movements often harness the power of media to influence public opinion and pressure government. As Woods (2003a) points out, media have also played the role of grouping diverse issues and giving a sense of unity to rural protests. Media reports highlighting the point that contention was located on the Moraine, rather than identifying only specific sites, served to give visibility and legitimacy to this ecological feature and a common frame to a plethora of local struggles. The role of pro-conservation media coverage, particularly by the *Toronto Star*, in swaying public opinion and applying political pressure is documented by Edey, Seasons, and Whitelaw (2006). Over time the *Star*'s coverage shifted from local site-specific protests about redevelopment to environmental issues and then to broader questions of sprawl and urban growth patterns (ibid.) Even after the

Figure 5.5: Raging Grannies on the Moraine

In their relentless campaign to gain media attention, Oak Ridges Moraine advocates relied heavily on famous people to support their cause. The Raging Grannies, an activist organization of women who dress up in stereotypical old dresses and sing protest songs, protested in front of the Ontario Legislature. The group was formed in Victoria, British Columbia, in 1986–7, but it has since become an international organization. Source: Earthroots, ca. 2001

passage of the *Oak Ridges Moraine Conservation Plan*, the *Toronto Star* continued its coverage of Moraine-related issues, publishing an average of thirteen items per month (ibid.).

Moraine Activists and the State: Institutionalizing the Agenda

Michael Woods (2003a, 2003b) argues that urban and rural space can become blurred as urban activists demand the extension of the scope of state regulation into land management in rural areas, and environmental movements become increasingly engaged in trying to influence land use policy and planning. When social movements require state action

Figure 5.6: Stand-off on the Moraine

A new protest tactic: picketing on the opening day of the presentation centre of a new subdivision on the Oak Ridges Moraine. Children spoke or were pictured in many protest situations in the Moraine battle. Source: *Toronto Star*, 19 October 2003: A1; Tony Bock and GetStock.com

to further their goals, this alters the relationship between the state and specific groups. States respond to social movements in diverse ways: they may embrace movements and seek their support; movements may gain routine access to the state; institutions of the state may even enforce movement policies; or they may shut out social movements.

During the past three decades environmentalist movements have struggled with the dilemma of being oppositional movements that take a confrontational stance towards government in attempting to influence public policy from the outside, and/or being interest groups that are part of a growing complex of environmental management (Schlosberg and Dryzek, 2002). Many follow a dual strategy, as we have seen in our analysis of Moraine activism. Activists worked from the outside to change the terms of political discourse, creating the Moraine as a landscape to be preserved, and disseminating a language borrowed from science that started to pervade the understandings of both ordinary citizens and policymakers, and ultimately they changed environmental and planning practices. The campaigns placed a heavy emphasis on gaining legislative protection for the Moraine lands. Activists helped shape the policy process that resulted in legislation and ensured the establishment of a special-purpose body – a provincially funded foundation, the Oak Ridges Moraine Foundation – to fund continued civil society engagement and monitoring. These processes and structures set precedents for subsequent provincial policy changes in the Toronto region (Wekerle et al., 2007).

Movements develop a relationship with the state because they want systemic change, often through legislation. They want resources from the state, often funding. And they want legitimacy through recognition or representation, thereby showing that they are influencing the state (Amenta and Caren, 2004). Social movements may become part of negotiations, gaining formal recognition and inclusion in policymaking; they may get legislation passed and ensure its enforcement; and they may receive appointments to state positions or representation in legislative offices and bureaucracies.

In the Moraine campaigns, running in parallel to the protests, the Federation of Ontario Naturalists engaged in negotiations that were directed at establishing a process of interest-based negotiation with the goal of achieving legislative change. According to Ric Symmes (2007), former executive director, the front-line combatants in the Richmond Hill and Ontario Municipal Board skirmishes played an important role. "In making the right conditions for success, in 'setting the table' for negotiations, the participants needed to be the more moderate, middle of the road folks to facilitate discussion and build up the discussion process. We had a process for keeping the other groups informed, and they got to comment on the draft solutions, and ultimately helped bring about further improvements in the final proposal to the Minister."

Symmes (ibid.) outlined a new approach to changes in land use policy that drew upon the experiences of the Partnership for Public Lands, culminating in the *Ontario Forest Accord* (based in northern Ontario), in which he and other environmental movement leaders had brought together the forestry industry, provincial government, and environmental groups to culminate in a negotiated settlement. As a result, Symmes observed, "A lot of the same people got together to try to solve the Oak Ridges Moraine problem."

Symmes recounts that a shift in political opportunities created an environment for a new approach to land use planning in the region. The

Conservative government was besieged by people whom it historically considered to be its supporters. The replacement in late 1999 of the Minister of Municipal Affairs and Housing, Steven Gilchrist, after he had offended developers by threatening limits to development, received a lot of media attention critical of the provincial government. The Richmond Hill OMB hearing on applications for development on the Moraine was protracted, expensive, and widely covered by the media. Public opinion was turning against the provincial government when the Tories conducted polls for a by-election and found widespread public discontent with land use planning on the Moraine. The Federation of Ontario Naturalists began discussions with the Minister of Municipal Affairs and Housing, Chris Hodgson (February 2001 to January 2003). Symmes describes him as "a person who wanted to get things done. He wanted to leave a legacy. He wanted to see the Oak Ridges Moraine Trail system maintained. He was ready to tackle a solution." A new process was put in place:

> We proposed interest-based negotiation with the municipalities and the development industry. The developers responded the same as the forestry industry. They said that they wanted clarity, i.e. clear rules, fairness and some certainty. They said they would come and talk. They wanted to be able to develop within the existing urban envelope and no takebacks of the approved 11,000 units that were at one point committed for development. Chris Hodgson (the Minister) made the call on the cutoff. Developers had to have some but not all of the permits. There was a transition period. Tony Clement (the previous minister) had made the mistake of claiming that there had been initial controls. Hodgson cut it off at 4,000 of the 11,000 units. He was trying to avert a huge court case. It (the number of housing units) was higher than we would have liked. (Symmes 2007)

On 28 June 2001 the provincial government appointed an Oak Ridges Moraine advisory panel comprising representatives of developers (Fred de Gasperis of Metrus, Peter Gilkin of Mattamy, and Mario Cortellucci of Cortel Group), politicians (Roger Anderson of Durham Region, Bill Fisch of York Region), academics (James McKellar of York University's Schulich School of Business), environmental groups (Debbe Crandall of Save the Oak Ridges Moraine Coalition, Ric Symmes of the Federation of Ontario Naturalists, Russ Powell of the Oak Ridges Moraine Foundation, and John Riley of the Nature Conservancy of Canada), and the aggregate industry (Dennis Smigelow). This body was given the mandate to hold public consultations and stakeholder group meetings and make recommendations for future land uses on the Moraine. Over the summer months the advisory panel held four public meetings in different locations across the Moraine, each of which attracted several hundred people. Each person was limited to five minutes for comments and presentations. At every location, half a day was allocated for *in camera* meetings with invited stakeholders, who were not publicly named, including developers, aggregate industry representatives, environmental organizations, and resident associations. The public meetings, extensively covered by print and electronic media, provided an opportunity for both ordinary citizens and social movement organizations to publicly make their claims and outline their visions for the future of the Moraine.

From the perspective of Ric Symmes (2007), an advisory panel member, the public participation process focused more on confrontation than did the stakeholder meetings, which emphasized an interest-based negotiation process:

> The town hall meetings attracted position holders, people who want the ideal outcome without regard to other interests; people who play to the grandstand. Not a constructive outcome. People who desire a higher profile, who are not good at problem-solving. They drive parties apart. There is no trust and mutual interest.
>
> We prefer strong, top of the house representatives to try to get a common resolution and draft in place. Then the public can come back in. You can miss things. Expose the draft to the public and you can tweak it up or down for a successful solution. I like it less confrontational.

On 14 August 2001 the Ontario Ministry of Municipal Affairs and Housing (2001b) released the *Share Your Vision* draft recommendations for land use planning on the Moraine and allocated thirty days for public consultation. This process involved further deputations from citizen groups and subsequent changes to the recommendations. The provincial government put together a technical panel to evaluate the recommendations of the Oak Ridges Moraine Advisory Panel and the public comments, coming back with a stronger proposal, which the advisory panel endorsed and recommended.

On 1 November 2001 the Province introduced Bill 122, the draft *Oak Ridges Moraine Conservation Act* and *Oak Ridges Moraine Conservation Plan*, which recommended protection of natural core areas and natural linkage areas of the Moraine, and the establishment of an Oak Ridges Moraine trust and foundation. The Oak Ridges Moraine legislation included provision for a ten-year review (extended to fifteen years). As required by law, there was a thirty-day posting of Bill 122 and the draft land use plan on the Environmental Registry. Over six hundred responses were received from the public.

The Province designed a land swap for the developers of contested sites on sensitive lands in Richmond Hill and Uxbridge (location of the so-called Gan Eden lands, where development had been challenged) for lands in north Pickering on the site of the proposed Seaton community outside the Moraine, in compensation for land frozen from development. (This land exchange was completed by the Province in August 2007 when 615 hectares were conveyed to four major developers: Metrus Development, Lebovic Enterprises, Mattamy Homes, and Joey Tanenbaum.) The Province appointed a review panel, the North Pickering Land Exchange Review Panel, led by former Toronto mayor David Crombie, to advise the government on the land swap. Debbe Crandall of Save the Oak Ridges Moraine Coalition, Ric Symmes of the Federation of Ontario Naturalists, Ron Christie of the Rouge Park Alliance, and John Riley of the Nature Conservancy of Canada also sat on the panel, along with two former members of the Ontario Realty Corporation. While there was some disagreement about the role of the review panel, the provincial government held that "the rationale is that negotiations involving the disposal of public assets like land are best conducted in private" (Gillespie quoted in Swainson, 2002c: B7).

In the end, very little was achieved from a conservation point of view in the swap of lands in Richmond Hill and Seaton. The developers came out of the conflict relatively well and admitted so publicly. Through top-down intervention by the provincial government, some of the outstanding disputes over development proposals on the Moraine at the OMB were resolved, and the security of investments was ensured for developers. However, the land swap was seen by many as a sell-out and a costly compromise.

While rural and environmental organizations and opposition politicians initially celebrated a victory, they soon had reservations. One set of concerns focused on the provision for the future review of the legislation and the power of the Minister of Municipal Affairs and Housing to override the provisions of the *Oak Ridges Moraine Conservation Plan*. Another apprehension surrounded the land swap, which many critics feared would give the developers even more land on better terms than those offered by the Richmond Hill lands. Pickering officials declared that they would fight the swap, claiming that the Pickering lands in Seaton were equally sensitive.

Another concern surfaced when it was revealed that some of the housing development in Richmond Hill would still proceed. In March 2002, rumours circulated that the Ontario legislature was negotiating a backroom deal that would guarantee Richmond Hill builders 7,495 new homes on parts of the Oak Ridges Moraine, prompting Glenn De Baeremaeker, executive director of Save the Rouge Valley System, to state that "everything the government promised is being violated in this sweetheart deal ... They've betrayed the public and given the developers everything they wanted" (quoted in Swainson, 2002b: A1). De Baeremaeker also added that none of the developments would be subject to public scrutiny because a provincial zoning order would give developers an automatic right to build that would supersede all other requirements (ibid.). Soon after, the Province confirmed that it had given developers permission to build 4,150 housing units in Richmond Hill (Swainson and Brennan, 2002: B1).

On 27 June 2002 a Minister's Order, which was final and binding, aborted the ongoing process of review for development proposals on the Moraine. The Order allowed development of the lands in Richmond Hill that were still before the OMB. This permitted an additional 6,600 houses to be built on the Moraine, prompting Save the Rouge Valley System to call the public consultation process "a sham" (Swainson, 2002a).

The approvals of all development applications made prior to the legislation were also secured and grandparented, thus guaranteeing continued public protests and contention as these developments came on stream. (To date, there is no publicly available list of the number and location of the development proposals that were grandparented on the Moraine.) This situation occasioned one local activist in Uxbridge Township to write: "Simply put, the moraine was exponentially being consumed by inappropriate planning applications that pre-date May 17, 2001 ... The 'grandfather' [sic] clause mocks us. We are back in the trenches, back before council, back at the Ontario Municipal Board. The Moraine developer is still our worst nightmare. This is not melodrama. This is how it feels to be on the front lines today in the wake of all the backslapping and handshaking that's going on over Bill 122" (Johnston, 2002).

Development approvals sanctioned by Minister's Orders whittled away some of the "saved" Oak Ridges Moraine lands, while new environmental conflicts surfaced in north Pickering where provincially owned land was given to developers in a land swap and where lands protected as an agricultural preserve were threatened by development when Pickering Council sided with developers in attempts to revise the Greenbelt boundaries. These changes, plus the prospect of a review of the Moraine protections after only fifteen years, make it difficult for environmentalists to claim an unequivocal victory.

The passage of the *Oak Ridges Moraine Conservation Act* and *Plan* is generally seen as a victory and an achievement for the campaigns that worked to save the Moraine. The hearings and appeals built into the planning system, and the creation of new structures for public consultation, opened up opportunities for homeowners associations and rural and environmental movements to organize and be heard. In Richmond Hill, despite a pro-development local council, the requirements for public consultations on rezoning applications and the standing for local organizations in challenging development in OMB hearings provided opportunities for greater public awareness and an upwelling of resident protests, for environmental groups to air their concerns, and for other agents, such as the City of Toronto, to lend their support to the protection of the Moraine. Another reason for the perception of the success of the Oak Ridges Moraine legislation related to the manner in which environmental non-governmental organizations framed the Moraine. These ways were both adopted and developed further in the media.

In the Wake of the *Oak Ridges Moraine Conservation Plan*

In the immediate wake of the Oak Ridges Moraine legislation, environmentalist and resident activism did not subside, but it was transformed. After the legislation was passed on 14 December 2001, Save the Oak Ridges Moraine Coalition declared that it had served its purpose and achieved its goals. At one point the coalition was even prepared to scale down or disband its operations. Instead, Save the Oak Ridges Moraine Coalition reassessed its assets as an umbrella organization with a well-known name, which was able to obtain funds and support from foundations (Oak Ridges Moraine Foundation and Metcalf Foundation) and state funders (Ontario Ministry of Natural Resources).

Save the Oak Ridges Moraine Coalition developed a new project to monitor the Moraine in partnership with Citizens' Environment Watch (now EcoSpark) and the Centre for Community Mapping. The mandate was to "design and implement an integrated ecological and policy monitoring program for the Oak Ridges Moraine" (Monitoring the Moraine, 2006) and facilitate and engage citizens in provincial and municipal land use planning and environmental protection on the Moraine. The project was an example of changing political priorities with regard to conservation policy, namely the increased emphasis on the privatization of conservation projects and ecological monitoring and on their delegation to civic and private organizations. While this change may be seen as bottom-up democratic participation, expecting citizen volunteers to monitor hundreds of well-funded development activities that fall under multiple jurisdictions across the broad Moraine was and remains a daunting task (Sandberg and Wekerle, 2010). Under the guise of partnership, the role of the provincial government has shifted to coordinating or providing limited funding for non-elected partners' monitoring activities.

The political opportunity structure for environmentalists and residents changed with the formation of the Oak Ridges Moraine legislation. A land-based legislative system was now in place that stipulated differentially restricted land uses for the four different zones on the Moraine: settlement, rural, natural linkage, and natural core areas. The legislation required that municipalities enforce the legislation, while the Ministry of Municipal Affairs and Housing would be the overall watchdog. The Oak Ridges Moraine Foundation, a provincial government–appointed body with a $15 million budget, was formed to dispense grants to community and environmental groups involved in promoting and monitoring the implementation of the objectives of the Oak Ridges Moraine conservation legislation, and to mobilize support for the provincial government's intervention in regional land use planning. The new legislation created a situation for environmentalist and resident groups to become much more dependent on the public purse for their activities. It also provided opportunities for activists to become involved in conservation projects that fit well within, rather than challenged, the Oak Ridges Moraine legislation. As attention shifted from preserving the Moraine to implementing the *Greenbelt Plan* and the *Growth Plan*, the Oak Ridges Moraine as an ecological and political project had less visibility.

With the institutionalization of the conservation agenda there was a new emphasis on partnerships and the dispensation of government largesse. Slogans such as "Save, Don't Pave, the Moraine" and "Protect the Moraine" gave way to other catchphrases such as "The Moraine for Life," "Caring for the Moraine," "Monitoring the Moraine," and "Sustain the Moraine." The Moraine was transformed into an object that is conserved and protected. The door thus closed discursively on continued challenges over the terms of the Oak Ridges Moraine legislation and some of its potential faults and weaknesses. Instead, protection or conservation became dependent upon and answerable to the terms of the legislation.

This situation has now been well accepted by environmental and other activist groups. At a symposium organized by the Oak Ridges Moraine Foundation in February 2007, for example, one of the long-term champions of the Oak Ridges Moraine, journalist David Lewis Stein, spoke positively about the current state of framing and funding for the Moraine. Recalling the fate of other state-sponsored agencies that had faced corruption charges and the cut-off of funding, he referred to the citizens' movement on the Oak Ridges Moraine as a "*de facto* government agency" that relieves the government of expensive bureaucrats by relying on citizens who are cheap. The way to sell such an arrangement, Stein (2007) argued, is for the citizens' initiatives to be transparent, accountable, self-disciplined, and self-disciplining by adhering to a master plan. Environmental Commissioner Gordon Miller, typically a vocal critic of the provincial government's environmental record, has endorsed a similar discourse of governance. Commenting on the Monitoring the Moraine project, Miller (quoted in the *Caledon Citizen*, 2006) stated: "The Ministry of Natural Resources and the Ministry of Environment are so under-resourced that they can't do the job that the public expects them to. They haven't got the troops, they haven't got the expertise, they haven't got the money … [Instead] the people must do it, because if the people do it, it tells the government that it matters to the people … It is absolutely the right thing to do. It is truly a noble thing for people in the community to monitor not only the ecology but also policy to make sure that the *Oak Ridges Moraine Conservation Plan* is successful."

Miller's statement acknowledges a situation in which gaining a victory through protective environmental legislation is not enough. Citizens are increasingly made responsible for conservation initiatives that are based on their individual engagements and on government funding that is filtered through targeted grant programs.

The lengthy process of protest, resistance, and ultimately negotiation and partnership of homeowner associations and rural and environmental movements with agencies of the state raises questions about the changing roles of the state, of planning, and of social movements. The environmental groups that were actively engaged in negotiating the terms of the legislative framework moved from a position as outsiders to become partners with the state through their roles in task forces and advisory bodies of newly created, quasi-autonomous, non-governmental organizations, such as foundations and land trusts that implement state policies. This position gave them legitimacy and prominence in the public eye. The links between government and certain environmental organizations may be further strengthened by the movement of key environmental actors into government as politicians, staff, and advisers. Erin Shapero, active in Save the Rouge Valley System, was elected to Markham Council. Glenn De Baeremaeker, president of Save the Rouge Valley System, was elected to the City of Toronto Council. Josh Matlow, Moraine organizer for Earthroots, ran unsuccessfully in a provincial by-election for the Liberals against Ernie Eves, leader of the provincial Tories, but he was subsequently elected as a school trustee in Toronto and then as a councillor in the City of Toronto. John Mackenzie, environmental planner for Save the Rouge Valley System, became a planner with the Ministry of Municipal Affairs and Housing, was later hired as the assistant to Municipal Affairs Minister John Gerretsen when the Liberals gained power in 2003, and subsequently moved to Ontario Realty Corporation, and then was hired as Chief Planner for the city of Vaughan.

Conclusion

From one perspective, the Moraine campaigns may be viewed as a success story of citizen activism against sprawl and the destruction of nature in exurban places. As Allen Scott (1990: 10) notes, "success is thus quite compatible with, and indeed overlaps, the disappearance of the movement as a movement." It can further be argued that activists learned from their experience of struggles for the Moraine and have been able to translate it into more sophisticated tactics in subsequent contestations over the Greenbelt. If, as Scott (1990) suggests, social movement success consists of integrating previously excluded

issues and groups into the "normal" political process, then the movements to save the Moraine may have far exceeded the expectations of
some activists. Large parts of the Moraine were saved from development, although Minister's Orders and grandparenting of developments
continued the building of thousands of homes on the Moraine. Provincial legislation and the *Oak Ridges Moraine Conservation Plan* clearly
set out the ground rules of where development can or cannot occur on
the Moraine in the future, subject to the future review of the Moraine
legislation.

The active engagement of environmental organizations in designing
an interest-based policy-negotiation process has effected a substantial
reframing of regional land use policies that does not stop with the Oak
Ridges Moraine legislation. Since its enactment the provincial government has passed new planning legislation regarding the bigger picture
of growth and land use in the Greater Golden Horseshoe. The *Greenbelt
Plan* protects countryside and prime agricultural lands. It followed the
model of the Moraine planning process to incorporate public consultations and an advisory group of appointed stakeholders, including environmental organizations. More important perhaps, the discourse of
ecosystem planning approaches was extended into the *Greenbelt Plan*.

As we have seen in this chapter, the movements on the Moraine engaged in both social protest and institutionalized political actions, strategies that Goldstone (2003: 7) suggests are complementary: "It may be
the ability of groups to combine *both* protest and conventional tactics
for influencing government actors that best conduces to movement
success." Goldstone argues that social movement actors should be portrayed not so much as insiders or outsiders but as enjoying a continuum
of access and influence on the state that is dynamic and contingent. A
continuum describes the social movement activism on the Moraine in
which a coalition of homeowners, rural activists, and environmental
movements sought to influence the state and gained its intervention in
the protection of places and nature on a regional scale in a process that
extended over several decades.

While media coverage often focused on the opposition to state policies regarding the Moraine, as Goldstone (2003: 21) suggests, "states
may actually embrace movements and seek their support," particularly
when it forwards the state's own agenda. Current research on governance and spatial planning (Nuissl and Heinrichs, 2011) suggests that
there is a need to focus on the way public affairs are regulated and
on the institutional frameworks in which interaction among collective

actors takes place and influences results. These questions are addressed in the next chapter, in which we consider the Oak Ridges Moraine legislation as a unique "conservation actor" that shapes environmental conflict resolution in subtle but strong and persistent ways that promote economic growth and compromise nature conservation.

Chapter Six

Conservation Planning in the Service of Growth

Changes in land use planning ·policies are often proposed as ways to address the problems associated with growth and conservation in fast-changing urban regional economies (figure 6.1). The professional skills of planners as experts, in consultation with relevant stakeholders, are expected to resolve defined problems. Yet critics question the claims of objectivity of an instrumental rationality in solving conservation and planning problems on a neutral and apolitical basis. These critics suggest that planning is political and that an often hidden power underpins its operation, execution, and outcomes (Flyvbjerg, 1998; Forester, 1989; Friedmann, 1998). Planning is a social practice in which the legal system, the natural sciences, and cultural norms and values shape, and are shaped by, powerful political, economic, and environmental priorities and interests. Planning is a politics by other means. Planning is partial in supporting capital accumulation and private property rights, be they based on growth or conservation objectives. On the one hand, planning may be framed to accommodate development, such as housing, manufacturing facilities, retail outlets, public infrastructure, and resource extraction. When development interests are challenged, proponents typically access legal provisions that support growth. In addition, the same interests engage and pay for expert witnesses, often natural scientists, who reference a permissive natural science that shows minimal impact and ecosystem adaptability, to permit development to take place.

On the other hand, planning can also favour environmental conservation, as in the case of the Oak Ridges Moraine. Using the precautionary principle, natural science may be highly supportive in mandating restrictions on the development aspirations of private residents and

Figure 6.1 Housing development on the Oak Ridges Moraine

The Oak Ridges Moraine conservation legislation is intended to protect a significant ecological, hydrological, and geomorphological area, yet it contains loopholes and provisions that promote growth. Source: the authors, 2003

landowners. The precautionary principle and the long-term and negative cumulative impact through wider ecosystem interconnections may trump the claims of a project's minimal and uncertain impact over the short term (Richardson, Sherman, and Gismondi, 1993). Within the planning process, then, the truth claims of natural science may be highly politicized, contingent, and subject to the tensions, contradictions, uncertainties, and ambiguities of specific situations (Bocking, 2005).

The Oak Ridges Moraine is a privileged residential environment, now supported by nature conservation measures, but that does not mean that the Moraine is immune to development pressures. We argue that the Oak Ridges Moraine planning legislation is by no means an absolute or definitive statement in favour of conservation but rather an ambiguous document shaped by distinct struggles, conflicts, and histories. Subjected to a dance of contestations, the Moraine legislation supports conservation in some instances while marginalizing it in others. In addition, the conservation of the Moraine heavily affects areas that lie beyond its boundaries. In order to assess the impact of the Oak Ridges Moraine legislation on nature conservation, the Act and the Plan need to be seen and evaluated as an actor in a larger context. The legislation, in other words, whether supportive of growth or conservation (or both), and the community of planners, politicians, and lawyers charged with its implementation are part of an episteme, a discourse, and a rationality that in themselves constitute an actor that confines thinking and acting to specific paths while excluding and marginalizing others.

The *Oak Ridges Moraine Conservation Plan* has been lauded as drawing a line in the sand – asserting the significance of, and protecting, habitat and green corridors in a landscape subject to intense development pressures. In this chapter we first explore the ways in which the Oak Ridges Moraine conservation legislation supports both conservation and growth. We show that while the legislation may be averting urban sprawl in some ways, it also accommodates, supports, and concedes to growth in other ways. We then focus on the manner in which the Oak Ridges Moraine is imagined and re-imagined conceptually, tactically, and strategically in conflict situations, as well as the way in which these dynamics generally affect nature conservation in the Greater Toronto Area. We point especially to the importance of considering the limitations of the Oak Ridges Moraine legislation and the role of other federal and provincial statutes in the routine management of the Moraine. These cases show that the conservation discourse surrounding the Oak Ridges Moraine is pregnant with inconsistencies and contradictions. Different spatial, thematic, legal, and scientific constructions of the Moraine are highly political and are invoked conceptually and differentially in disputes and challenges over the environmental impact of growth. We maintain that the growth and conservation provisions that underpin the Oak Ridges Moraine legislation colour natural science evidence and legal procedures, making such evidence and procedures political vehicles in promoting development and conservation objectives on the Moraine.

Conservation in the Service of Growth

As illustrated in chapter 3, recent decisions at the Ontario Municipal Board show that the *Oak Ridges Moraine Conservation Act* and *Plan* can make a difference in the routine conservation management of the Moraine and in the setting of precedents for future decisions. Even so, there are other elements of the Act and Plan that are less supportive of conservation. However strong the conservation objectives and intentions of the Oak Ridges Moraine legislation are, all the policy documents and legislation governing nature conservation in relation to the Moraine make generous provisions for growth. These growth provisions are consistent with the *Provincial Policy Statement* and the *Ontario Planning Act*, which consider economic prosperity as a key consideration when balancing provincial interests (Ontario Ministry of Municipal Affairs and Housing, 2005: 1994). The *Places to Grow Act, 2005*, the leading growth plan for the Greater Toronto Area and surroundings, similarly has as its goal "support for infrastructure which achieves the social and economic aims," while seeking only to "minimize environmental impacts" (Ontario Ministry of Public Infrastructure and Renewal, 2006: 6).

In the Oak Ridges Moraine legislation a prominent goal in support of growth is to promote "land and resource uses and development that are compatible with ... continued development within existing urban settlement areas" (Ontario Ministry of Municipal Affairs and Housing, 2001b: 4). The Oak Ridges Moraine legislation endorses the Ontario government's so-called smart growth strategy, defined as explicitly promoting and managing growth in ways that build strong communities, sustain a strong economy, and promote a healthy environment. *The Oak Ridges Moraine Conservation Plan* "involves integrating decisions on development, infrastructure and the environment and making sure those decisions are economically sound" (Ontario Ministry of Municipal Affairs and Housing, 2002a: 4). Clearly, the Oak Ridges Moraine legislation is not only about nature conservation but also about development policy, of which the basic premise of growth is an integral ingredient.

The support of growth is illustrated by the continued construction of some housing developments, with respect to grandparented housing developments approved prior to the Oak Ridges Moraine legislation as well as developments within "settlement" and some "countryside areas." But the support of growth is also apparent in the provisions made for aggregate extraction and for infrastructure development in the form of sewer and road constructions. The support of such infrastructure, which draws new housing development, permits conventional development on the southern flank of the Moraine, as well as facilitating leapfrog development in the areas to the east, north, and west of the Moraine. In this chapter the treatment and resolution of conflicts surrounding some housing development and public sewers and roads on the Moraine illustrates the way in which support of the Oak Ridges Moraine legislation channels debates and conflict in the direction of spatially based, technocratic, and growth-accommodating solutions.

Housing Development as Actor

The Oak Ridges Moraine conservation legislation contains provisions for the continued growth of housing on the Moraine. The demand for housing becomes elevated to a powerful and unquestioned component of provincial policy that is deferred to in planning legislation. With regard to the settlement and countryside areas, the rules are relaxed because there has been a lot of planning, investment, and infrastructure already made in these areas. Developments on the Moraine that were approved or were in the approval process before the Oak Ridges Moraine legislation came into place have also been planned or are being built, making the Oak Ridges Moraine a construction site in many locations. In 2002 the Save the Oak Ridges Moraine Coalition estimated that the ongoing construction comprised 25,000 homes, some of which were being built within the most restricted zone, natural core areas. However, as an active partner in negotiating the terms of the legislation, Save the Oak Ridges Moraine Coalition (2002a) was resigned, commenting that "while this may seem unfair, this 'grandfathering' of approved applications is consistent with existing legal principles." A similar deference to growth based on legal principles is illustrated in the housing developments in Richmond Hill that figured so prominently in chapter 5, where the Liberal government reneged on the election promises to cancel them, claiming it "had no choice." "Keeping its promise would have cost 'billions'" and resulted in "a financial and legal nightmare" (Abbate, 2003). The government thus proclaimed that it "had obtained legal advice that ... to freeze all of the land ... would result in a lengthy and costly legal battle" (ibid.) (figure 6.2). Grandparented developments continue to sprout over the Moraine, although the location and number of these developments has not been made public. In 2011, grandparented or transitional developments had occurred on such a scale that the Oak Ridges Moraine Foundation called for the government to set a sunset date for all such developments (Oak Ridges Moraine Foundation, 2011a, 2011b).

Figure 6.2: Bulldozing the Oak Ridges Moraine in Richmond Hill

Immediately prior to the 2003 provincial election Moraine activists demanded that the Liberal government halt further development on Moraine lands. On development sites across the Moraine development activity intensified as bulldozers worked overtime to clear lands and lay sewer pipes. During the election campaign the Liberals ran on a platform that called into question the development approvals in Richmond Hill. When elected, however, they reneged on the promise and allowed for development of sites that had already received some level of planning approvals. Source: the authors, 2003

There are also provisions built into the Moraine legislation for housing developments. They are well expressed in some recent Ontario Municipal Board cases in Richmond Hill in which housing subdivisions were contested. The OMB referred to the *Oak Ridge Moraine Conservation Plan* as the definitive frame through which it made its decision to allow the subdivisions to proceed. The Oak Ridges Moraine legislation contains stipulations that frame and ultimately determine the outcome of such contestations. In an area of Richmond Hill bounded by Bayview

Avenue to the west, Bethesda Sideroad to the north, Leslie Street to the east and Stouffville Road to the south (Ontario Municipal Board, 2006a), the planned subdivisions were located completely within the Oak Ridges Moraine, placed on settlement areas, but backing on to natural core and linkage areas (Athanasiu, 2005) (figure 6.3). At the onset of the contestation all the sensitive lands were included, but all parties eventually agreed that no development would occur in the natural core and linkage areas. There nevertheless remained several objectors who advocated for the protection of an extended area, as well as protesting the potential building of infrastructure lines across the natural core and linkage areas. The Richmond Hill Naturalists feared that the development of six high-density buildings (one having eighteen storeys), 1,450 homes, and commercial buildings was "premature": "It lacks servicing and this is 'urban sprawl,' contrary to good planning" (Richmond Hill Naturalists, 2006: 7). However, such interventions were legally and discursively written out of the Plan, and the Ontario Municipal Board (2006a: 4) resolved: "all of the senior policy documents [the *Oak Ridges Moraine Conservation Act* and *Plan*] with which this Secondary Plan must conform have delineated and defined the natural areas. The Secondary Plan which is before the Board does nothing to change those designations, but simply provides policies as to how development in the urban areas shall take place."

The reference to the lack of authority on the part of the OMB to intervene in the spatial categories of settlement area, countryside area, natural core area, and linkage area set down by the Oak Ridges Moraine conservation legislation illustrates the disciplining role of the legislation towards the Moraine, and the marginalization of dissent that falls outside the terms of the Plan. The Plan silenced the environmentalists' voice and vision, and it became the prime basis of the approval of the development. The Plan also deferred to other legislation to deal with the objections raised by the dissenters.

A similar process of approving subdivision development and silencing dissent occurred in the extended conflict from 2002 to 2006 over the development on a 620 hectare parcel of land, collectively known as the North Leslie lands, which is a few kilometres to the south of the above-mentioned case; the area is bounded by Bayview Avenue to the west, Highway 404 to the east, Elgin Mills Road East to the south, and Nineteenth Avenue to the north and includes an area of land north of Nineteenth Avenue, east of Leslie Street, in Richmond Hill (Ontario Municipal Board, 2006b). Although the area only contains a small part

Figure 6.3: Contested development at Bethesda Sideroad, Leslie Street, Stouffville Road, and Bayview Avenue

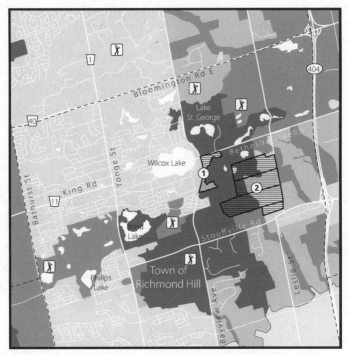

Contested development at Bethesda Sideroad, Leslie Street, Stouffville Road and Bayview Avenue

☐ Oak Ridges Moraine Conservation Plan Area   ① Casa Developments
■ Natural Core Area   ② West Gormley Secondary Plan
■ Natural Linkage Area
▨ Countryside Area   🏌 Golf Course
▨ Settlement Area

In spite of vocal and conspicuous protests covered widely in the media, many subdivision developments on the Moraine have been approved by the Ontario Municipal Board. In such instances, the OMB has often referred to the *Oak Ridges Moraine Conservation Plan* as an endorsement of the development. The stipulations in the legislation typically only pertain to the immediate sur-roundings of contested developments. and they obscure any potential syner-gistic and cumulative effects of the developments. The choke point of the Mo-raine along Yonge Street is seen to the west in the map. Source: York Region School Board, 2006; Rajiv Rawat and the authors, 2011 of the officially designated Moraine at the northern edge, the Green-belt Alliance referred to this site as one of the top ten hot spots for en-vironmentally sensitive developments in Ontario. The protests against the development received a very sympathetic treatment in the media. The Town of Richmond Hill refused to enact a proposal to redesignate lands for development. But a group of landowners appealed the Town's decision to the Ontario Municipal Board, and the OMB approved the housing development, paying little attention to the evidence of Save the Rouge Valley System, the environmental group that had been at the forefront in fighting for the Oak Ridges Moraine legislation. Save the Rouge Valley System had argued that the applications were premature, the "natural heritage system" was incomplete, and the development of the headwaters of the Rouge River, above a 10 per cent permeability threshold, was inappropriate. In pondering its decision and the role of Save the Rouge Valley System at the hearing, the OMB stated: "The Province's aggressiveness in enacting the Oak Ridges Moraine Act, 2001 and the Greenbelt Act 2005 and their regulations appears to have substantially changed the positions of the parties such that many of the once disputed areas are now protected by one or other of these respec-tive plans. This may also be the reason for Save the Rouge Valley Sys-tem's lack of presence at this hearing and the ability of the parties to settle many of the issues that were outstanding at the commencement of this hearing. It is unfortunate that some of these issues could not have been settled earlier" (Ontario Municipal Board, 2006b: 8).

OMB members may well be correct in asserting that the aggressive enactment of the *Oak Ridges Moraine Conservation Act* was responsible for the lack of concern of Save the Rouge Valley System at the hearing. The organization, it may be presumed, had achieved a large part of its conservation goals by the formation of the Oak Ridges Moraine leg-islation, and it was, at the time, according to the OMB, a mere "small group of private interests" (ibid.: 4). However, the example also shows a formalization and institutionalization of the planning process that excluded some of the broader concerns articulated by the environ-mentalists and residents, concerns that echoed the objections heard in events leading up to the Oak Ridges Moraine legislation. These con-cerns included the issue of challenging or questioning the conservation divisions and exclusions of the Moraine, infrastructural development crossing natural core and linkage areas, and the well-being of the Mo-raine as a whole, rather than of the isolated points of development. The formalization of the spatial divisions of the Moraine, and the various activities allowed in each, aided and abetted the allowance of housing subdivisions in certain parts of the Moraine.

The challenge by Westhill Redevelopment of the Town of Aurora's rejection of a proposed golf course complex and a condominium illustrates more recently the power of conservation legislation in shaping development outcomes (Ontario Municipal Board, 2011). Westhill, owned by Lebovic Enterprises Ltd., proposed the development on 200 acres (81 hectares) situated north of Bloomington Road and east and west of Leslie Street (ibid.). The project was opposed by the Town, some local residents, and the environmental organization Earthroots, but supported by the Regional Municipality of York and the Town's mayor. The key issue for the contestants was whether the quantity of water required to serve the development would negatively affect water levels in wells locally and the Town and the Region generally.

The origin of the application to the Region and the Town dated back to 1988 and 1989. After many legal complications and delays, the hearing on the proposal commenced in September 2010 and lasted approximately seven weeks. For the opponents, the most fundamental issue was that the development threatened to set a precedent for the acceptance of three silos of regulatory approvals: land use, environmental assessment, and water. According to the presiding judge, the Town's "position was that each of the required approvals represent a 'silo' because each involves different legal regimes that traditionally do not 'meet up'; environmental assessment addressed separately from land use, and water approvals approached separately from land use and environmental assessment" (ibid.). The Town argued specifically that Westhill had failed to demonstrate that groundwater would be maintained if a golf complex were developed; the water-taking provisions were premature in light of the development of the pending *Clean Water Act*, which was to deal with water issues in the province generally; and the development did not take into account cumulative impacts. In making these arguments, the opponents placed the development on a broader spatial, temporal, and conceptual scale, a procedure that garnered wide support among local residents, the Town, and the media.

The judge, however, rejected the opponents on all substantive grounds, scaling and basing her judgment on a narrower spatial and conceptual level consistent with the conservation legislation. Considering all the evidence, she stated, "I find that the planning instruments under appeal are consistent with the Provincial Policy Statement and conform to all applicable provincial plans" (ibid.). In her single-spaced, thirty-three-page statement, she thus weighed the evidence within the frames of existing legislation and procedures, on very different spatial and temporal scales than those of the opponents.

The reaction to the OMB decision reflected different frames of interpreting the environmental challenges raised by the situation. The mayor lamented the cost of a $650,000 legal battle, a challenge that his staff did not feel was warranted in the first place, so he claimed. He also opined that the town council should only resort to an OMB hearing if it had "a truly compelling, reasoned and defensible position ..." (Pearce, 2011). The mayor further argued that it "is the first duty of an elected official to follow the legislation that is in place, not make our own laws simply because we disagree with those already in place" (ibid.). By contrast, councillors who supported the case, along with Earthroots senior campaigner Josh Garfinkel, took the wider perspective. They referred to the unknown number of applications for development that remained in the pipeline and felt that rejecting the Westhill case could have set a precedent for putting a stop to them. Garfinkel referred to the OMB as an inadequate institution to "assess the impacts of *all* [emphasis added] of the water taking on the moraine" rather than limit itself to the spatially and temporally confined parameters set by the hearing (ibid.).

As we have noted in previous chapters, the uses of natural science to frame debates about conservation and the curtailment of urban growth constituted a focal point in the debates leading up to the identification of the Oak Ridges Moraine as an object of conservation. Scientific discourse and evidence also give insights into the ways in which a contested land use conflict is alternately challenged and supported. Substantial scientific research has accumulated on the impacts of development on natural areas. This discourse illustrates a new trend in land use battles: to engage natural science and scientists in making a case for slowing urban growth.

The Oak Ridges Moraine legislation has shaped and scaled the natural science evidence that is considered in evaluating the environmental impact of housing developments. We use the word *scale* as a verb denoting the variable and subjective ways that the Moraine is defined and conceived spatially and the ways that these spatial narratives are invoked in struggles over conservation and growth (Chambers and Sandberg, 2007; Wekerle, Sandberg, and Gilbert, 2009a). Hydrogeology in particular has been central in resolving issues pertaining to housing development. A Google Scholar search for the keywords *Oak Ridges*

Moraine yields almost five hundred entries, most of which are based in the hydrological and hydrogeological sciences. These studies deal with topics that include groundwater, seismic facies, water wells, surficial geology, regional aquitards, three-dimensional stratigraphic modelling, chromo-enhanced digital elevation modeling, and geostatistical mapping.

Most of the research on the Moraine took place at the Geological Survey of Canada and the University of Toronto's Groundwater Research Group in the 1990s, led by Ken Howard and Nick Eyles (Howard, 2008). Various consulting firms have also made contributions, such as those commissioned by the Oak Ridges Moraine Technical Working Committee in the mid-1990s, as well as private developers, municipal governments, and environmental groups (Hunter Geographic Information Systems, 2008). In the early 1990s hundreds of thousands of dollars were poured into research on modelling and mapping the hydrogeology of the Oak Ridges Moraine; consequently, it is now the most well-documented landscape feature in Canada in this regard. Schuurman (2004: 79–80) describes the standardization of well-log data for the Moraine as an example of a database being used for planning the siting of subdivisions, landfills, and other developments as well as providing scientists and planners elsewhere with a standardized scheme for developing similar plans. According to Schuurman (2004: 79), for example, the most successful attempt to classify water-well-log data in Canada has been on the Oak Ridges Moraine. The hydrogeological data for the Oak Ridges Moraine are now the most detailed and sophisticated of any other landform in Canada.

These hydrogeological studies are inconclusive and highly political. Most natural scientists conclude that they need to do more research and have more research funding to understand and eventually manage the complexity of the Oak Ridges Moraine. At the same time, the continued human-made changes to the Moraine as well as surrounding areas add to the complexity. Schuurman (2004: 80), for example, argues that the standardized well-log data for the Moraine constitute not absolute and unchanging spatial data "but spatiotemporal entities that represent a snapshot in time." This argument implies that the data are continually changing not only because of "independent" hydrogeological dynamics but also because of the continuing human impact and stresses under which these dynamics operate. A second political consequence, flowing from the assumption of complexity, is that inconclusive natural science data are open to interpretation. Schuurman suggests that developers "take the view that more data are dangerous" and that data "do not necessarily help them achieve their objectives." More natural science data, however, as we will see below, can also support development projects.

In the history of the Moraine two competing natural science–scaled conceptions have prevailed. In the early 1990s the Geological Survey of Canada conveyed the image of the Oak Ridges Moraine as a whole landscape feature that served essential hydrological functions. In the case of housing developments, the Survey was critical of the use of water-well drillers as a fundamental source of water information and measure of development impacts, arguing that it yielded limited hydrostratigraphic data regarding groundwater on the Moraine. The Survey advocated instead for a regional tridimensional mapping of the Moraine in order to understand aquifer connectivity, capacity, and protection on a larger scale across and beyond the boundaries of the Moraine (Natural Resources Canada, 2009). Geological maps synthesize and communicate earth science information, revealing that there is both architectural and sedimentological variation within the region (Sharpe et al., 1999). On the basis of that variation, Sharpe et al. (2002) called for a basin analysis for understanding the Moraine, which includes a complex combination of data compilation and modelling, including geological, hydrostratigraphic, and groundwater flow models.

The work of Ken Howard of the Groundwater Research Group, who published several anti-development articles concerning the Moraine between 1995 and 1999, similarly called attention to the Moraine as a threatened sensitive water repository, labelling it a landform "at risk" (Howard et al., 1995). In 1997, working with federal government funding, Howard argued that the Moraine is a "nationally significant groundwater resource that has become increasingly threatened by urban growth. The results of the hydrochemical and hydrogeological studies confirm that urbanization represents a serious threat to local groundwater quality" (quoted in Swainson, 2000c). Prominent hydrogeologist Nick Eyles has also argued that groundwater protection throughout the Moraine "should be an urgent priority of municipal planners if the resource is not to be degraded to a condition that precludes its use" (Meriano and Eyles, 2003: 302). Eyles's research was also driven by concerns over leaking landfills in old sandpits on the Moraine. Hunter and Associates, a private environmental consultancy, also played a key role in articulating the threat to groundwater. On development impacts, the firm's scientists held that "urban development, even when serviced with sanitary sewers, is a source of a wide variety of contaminants conveyed and recharged in storm runoff. In general, large communal sewage disposal systems are considered environmentally inappropriate for new residential development in the Oak Ridges Moraine upland area and headwater catchments above 275 m asl [metres above sea level]. There is little evidence to suggest that existing dispersed private individual soil effluent absorption systems in low density residential developments are adversely affecting the Oak Ridges Moraine aquifers" (Hunter, Beck, and Smart, 1997).[1]

Resident activists, environmentalists, developers, and government institutions largely accept natural science criteria as a basis for the scaling of the Oak Ridges Moraine as a landscape feature that deserves full protection. Environmental activists have adopted the terms *rain barrel* and *sponge*, metaphors for a retainer and a filter of water, to characterize the significance of the Oak Ridges Moraine (Bocking, 2005; McElhinny, 2006; International Association for Great Lakes Research, 2002). The Greater Toronto Home Builders' Association (2001), the representative of the development industry, similarly acknowledges the importance of the Oak Ridges Moraine as a provider of ecosystem services and supports the conservation legislation. The largely natural science-staffed provincial network of conservation authorities that share parts of the Moraine within their jurisdictions has similarly formed a larger organization, the Conservation Authorities Moraine Coalition (2012), "to advocate for and protect the Moraine along its 160-kilometre length. The Coalition was formed in response to the need for a comprehensive policy, planning and management approach geared to sustaining the health of the entire Oak Ridges Moraine." Various stakeholders are thus united in their appeal to science to conserve the Moraine as an identifiable and distinct landscape, and scientists themselves are largely united in defence of the Moraine.

Another conception of the impact of development on the Moraine, however, scales natural science at the level of the sites of development rather than at the level of the Moraine as a whole. This conception has its origin in the evaluations of hydrogeological evidence in some of the housing developments that preceded and followed the Moraine legislation. In his capacity as expert witness to the development industry (in the late 1990s and early 2000s), Ken Howard cogently articulated in 1999 the position that housing subdivisions in Richmond Hill and Uxbridge could accommodate adequate water recharge to the Moraine if proper hydrogeological designs were applied on urban subdivisions. He then stated, "I've been working on groundwater for 25 years ... and I believe development can take place in ways that minimize the impact on water quantity and quality. And I find that developers are actually listening" (quoted in Stein, 1999: 01).

A year later, Howard testified in the OMB hearings on the controversial housing developments at Richmond Hill that precipitated the Moraine legislation. At the hearing he argued that only a small percentage of the water recharge to the Moraine came from the Moraine itself and that the Moraine could sustain more housing subdivisions if only these subdivisions were built with the proper technology to allow water recharge. He argued further that the housing developments in Richmond Hill "would be acceptable within an acceptable limit" and that "dumps, septic systems, road salt and fertilizers on golf courses and farmland are more serious sources of groundwater contamination than housing" (quoted in Levy, 2000: 1).

Under cross-examination, Howard acknowledged there were cracks in the Moraine's upper aquifer that might cause polluted groundwater to penetrate into the lower aquifer, but he had seen no evidence that these cracks would admit enough contaminated surface water to threaten the water quality in the important lower aquifer (in Swainson, 2001a). In the end, Howard did not base his assertions on definitive evidence, stating on another occasion that the models used by developers to protect the water regime were incomplete, "transient," and untested. He nevertheless concluded that, in his "best opinion," "the case for safe development on the moraine has been made judging by the work done to date despite not being subjected to rigorous testing or peer review" (quoted in Swainson, 2000d: B2).

At the conclusion of Howard's evidence the Province, the Town of Richmond Hill, the Toronto and Region Conservation Authority, York Region, and two environmental groups lined up to challenge Howard's position. However, the OMB rejected a key Provincial witness, civic engineer Garry Hunter of Hunter Associates, on the basis that he lacked the professional credentials to give an authoritative opinion in evidence (Swainson, 2000c). Four other witnesses of the Province had their credentials questioned and their ability to give testimony restricted (ibid.). Shortly thereafter the Province aborted the OMB hearing and commenced the process leading to the Oak Ridges Moraine legislation.

It may perhaps be plausible to argue that a politics of science driven by self-interests may have shaped some of these conceptions of science in the context of development on the Oak Ridges Moraine. In addition, the challenges to Garry Hunter's credentials may be considered frivolous and driven by the developers' desire to build houses for profit. Hunter had, after all, headed up the extensive studies leading to the reports on the hydrogeology of the Moraine for the Oak Ridges Moraine Technical Working Committee in the mid-1990s. Moreover, in February 2001 the Ontario Supreme Court directed the Ontario Municipal Board to accept Hunter's evidence in the fields of geology, hydrogeology, and hydrogeochemistry (Hunter and Associates, 2001).

The picture is more complicated, however. It shows that evaluations of the environmental impact of development on the hydrogeology of the Oak Ridges Moraine were driven by two different conceptions or scales. The Geological Survey of Canada, Hunter and Associates, Nick Eyles, and earlier statements by Ken Howard considered environmental impacts on the scale of the Moraine as a whole, while Howard's later positions allowed for impact assessment on individual sites across the Moraine. The passing of the *Oak Ridges Moraine Conservation Act* and *Plan* obviously played a considerable role in acknowledging the Oak Ridges Moraine as a full and continuous landform, but the legislation marginalized or occluded the very same conception by its spatial divisions, degrees of conservation and development, and exemptions for development.

The aborted OMB hearing on the building of several housing subdivisions on the Moraine in Richmond Hill in May 2001 closed the door to wider consideration of the Moraine's protection. After the Oak Ridges Moraine legislation had been passed, the questioning of the housing developments in Richmond Hill continued, but it was now disciplined, framed, and constrained by both the legal supports for conservation and the exemptions for growth. In subsequent OMB hearings that challenged these subdivisions, the variety of ecological and hydrogeological evidence that supported the value of the Oak Ridges Moraine as a complete landform was dismissed in favour of detailed information pertaining to the specific sites. Experts for the developers typically weigh heavier than do those for the environmentalists and residents. In Richmond Hill's North Leslie lands, referred to earlier, the arguments of Save the Rouge Valley System were that "the environmental features, taken together, present wide areas of environmental vulnerability that exclude development on the major part of the secondary plan area" (Ontario Municipal Board, 2006b: 11). At that hearing, in April 2006, Garry Hunter presented evidence for the same organization and had some of his recommendations for mitigating (not preventing) development accepted by the OMB (ibid.: 17). Overall, however, the OMB found "that the extensive and current fieldwork and analysis under-taken by the owner's and public agencies' witnesses in establishing the proposed Natural Heritage System is to be preferred over [that of] the Save the Rouge Valley System witnesses" (ibid.: 14).

Sewer and Road Infrastructure as Actors

In provincial legislation the generous provisions for public sewer and road systems have also supported a growth agenda. The *Provincial Policy Statement*, while mindful of the environmental impacts of development, stipulates that a road and sewer infrastructure be in place to direct and accommodate expected growth (Ontario Ministry of Municipal Affairs and Housing, 2005: 10–12). The privileging of growth is also well illustrated in the *Oak Ridges Moraine Conservation Act* and *Plan* by the legal construction and extension of the provincial sewer and road networks as "provincial necessities." The technical legal language in the Plan contains some seemingly strong words on the conditions for the establishment of roads and sewers. It states: "New transportation and utility corridors or facilities shall only be allowed in Natural Core Areas and Natural Linkage Areas if they are shown to be necessary and there is no reasonable alternative. They shall also have to meet stringent review and approval standards" (Ontario Ministry of Municipal Affairs and Housing, 2002a). The term *necessary* is of most significance in this provision, a point we will return to in the context of two development projects covered in the next section of this chapter.

The case of the expansion of the York Durham Sewage System, the so-called Big Pipe, provides a good study of the different social constructions and of the narratives of growth, natural science, and technology that played a crucial role in determining the outcome of the disputes over the construction or expansion of sewer pipes on the Oak Ridges Moraine (McMahon, 2003; Macaraig and Sandberg, 2009). The Big Pipe has been developed as a carrier of sewage from settlements that are increasingly distant from the shores of Lake Ontario to a treatment plant at the Duffin Creek Water Pollution Plant in Pickering (figure 6.4).

The Big Pipe serves relatively dense urban and suburban settlements. This system contrasts with the wells for drinking water, and the septic tanks and smaller local facilities for sewage treatment, which characterize rural and less dense settlement patterns. The majority of residents on the Oak Ridges Moraine rely on the latter system, though this is now changing as the growing supply of housing creates new demands.

Figure 6.4: Toronto's Big Pipe

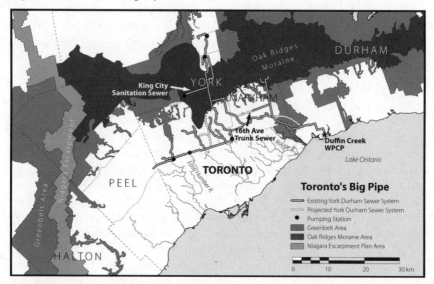

The York Durham Sewer System, known as the Big Pipe, is both a cause and an effect of urban sprawl that is sanctioned as a necessary public good in the Oak Ridges Moraine legislation. The latter has thus assisted the advocates in favour of pipe extension on the Oak Ridges Moraine and has formed an obstacle for the community groups that have fought it. Source: Rajiv Rawat and the authors, 2009

In the period before the Oak Ridges Moraine legislation the aspirations of the municipalities, and the provincial demands on them, especially along the Yonge Street corridor, were to build more housing on or near the Oak Ridges Moraine. Such growth aspirations put pressure on the municipalities along the Yonge Street corridor to connect to the Big Pipe in order to accommodate the increased demand for sewage disposal. Big Pipe hook-ups in Richmond Hill and Vaughan were in part a response to and in part a cause of the establishment of large subdivision housing developments. Once sewer pipes were built, they induced further development that would raise the revenue to meet their cost; environmental groups refer to this process as "pipe-driven urban sprawl" (McMahon, 2003). The Big Pipe now pierces the Oak Ridges Moraine in half along the Yonge Street corridor and is largely responsible for the concentration of settlement areas in this part of the Moraine.

The Big Pipe is both a cause and an effect of the housing developments that exist and are planned for the area.

The proponents and opponents of the Big Pipe use different narratives of growth, nature, and science to promote their positions (Macaraig and Sandberg, 2009). York Region has been the most aggressive promoter and defender of growth in the Greater Toronto Region. The Region has pictured the Big Pipe as critical to ensuring adequate wastewater treatment for current and future York Region residents and businesses and for the expected growth in the Region's population, which was 950,000 in 2006 but is projected to reach more than 1.5 million by 2031 (York Region, 2007: 9). The Region and its supporters have also claimed that existing septic tanks are polluting, smaller sewage treatment plants are impractical, and any potential environmental problems associated with expanding the Big Pipe are only temporary or can be mitigated (Macaraig and Sandberg, 2009).

These narratives have been countered by prominent groups of residents and environmental groups who have concentrated their fight against the Big Pipe in King Township on the Humber River watershed. These groups include Concerned Citizens of King Township Inc., King City Preserve the City Inc., Nobleton Alert Residents' Association Inc., Save the Oak Ridges Moraine Coalition, and the bi-national Great Lakes United, which have worked against the expansion of the Big Pipe since the early 1990s. They have alleged infringement on their democratic right to determine their own fate and to support moderate levels of growth that the local environment can sustain. They have also commissioned "independent" scientific assessments to show that the prevailing septic systems help to replenish base flows to the Humber River and that local sewage treatment plans are a viable option (Underhill, 2005). The groups have also charged that the dewatering associated with building extensions of the Big Pipe would upset water availability and disturb fish habitat.

The residents have also appealed to federal and provincial environmental assessments and charged violations of the federal *Fisheries Act* (Athanasiu, 2005). On the latter point, the environmental groups even cited Karen Gray of the Department of Fisheries and Oceans who conceded that "frankly, I am concerned that a 5–10% reduction in base flows to the Humber River may have a devastating impact to fish and fish habitat and there may also be high costs associated with impact studies and monitoring" (quoted in Richmond Hill Naturalists, 2004: 8). The groups also showed concern over the confined focus of environmental assessments, arguing that they were kept separate from each other deliberately. One activist argued that a combined assessment of the overall extension of the Big Pipe would have shown the true environmental impact and that the current assessments were based on misinformation and were vulnerable to legal challenge (Macaraig and Sandberg, 2009).

At one level, the activism in King Township against the incursion of the Big Pipe reflects the local concerns of those immediately involved in the struggle. Fundamentally, however, it illustrates a broader narrative of the rejection of growth as a strategy for continued local prosperity, a distrust in the science that suggests that the Big Pipe technology is safe, and a profound belief that the Oak Ridges Moraine is unable to withstand further ecological disruption. Yet the federal and provincial governments have consistently ruled against the local scientific evidence presented by groups of community members. All the conservation campaigns have been trumped by the policies of the Region and the Province to upgrade infrastructure and by their insistence that they were meeting the requirement to protect water, wetlands, and fish habitats. This position is underpinned by a different narrative that sees growth as inevitable, the Big Pipe technology as desirable and trustworthy, and nature as resilient and subject to remediation (ibid.).

The Oak Ridges Moraine legislation was prominent by its absence in the contestation over the Big Pipe. The legislation provided largely no assistance in the broader consideration of its environmental impact on the Moraine. The *Oak Ridges Moraine Conservation Plan*, as we have noted, exempts the building of "necessary" infrastructural developments. The exempt provision for the Big Pipe in fact endorsed the consideration of impact confined to the immediate sites of construction rather than the cumulative impact of its expansion across the Moraine as a whole.

The fight of local residents and environmentalists against the Bayview Avenue extension, the public road extension in Richmond Hill referred to in chapter 3, experienced a similar fate. Local activist and biologist Natalie Helferty was part of the leadership protesting the extension of the road in the late 1990s. The extension had already passed a provincial environmental assessment in 1998, but, in 2000, Helferty (2004a, 2004b) argued, ecological matters had changed sufficiently to warrant a reconsideration of the assessment. Helferty had then found the colony of yellow-spotted and Jefferson salamanders in the Jefferson Forest that the consultants of the original assessment had missed. With the much anticipated Oak Ridges Moraine legislation in the works,

Helferty (2001) articulated a firm position: "I can't stand by as a biologist who knows and loves these critters and do nothing, especially in the name of science, whose purpose is to seek and speak the truth about life."

In spite of the militant activism and the natural-science-based evidence garnered against the building of the Bayview Avenue extension, it was built. As with the Big Pipe, the Oak Ridges Moraine legislation's provision for public roads prevailed or made the legislation irrelevant for the opposition of the road. In 2002 the Save the Oak Ridges Moraine Coalition was exasperated over the lack of action to stop the extension in spite of the detrimental impact on natural life. Save the Oak Ridges Moraine Coalition (2002b) wrote: "Despite the fact that the Bayview Extension paves over a designated 'natural core area,' despite the fact that the nationally threatened Jefferson salamander and Yellow-spotted salamander call the area home, despite the fact that this thoroughfare will contribute to the worst kind of urban sprawl, and despite the residents and Save the Rouge's valiant legal efforts to stop the road, the economic engine bulldozes on."

The Province, by contrast, countered with its own measures, which consisted of reference to traffic flows and the necessity to accommodate growth in the region. The building of culverts and underpasses under the Bayview Avenue extension was considered sufficient to accommodate the movement of the salamanders from one side to the other of the road extension. Although some have argued that the culverts and the underpass have proved a pyrrhic victory for wildlife, since the underpass connected two housing subdivisions, some scientific accounts have suggested the opposite (Swainson, 2001d, 2002e). The natural science of the local situation, then, when filtered through the growth provisions of the Oak Ridges Moraine legislation, did little to prevent the Bayview Avenue extension and will likely do little to prevent the building of other "necessary" public infrastructure in the future, including the extension of Highway 404, which has destroyed six woodlots. (One change has been that the Ministry of Transportation invited conservation organizations to organize plant rescues from these woodlots prior to construction.) Overall, environmentalists have had a poor record in invoking natural science in the protection of nature from public sewer and road networks.

Given the power of the growth provisions in the Oak Ridges Moraine legislation, challenging them is seldom successful. When environmental disputes occur at the local level, and the ecological and geological impacts are scrutinized separately, it is relatively easy to shed doubt on environmental concerns. In a recent assessment the Oak Ridges Moraine Foundation identified the generous provisions for infrastructure as a major weakness in the Moraine legislation that needed attention (Oak Ridges Moraine Foundation, 2011a, 2011b). In this context an uncertain science tends to rationalize and legitimize the power and the development bias that underpin the same process (Flyvbjerg, 1998). A malleable ecological science in a flexible legal system ends up supporting growth and development rather than conserving nature.

We conclude that in the case of the infrastructure provisions in the form of sewers and roads, the compartmentalized views of ecology, the uncertain and malleable findings of natural science, and the costs involved in legal challenges typically facilitate rather than hinder such development. Public infrastructure is deemed "necessary" and is therefore given approval. A compartmentalized conception of hydrogeology and ecology becomes an important vehicle or tool in defence of development projects; relevant natural science data are either called into doubt in the legal process or simply ignored in the political process. A full conception of the Oak Ridges Moraine has become confined to the enforcement of conservation measures, which are implemented and monitored by conservation organizations, municipal governments, and civic organizations. While the enforcement is strict in some cases, underfunding and the high volume of data and technical nature of the enforcement are likely to compromise these efforts.

Leapfrog Development as Actor

The provision for public infrastructural development in the Oak Ridges Moraine legislation, its deference to other federal and provincial laws that evaluate the environmental impacts, and the weak nature of such laws work in unison to support a growth agenda not only within parts of the Moraine but also beyond. An added incentive that fuels development beyond the Moraine is the provincial requirement that municipal official plans have to maintain at least a ten-year supply of land for new residential development and a three-year supply of serviced land for development (Rowe, 2004; Melling, 2004). These provisions are sometimes referred to as escalator clauses because they require municipalities to facilitate urban growth by maintaining supplies of developable lands (Winfield, 2004). Municipalities are also under provincial government pressure (owing to funding cutbacks and downloading) to permit new development because a considerable amount of their budget comes from property taxes and development charges. Such fiscal policy tools are considered by some to be potentially powerful planning measures, though they are typically only used to raise revenue (Slack, 2002; Tomalty and Skaburskis, 2003). And while it is true that development is restricted on the Oak Ridges Moraine, these growth provisions put increased pressure on the lands adjacent to the Moraine for development.

Both the Oak Ridges Moraine legislation and the subsequent *Greenbelt Act* and *Plan* have caused so-called leapfrog development to occur outside their respective boundaries. References are often made to leapfrog development as being an "unintentional" consequence of the conservation legislation, but, as we have seen, it is a mechanism built into the *Oak Ridges Moraine Conservation Plan*. As we have suggested elsewhere, conservation can be a cornerstone of growth, and one way in which this is expressed is through leapfrog development (Wekerle et al., 2007).

Simcoe County, which is located to the north of the Oak Ridges Moraine and easily reached by Highway 400, is a prime example of leapfrog development. A 2004 Neptis Foundation study showed a substantial expansion of development into Simcoe County (Birnbaum, Nicolet, and Taylor, 2004). The study attributed the growth to the perception of there being a limited amount of land available south of the Oak Ridges Moraine and continued population and employment growth in the Greater Toronto Area. An additional factor, however, was the proposed highway expansions across the region that would allow for closer and quicker spatial integration.

Subsequent to the Neptis Foundation report on Simcoe County and critiques from environmentalists over leapfrog development, the Liberal provincial government passed the *Greenbelt Act* and *Plan* in 2005, legislation that extended the boundaries of nature conservation beyond the formal boundaries of the Oak Ridges Moraine. But such an extension has not stalled leapfrog development. In 2007 the Pembina Institute warned of continued leapfrog development and also identified its link to the provincial government's massive investment in the expansion of the provincial highway system, stating that all these projects present serious challenges to outlying regions of the Oak Ridges Moraine and the Greenbelt: "The northern and eastern expansion in particular will encourage 'leapfrog' urbanization of rural areas beyond the Greenbelt and Oak Ridges Moraine, far from existing employment centres" (Pembina Institute, 2007: 2). The provisions in the Oak Ridges Moraine legislation for building public highways make such leapfrogging possible, suggesting that the legislation is as much a development as a conservation act.

In 2008 the Grand River Conservation Authority, located west of the Moraine, also called attention to the fact that the Greenbelt "is causing a 'leapfrog' effect, attracting land speculation and spurring growth in the Grand River watershed." The authority continued by pointing to the ecological sensitivity of its own area, which includes moraines, and appended a map entitled "Moraine and Natural Heritage Systems in the Grand River Watershed" (Grand River Conservation Authority, 2008).

In 2007 a coalition of environmental groups summed up the collective problems of loopholes, such as leapfrogging, in the Oak Ridges Moraine and Greenbelt legislation:

> Outside of the Greenbelt, the protection of prime agricultural lands (with the exception of specialty crop lands) and natural areas remains weak, making them vulnerable to the ongoing expansion of highway and sewer infrastructure. Sensitive and increasingly rare landscapes, such as woodlands, wetlands and prairies, continue to disappear under the bulldozer. This trend is laying the foundations for even more automobile-dependent sprawl, the biggest driver of increasing greenhouse gas emissions in Ontario. At the same time, both inside and outside the Greenbelt, the ability of aggregate operations (rock quarries and sand and gravel pits) to trump protective measures poses a large threat to the integrity of natural areas. And despite overwhelming public support for its expansion, the Greenbelt boundary is arbitrarily frozen until 2015, leaving rural municipalities around the GTA (like Simcoe, Dufferin and Northumberland Counties) vulnerable to "leap-frog" development. Meanwhile, many municipalities are struggling to find the resources they need to properly implement the new planning directions and make them work. Ontario has started down the right road, but it still has a long way to go. (Priorities for Ontario, 2007)

A 2008 document commissioned by the Friends of the Greenbelt Foundation, praising the Greenbelt as "positioned to be the most useful greenbelt in the world," nevertheless concluded that leapfrog development was a problem (Carter-Whitney, 2008). However, the recommendation to alleviate the problem was merely to expand the Greenbelt (ibid.). While one may take issue with former Liberal Member of Parliament Jason Cherniak's (2005) position on development generally, his assessment of the effects of the conservation of parks is instructive: "These parks [the Oak Ridges Moraine and Rouge Park] include not only environmentally sensitive areas, but also vast spaces where the only 'sensitivity' is that houses have not yet been built there. Instead, we could have built houses and apartment buildings so that people could live closer to Toronto. Now, roads and traffic, sewers, sewage, hydro lines and more run through those parks just to get to the other side. It is infrastructure without development. It is urban sprawl."

As conservation plans, then, the Oak Ridges Moraine and Greenbelt legislations are clearly sieves, as permeable as the sands of the Moraine, through which many development projects escape.

Aggregate Demand as Actor

While exurbanites have been attracted to the Oak Ridges Moraine for its scenic beauty, corporate investors continue to be attracted to the Moraine for its geological features that offer the promise of profit. The extraction of stone, gravel, and sand, collectively referred to as aggregate resources, sustains much of the growth of the house subdivisions and utility infrastructure of the Greater Golden Horseshoe. The Oak Ridges Moraine and Niagara Escarpment constitute important sources for such material. Provincial peak extraction of aggregates occurred in 1987 with 197 million tons. In recent years extraction has hovered around 160 million tons per year. Most of this material is extracted and consumed in the Greater Golden Horseshoe, with aggregates being largely used in foundation drainage beds for buildings and sewer and transportation infrastructures. Up to 60 per cent of the total production is consumed by the provincial and municipal governments for the construction of public roads and utilities (Chambers and Sandberg, 2007). The Oak Ridges Moraine provides over 50 per cent of the aggregates supplied to the Greater Toronto Area (figure 6.5). The rest comes from the Niagara Escarpment as well as other limestone and sand and gravel deposits in proximity to the area.

The Oak Ridges Moraine is indelibly shaped by the international business structures that control the aggregate sector. These structures include primarily horizontally and vertically integrated transnational cement companies that, as a consequence of the competition to sell cement powder, own most aggregate firms. The cement industry is dominated by large multinational firms, such as Holcim Ltd. (Switzerland), Lafarge (France), CEMEX (Mexico), HeidelbergCement (Germany),

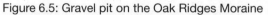

Figure 6.5: Gravel pit on the Oak Ridges Moraine

There are liberal provisions for the extraction of sand and gravel in the Oak Ridges Moraine legislation. This gravel pit is one of many located in the Township of Uxbridge. Other extensive pits are located in the Township of Adjala-Tosorontio, the Municipality of Clarington, and the City of Kawartha Lakes. Source: the authors, 2011

and Italcementi (Italy). Each multinational firm operates in upwards of thirty countries and rose to prominence by acquiring formerly domestically owned plants throughout the world, from North America to Latin America, Eastern Europe, and Asia.

The cement companies have been particularly capable of exerting their power in Canada. In 1992, Lafarge, Holderbank (now Holcim Ltd.), Ciments Français (a subsidiary of Italicementi), and CBR (a member of HeidelbergCement) held nearly 90 per cent of Canada's cement market. According to Ferguson (1992), Canada's weak antitrust laws and governmental indifference allowed the industry to set the highest prices in the world and to buy up most of its cement customers. The

kind of cement that was consumed in Canada was sold in the United
States for less than half the Canadian price. Ferguson (ibid.: 130) reported that in the Greater Toronto Area "almost all ready-mix concrete makers, cement-block makers, cement-pipe makers and sand and
gravel suppliers ... are owned by Holderbank, Lafarge, Ciments Français subsidiaries and the one large independent cement maker in the
area [James Dick Construction]. Almost total vertical integration makes
price fixing and bid rigging an easy exercise in the Toronto-area market." Swiss transnational Holcim operates under the name St Lawrence
Cement in Canada, and Dufferin Aggregates in Ontario. On the Oak
Ridges Moraine its major operations are at Mosport in Durham region,
shipping 1.8 million tons of sand and gravel to various destinations.
However, in 2001, operators on the Oak Ridges Moraine worked three
of Canada's twenty largest pits (see table 6.1). Lafarge operated the sec-
ond- and eighth-largest pits, in Mosport and Stouffville (in York Region). Dufferin Aggregates' Mosport pit was ranked tenth. Six other
of the twenty largest sand and gravel pits in Canada bordered the Moraine. Of course, there are many smaller pits operating on the Moraine.
Parkin (2003) states that there are approximately one hundred licensed
pits on the Moraine within the Greater Toronto Area, and they supply
about one-third of the total aggregates within the area.

At the same time as the aggregate companies exert their economic
power, they have a global and national network that promotes an environmental and social sustainability perspective from the industry's
point of view (Cement Sustainability Initiative, 2002; Cement Association of Canada, 2004). In Ontario, aggregate firms also operate a powerful public relations apparatus that promotes their image as good
community citizens and environmental stewards. A long-established
industry organization, the Ontario Stone, Sand, and Gravel Association (previously known as the Aggregate Producers Association of Ontario), serves this function centrally while also operating as a powerful
lobbyist for the industry and the administrator of pit and quarry rehabilitation schemes (Patano and Sandberg, 2005). Recently the industry
has been involved in forming two organizations that promote "green
gravel" and aspire to develop standards that assign a green and socially
conscious label to aggregate products. Socially and Environmentally
Responsible Aggregate Canada is a collaborative effort between Environmental Defence Canada and Holcim (Canada) Inc., while Aggregate
Forum of Ontario is a cooperative venture between the Ontario Stone,
Sand, and Gravel Association and six environmental organizations,

Table 6.1 Canada's top twenty producers of sand and gravel, 2001

Rank	Company and location (extracting on the Oak Ridges Moraine shown in bold)	Production in millions of tons
1	Construction Aggregates, Sechelt Pit, BC	3.05
2	**Lafarge Canada, Mosport Pit, Ontario**	**2.30**
3	Inland Aggregates, Villeneuve Pit, Alberta	2.14
4	Lafarge Canada, Spy Hill Pit, Alberta	1.91
5	Construction Aggregates, Producers Pit, BC	1.51
6	CBM Aggregates, Aberfoyle Pit, Ontario	1.50
7	James Dick Construction, Caledon Pit, Ontario	1.49
8	**Lafarge Canada, Stouffville Pit, Ontario**	**1.39**
9	Lafarge Canada, Earle Pit, BC	1.30
10	**Dufferin Aggregates, Mosport, Ontario**	**1.20**
11	Dufferin Aggregates, Mill Creek Pit, Ontario	1.15
12	Lafarge Canada, Central Pit, BC	1.10
13	Jack Cewe, Pipeline Road, BC	1.00
14	Inland Aggregates, Spy Hill, Alberta	1.00
15	Lafarge Canada, Onoway, Alberta	1.00
16	Lafarge Canada, Caledon Pit, Ontario	0.99
17	CBM Aggregates Sunderland Pit, Ontario	0.96
18	Lafarge Canada, Villeneuve Pit, Alberta	0.93
19	Inland Aggregates, Pine Ridge Pit, Manitoba	0.90
20	Dufferin Aggregates, Aberfoyle Pit, Ontario	0.75

Source: *Aggregates and Roadbuilding Magazine*, 2001

among them Gravel Watch and Ontario Nature. While both Socially and Environmentally Responsible Aggregate and Aggregate Forum are working to develop standards that certify aggregates as produced sustainably, a similar process to the one through which the forest industry went a couple of decades ago, they are proceeding differently (Shuff, 2011a, 2011b). Socially and Environmentally Responsible Aggregate's initiative is based on a best-practices approach where Holcim (Canada) as an industry leader is charged with setting the standard for the industry as a whole. Aggregate Forum is proceeding more cautiously, even to the extent of considering whether certification may be a good thing in the first place (Shuff, 2011a, 2011b).

The aggregate industry has built several efficient scale narratives in support of its operations. One such narrative argues that the siting of an aggregate operation must be sufficiently close to the point of consumption to make extraction economically feasible and environmentally sustainable. Allegedly, the low value and bulk nature of its products dictate that transportation costs have to be kept down (Cowell and Owens, 1998: 800). In Canada, for example, the industry claims that transporting aggregates over thirty kilometres doubles their cost (Baker, Slam, and Summerville, 2001: 464; Ontario Ministry of Natural Resources, 2009a). The industry is also fond of invoking the argument that a longer distance for transporting aggregates has severe impacts on greenhouse gas emissions and acts against the current trend towards bioregional consumption, such as the promotion of the consumption of local foods. Lower transportation costs also mean lower-cost cement, which keeps costs down for government-funded infrastructure and private home building. Keeping the costs low for cement is, in turn, framed as "saving money" rather than imposing an unnecessary burden on the taxpayers to please a "not in my backyard" demographic in select areas. As a consequence, the aggregate companies typically fight opponents until proven reserves in the areas closest to the market are completely exhausted.

There is more to this story, however. The industry has also helped to construct the Oak Ridges Moraine as an essential source of aggregates. It is persistent in its lament of the pending scarcities of local aggregates and calls for continued open access to the Oak Ridges Moraine and elsewhere (Miller, 2005; Aggregates Manager, 2005; Ontario Ministry of Natural Resources, 2010a; Binstock and Carter-Whitney, 2011). In the process of constructing such a dire situation with regard to aggregate supply and the Oak Ridges Moraine's central position therein, the industry's story obscures a series of other considerations. These considerations include redirecting the substantial volume of presently exported aggregate material to local uses; using other substances (for example, nickel and copper slag, shingles, tires, and glass) as substitutes for aggregate; channelling more resources towards recycling; and designing in ways that require less aggregate (Winfield and Taylor, 2005; Toronto Environmental Alliance, 2009). The industry is highly active in the extraction and exploration of deposits at large distances from the

Greater Toronto Area. Huge extraction sites on Manitoulin Island in Lake Huron, and the Superior Aggregates superquarry on the eastern shore of Lake Superior, already supply or could supply more aggregate to the Greater Toronto Area market (Miller, 2005). There are also different modes of transportation than trucks, such as trains, freighters, and barges, which could be used to move aggregate or substitutes (for example, waste rock from northern metal mines) from distant and large regional quarries (Drake, 2002; Miller, 2005). Finally, the demand projections of aggregates can be challenged – if one recognizes that such demands are constructed by industry consultants whose interests are closely vested in the continued growth of a suburban, ex-urban, road- and automobile-dependent society and economy (Cowell and Murdoch, 1999). The most recent state-of-the-resource studies for the Ontario Ministry of Natural Resources (2010a) were all done by such consultants. This kind of growth refuses to conceive of a different economy based on higher levels of urban intensification and different means of transportation that consume less aggregate (Binstock and Carter-Whitney, 2011).

The provincial government is keenly linked to and complicit in the aggregate industry's narrative with regard to resource protection and the distance-cost relationship discussed earlier. This situation is by no means predetermined. Prior to the 1970s the aggregate policy regime in Ontario was relatively decentralized, and municipalities had considerable control over the presence of pits and quarries. Municipalities could use by-laws or their official plans to exclude and regulate aggregate extraction within their boundaries (Baker, Slam, and Sommerville, 2001: 467). The late 1960s and early 1970s, however, proved a watershed time for aggregate policy, as the Province, at the behest of the producers, began to regulate aggregate extraction centrally. During this time the interests of the provincial government in satisfying the increasing demand from growing urban centres coincided with those of the industry, the result being the marginalization of anti-aggregate municipalities and their loss of control over the siting of pits and quarries (ibid.: 468).

In 1986 the Province of Ontario passed the *Mineral Aggregate Resources Policy Statement* by Order in Council under its *Planning Act* (ibid.: 470–1). The statement is based on a detailed inventory of aggregates in the province, projected demands for aggregates, and stipulated volumes mandated by the Province to be produced by local jurisdictions. The Province also states that mineral aggregate extraction on prime agricultural land is permitted as an interim use and as long as prescribed rehabilitation occurs (Ontario Ministry of Municipal Affairs and Housing, 2005). The Ontario Ministry of Natural Resources has prepared several research papers coordinating such uses over the past thirty years (Mackintosh, 1982, 1985).

Although the statement and recent legislation have made aggregate producers more accountable for their social and environmental impacts, policy outcomes favouring industry interests and the Province's desire for access to low-cost aggregate are assumed (Baker, Slam, and Sommerville, 2001). Aggregate extraction fees and royalties in Ontario remain extremely low in comparison to those of other jurisdictions (Binstock and Carter-Whitney, 2011: 49–54). This favouritism is well reflected at the Ontario Municipal Board which routinely favours the aggregate industry, whose members have stated that "regrettably, gravel is where you can find it" (Estrin and Swaigen, 1993: 753). There is, then, little doubt that the municipalities and citizens opposed to aggregate development have lost control over pit sitings as a result of aggregate policy being scaled at the provincial level via the *Mineral Aggregate Resources Policy Statement* (Baker, Slam, and Sommerville, 2001: 478). This situation has been strengthened by the policies of financial cutbacks to the provincial bureaucracies that have been pursued by the provincial government since 1995. The industry basically obtained self-regulatory and self-monitoring powers with regard to legislative compliance and the disbursement of a fund for the rehabilitation of abandoned aggregate pits; the fund is maintained by a small fee charged on each ton of aggregate produced (Lindgren, 1996; Winfield and Jenish, 1997). The provincial government has also incorporated the *Mineral Aggregate Resources Policy Statement* into the *Provincial Policy Statement*, which unequivocally states that any analysis of supply and demand of aggregate shall not be a consideration in the siting of new aggregate operations (Ontario Ministry of Municipal Affairs and Housing, 2005: 19). In other words, wherever aggregate exists in economically feasible quantities, regardless of whether there are other sources of licensed aggregate available nearby, the industry is entitled to mine it. The prevalence of an international and localized aggregate industry network and the construction of scale efficiency narratives by that network and the provincial state in support of aggregate protection and extraction clearly have the effect of positioning the Oak Ridges Moraine as an essential and public source of aggregates.

The *Provincial Policy Statement* contains several clauses that facilitate current and future extraction of aggregates throughout the province. It puts primary emphasis on aggregates as a natural resource that should meet the growth demands of the province, proclaiming that these resources "shall be protected for long-term use." It also stipulates that as "much mineral aggregate resources as is realistically possible shall be made available as close to markets as possible" (Ontario Ministry of Municipal Affairs and Housing, 2005: 19). The same section reinforces the industry's carte blanche to expand, irrespective of provincial need. It states, "Demonstration of need for mineral aggregate resources, including any type of supply/demand analysis, shall not be required, notwithstanding the availability, designation or licensing for extraction of mineral aggregate resources locally or elsewhere" (ibid.). Environmentalists have called this a "gravel plunder" clause as it essentially states that sand and gravel pits should be extracted as close to markets and as cheaply as possible, regardless of a demonstrated need (Parkin, 2003; Rowe, 2004; Patano and Sandberg, 2005).

The *Oak Ridges Moraine Conservation Act* similarly constructs aggregates as necessary resources for the provincial economy. Although the Act does not allow for aggregate operations in natural core areas, extraction is permitted in all other zones, constituting 68 per cent of the Moraine area, if it meets certain conditions. These conditions are fuzzy, stipulating that aggregate extraction should avoid affecting the environment "where possible" and that ecosystem functions should be restored "as soon as possible" (Ontario Ministry of Municipal Affairs and Housing, 2002a). Under the pressure of perceived resource need, the Moraine is clearly subject to future aggregate licences, given its proximity to the markets of the Greater Toronto Area (Chambers and Sandberg, 2007; Patano and Sandberg, 2005).

In addition, the extraction of aggregates in natural core areas is not always prohibited. At the time of the enactment of the *Oak Ridges Moraine Conservation Plan*, there were already hundreds of aggregate pits operating on the Moraine, with many abandoned pits and even some operating pits in natural core areas. In the Township of Uxbridge alone there were forty-five operations, some of them in natural core areas (Township of Uxbridge, 2005). The supply of aggregates licensed in these areas is estimated to last over a hundred years (Fraser, 2001), leaving the industry plenty of resources to exploit before it is necessary to license new pits. In June 2011, Matt Binstock (2011), using a GIS database of *Aggregate Resources Act* licences kept by the Ontario Ministry of Natural Resources, found forty-one pits, most of them active, either within or bordering the natural core areas of the *Oak Ridges Moraine Conservation Plan*. *The Oak Ridges Moraine Conservation Plan* is only in effect until 2015, at which time the current boundaries of the designated natural core areas can be renegotiated and changed.

However, in spite of the political, legal, and economic deck being stacked in favour of the aggregate producers, the industry has recently come under considerable criticism from several quarters. There are an increasing number of communities that are fighting local quarry and pit developments in Ontario. Although there are no current disputes over pit operations on the Moraine, there are several that have occurred in close proximity at Melancthon, Milton, Mount Nemo, and Acton on or near the Niagara Escarpment and at Caledon in the west and Shelter Valley in the east. Some of these local battles have been successful in stalling and even stopping the extension of old pits and the expansion of new pits and quarries (Shuff, 2011a, 2011b). The protests often take on a "not in my backyard" character where the local protest groups strive to identify some unique natural characteristic of their locale that warrants the exclusion of aggregate operations. But there are also wider appeals. The everyday practices of the aggregate industry are contested because of the health impacts from intense noise and vibrations and dust emissions and because of the safety issues related to heavy truck traffic on local roads along the haul routes to markets. The Pembina Institute, the Environmental Commissioner of Ontario, the now-defunct Canadian Institute for Environmental Law and Policy, and a small environmental organization called Gravel Watch have provided such critiques of the industry, questioning its demand projections and its recycling and rehabilitation efforts (Miller, 2005; Winfield and Taylor, 2005; Gravel Watch Ontario, 2006; Binstock and Carter-Whitney, 2011). In the next chapter we note that the industry and its consultants are countering such critiques by building a nature and ecological aesthetic that is commensurate with environmental values.

Conclusion

The efforts to conserve nature on the Oak Ridges Moraine are genuine but tenuous. The nature conservation exercise on the Moraine is typically perceived and portrayed as a rational exercise based on planning expertise, assessments, and prescriptions. The use of expertise seeks to mediate a contested ground through careful conservation legislation, natural science expertise, close monitoring, public participation, new governance structures, and policy instruments. The housing development industry, the infrastructure complex that depends on it and is part of it, the aggregate industry, the provincial government, regional and local governments, local residents, and environmentalists thus struggle to advance particular interests, but the use of a rational policy keeps the interests of each actor in check. In many ways there is a consensus that the Oak Ridges Moraine legislation is a step in the right direction of nature conservation.

We propose as a more plausible explanation that conservation planning is linked intimately to the exercise in political power, which is shaped by divergent material interests. The planning rationality in the Oak Ridges Moraine legislation may therefore compromise conservation objectives. First, there are conceptual frames that favour growth in the form of new industrial, commercial, housing, transportation infrastructure, and extractive (especially aggregate) activities over conservation prerogatives. Second, the variable scaling of natural science data on the Oak Ridges Moraine typically favours development over conservation in legal conflict resolutions.

When the Oak Ridges Moraine is scaled as a conservation object, and natural science is the preferred means to assess the impact of development projects, such development projects are typically approved. Scientific studies are sometimes based on uncertain conclusions that favour elements of growth. When conflicts arise over that growth, interventions typically support development actors, who have the law on their side. Their substantial financial resources are a bonus rather than a determinant in the defence of their position. Environmentalists' engagement in these conflicts is invariably covered dramatically in the media, but is ultimately compromised. The odds of winning are generally low, while at the same time the conflicts obscure conservation options that are based on different social and political arrangements where the boundaries of growth and conservation are erased. Growth impacts on specific areas and on flora and fauna are considered separately rather than collectively, cumulatively, and synergistically. Such areas include housing subdivisions, road systems, sewer pipes, and aggregate sites.

The Oak Ridges Moraine legislation, then, contains and acts out a taken-for-granted concept of economic growth, and hides or refuses to interrogate a spatial view of ecology and a permissive view of hydrogeological evidence when evaluating the impact of development projects. The legislation does not acknowledge the political nature of expertise or question the assumptions that underpin the legal, scientific, and private measures used to mediate and balance growth and nature conservation. These processes leave a suburban and/or exurban landscape simultaneously infused with both growth and nature conservation. Conversely, growth and nature conservation are infused with suburban and exurban values, leaving marginalized or obscured any other ways of knowing, thinking, and acting out human or non-human relations.

Chapter Seven

Producing Exclusive Landscape Aesthetics

As emphasized throughout this book, many urban dwellers are attracted to suburban and exurban locations because they value a landscape aesthetic of scenic views, woodlands, and water features. The countryside has transformed from a space of production to an exurban space of consumption, where the old primary production activities (such as mineral extraction, forestry, and farming) are either challenged to make room for new consumption-oriented activities (such as housing, recreation, and environmental conservation) or transformed to correspond to these new values (Cloke and Little, 1997; Haan and Long, 1997; Furuseth and Lapping, 1999; Walker, 2003).

In the transformation of the countryside from spaces of production to spaces of consumption, myriad tensions and conflicts are pitting a productive class of farmers and of workers in resource extractive sectors against a service class of professionals and/or retirees (Phillips, 1998) (figure 7.1). Marsden et al. (1993: 188) define the rural landscape as a "preserved landscape" where the reconstitution of rurality is highly challenged and often controlled by articulate consumption interests that use the political system to protect their positional goods. They describe the productivist rural landscape as a "contested landscape" where decision making reflects local economic priorities, and "development projects" are likely to cause less contention (ibid.).

Such a conceptualization corresponds closely to the tensions on the peripheries of the Greater Toronto Area and on the Oak Ridges Moraine, though the full picture is more complicated. There are difficulties, for example, in classifying the housing sector because it is both a production- and a consumption-oriented activity fractured along social, spatial, and temporal lines. There are exurban residents who live

Figure 7.1: Equestrian landscape on the Moraine

Equestrian estates are a common aesthetic feature of the Moraine landscape. Horse breeding, riding, and showjumping are common activities, especially in the western and central parts of the Moraine. Source: the authors, 2007

on large or estate lots, and there are people who live in suburbs. Both resist development in their own backyards, insisting that the nature that attracted them to settle there in the first place now be protected. Such local residents may also support certain forms of farming that maintain an open and idyllic landscape. Some are hobby farmers; some are organic farmers who have found a small and exclusive market niche. Most farmers, however, who are caught in the increased cost of farming and in falling agricultural commodity prices, support the continued right to sell their lands to the highest bidder, no matter what their future use. There are also differences across the Moraine, with some political jurisdictions, especially in the eastern sections of the Moraine, being more accommodating to house subdivision developments and resource-extractive activities than to environmental and nature conservation activities.

In spite of such complications, we propose that there are two distinct dominant landscape aesthetics on the Oak Ridges Moraine that coexist in frequent tension and contradiction: one associated with amenity and the other connected to resource extraction. We understand aesthetics as something that goes beyond a position grounded in materiality or material conditions and that is associated with more than one particular group or social class. Instead, aesthetics comprises a shared value, an outlook, or an imaginary that is common to a cross-section of groups and individuals from a variety of professional, social, and economic categories. It can thus be shared by federal, provincial, and local politicians, exurban elites, environmentalists, naturalists, state bureaucrats, and ecologists.

The first aesthetic is based on exurban amenity and post-productivist rural values that emphasize the environmental, natural, scenic, recreational, and life quality aspects of the landscape. It is based on the stories and historical constructions of the Moraine as an amenity and a naturally significant area, the emotional connections to its space and place, and the shared struggles of its conservation by residents, environmentalists, politicians, and bureaucrats. It is also based on the story of a privatized nature and a process of private rather than public conservation measures.

The second landscape aesthetic is based on the resource- and infrastructure-based values that emphasize the resources necessary for a continued prospering provincial economy. Roads, aggregates, housing, industry, warehousing facilities, and farm products are crucial ingredients of this aesthetic. There is a belief in so-called win-win situations in which planning and expertise can yield natural resources, natural amenities, and biodiversity values.

However, there is a twist to both these aesthetics. The nature aesthetic is often dependent on the very resource development that it resists. This is perhaps most obvious with regard to those residents who already live on the Moraine, who commute and travel on the roads that intersect it, and who now resist further development. Similarly, the resource sector presents itself as an environmental steward with heightened awareness and uses ecological language and methods to claim a deep attachment to nature as well as an expertise in producing win-win ecologies that yield a combination of amenity, biodiversity, resource, and infrastructure values. We explore in particular the aggregate industry and its production of a landscape that it claims gives win-win results with respect to promoting resource, nature, and amenity values. This industry is of particular interest, we suggest, because it lies at the very heart of an urban economy built on sand, gravel, stone, cement, and concrete, the building material for which the Moraine constitutes a crucial source of raw material (Sandberg and Wallace, 2013).

We arrive at a paradox and contradiction: the amenity aesthetic and the resource-necessity aesthetic have a lot in common. The amenity aesthetic is in large part dependent on the resource aesthetic, though it refuses to acknowledge it, while the resource-necessity aesthetic, though claiming to live up to the amenity aesthetic, routinely fails to do so. The implication of this critique is far reaching. It calls for a rethinking of the social divisions that are in place and of the very levels of consumption and quality of life that are sought in general.

"The Irresistible Lure of Risk, Real Estate, and Romance"

In an article in *House and Home* (Sgroi, 2005: 75) two "city people" are featured as pioneers, living in a rebuilt log cabin in Northumberland County on the Oak Ridges Moraine. Driven by "the irresistible lure of risk, real estate, and romance," the couple represents the invasion of exurbanites on the Moraine. Duncan and Duncan (2004), in a study of Bedford, New York, argue that such exurbanites subscribe to a specific nature aesthetic based on amenity values (see also Cadieux, 2010). The emphasis is on visual values, such as topography and an open landscape, that enhance scenic vistas. The Duncans show that a nature aesthetic can be used as a front that conceals an exclusionary politics. Wealthy residents may not only resort to exclusionary zoning practices that openly keep out houses and properties of a certain size; they may also classify and define the nature associated with estate living as of key ecological importance and then assign that nature as deserving of protection. Exurbs have been portrayed as stockholder belts, cocktail belts, gentleman or estate farming areas, or rural estates (Punter, 1974: 8; see also Spectorsky, 1955). A recent review of the exurbs of large metropolitan areas in the United States, however, reveals considerable diversity, stating that "just 6 per cent of large metropolitan area residents live in an exurb, and these exurbs vary from affordable housing havens for middle-class families, to 'favored quarters' for high-income residents, to the path of least resistance for new development" (Berube et al., 2006).

The Development of an Exurban Amenity Aesthetic

Prominent parts of the Oak Ridges Moraine have a long history of being socially constructed or aestheticized as amenity landscapes for the elite (Punter, 1974; Walker, 1987). Wealthy families of the Toronto elite, such as the Sir John Pellatt, Baldwin, Eaton, St George, Strathy, and Flavelle families, bought properties on the Moraine from the late 1890s into the 1920s. They were the only ones who could afford to develop second estate homes in the pastoral and wooded hills of the Moraine. They were highly selective in their choice of properties and targeted prime locations where there were lakes, or the possibilities of constructing lakes, along with a varied topography and spectacular scenery. Typically the land acquisitions were large enough to protect vistas and prevent the incursions of neighbouring buildings. As Punter (1974: 107) points out, "only prime locations were selected, normally with a lake (or an obvious site for a lake) and with a topography tailor-made for 'Capability Brown' landscaping. Further purchases were made generally to ensure privacy and to prevent potential development on land abutting their estates." The Eaton family, owners of the former chain of Eaton Company stores, for example, acquired lands surrounding a kettle lake in King Township and built Eaton Hall; it was completed in the 1930s, and Lady Eaton lived there periodically until her death in 1970. The Eatons were not the first to build country estates in King. Their purchase came on the recommendation of their Toronto neighbour, financier Sir Henry Mill Pellatt, owner of Casa Loma in Toronto, who already owned land in the township (Eaton Hall, 2012).

John Punter (1974) initially documented the exurban invasion of the Oak Ridges Moraine in the 1960s and 1970s. Gerald Walker (1987) has described these exurbanites as upper-middle-class individuals of British derivation who saw the Moraine as a "conservative refuge": "They wished for an environment where natural prospects, woody vegetation and running water were visually available. They had strong and well defined landscape preferences and the financial ability to live where these visual characteristics were present ... The Moraine was ... the romantic image of a pastoral countryside" (Walker, 1987: 135).

So-called country or rural estates are a common category of housing development among these exurbanites. According to one builder, such rural estates possess four criteria: they have a scenic site, they are accessible by roads, they are coherent and self-contained with regard to water provision and sewage disposal, and they possess a backdrop of trees (Allemang, 1985). Developments of this type have been common in the housing market on the Moraine from Caledon to Uxbridge since the 1970s (ibid.). One frequent element of these estates is the presence of horses associated with equestrian competition and hunting clubs. The mayor of King Township commented, for example, that "it's been said that there are more horses than people in King" (quoted in ibid.).

The beginning of exurban settlements on the Moraine, however, only started in earnest after the Second World War. At that time the *Provincial Planning Act* put restrictions on severances and subdivisions of farmlands, yet provided opportunities and loopholes for exurban large-lot estate development. Punter (1974: 133) argues that the previous ethic guiding land disposal was "that an individual was free to dispose of his land in any way he chose." As a result, *permissiveness* was the watchword of municipal planning, farmers readily receiving consents from local planning boards to sever lands for purchase by middlemen or exurbanites. In 1949 an amendment to the *Planning Act* further reduced the power of planning boards to control development, by removing all lots exceeding four hectares (ten acres) from their control. The intent of the amendment was to avoid hardships in the countryside and to facilitate the creation of new farms. However, the liberal consents and the four-hectares loophole "became the floodgates through which the demand for building lots in rural areas was filled" (ibid.).

An additional element that shaped exurbia was the designation of the townships as the area of subdivision control, followed by the passage of by-laws regulating the sizes of lots (depending on the lot being serviced by septic tanks or sewer pipe systems) and of setbacks and floor space in order to ensure that those living there would not be a drain on the municipal tax base with regard to services. Services, Punter (ibid.) argues, "were increased to arbitrarily high levels to ensure that only the middle income group and above could afford these homes."

The emphasis on the amenity, scenery, and recreation values of the Moraine developed in tandem with a community of wealthy exurbanites in the 1970s and 1980s. The planning department of the Regional Municipality of York, for example, noted the significance of the exurban invasion of its rural areas in the early 1970s: "The pressures for rural-residential subdivisions (and consents) increasingly are symptomatic of a shift in emphasis from the fully serviced, urban residential lot to the larger, unserviced lot in the Region's extensive rural areas" (Regional Municipality of York, 1972: 3).

John Punter's assessment of the *Toronto Centred Region Plan* corresponds closely to the development of an exclusive exurbia on the Oak Ridges Moraine. Punter (1974: 514) argues that the provincial government and its planners congratulated themselves on an "overwhelmingly favourable public response to their proposals for maintaining the Oak Ridges Moraine and surrounding areas in their natural state and confining urbanizing influences to the lakeshore." Yet this vision restricted public recreational use and did "nothing other than grossly inflate the property of those exurbanites who 'beat the freeze.'" These results, Punter further argues, were not naturally given. Instead they could have been substituted with policies that would have accommodated both public recreational demands and more varied residential needs in the area.

The status of large parts of the Oak Ridges Moraine as an upper-middle-class preserve at such an early stage reflected its desirability as a place for homes in a pastoral setting and as a site in close proximity to Toronto for the daily car commuter. These residents also exhibited the traits of an incipient cadre of conservationists fighting to defend and maintain their pastoral refuge in the midst of a growing metropolis. Punter (1974: 15–16) writes: "Increasingly too the exurban voice is being heard on issues that vitally affect the countryside of Southern Ontario, and exurbanites are marshalling their considerable resources to fight Federal airports, provincial new-towns, municipal garbage sites, crown corporation hydro-lines, and corporate gravel pits. These are all sure signs that exurbia is coming of age, that it has become an established way of life in certain well-defined areas of the province."

Debbe Crandall, prominent spokesperson for Save the Oak Ridges Moraine Coalition, grew up and currently lives in one of these exurban areas. She refers to it as a place in which an environmental consciousness existed long before the Oak Ridges Moraine legislation. The Town of Caledon in the late 1970s transformed rural areas into estate community areas, in which lots varied from 0.8 to 6.0 hectares (2 to 15 acres) per house. These measures, Crandall (2004) claims, were developed from "complex geotechnical work that based the density of houses on the ability of the soil to attenuate private septic effluence." Her activism was triggered when local politicians sought to circumvent these provisions by selling lands for higher-density housing development, for personal gain. Although Crandall insists that this was not a "not in my backyard" intervention, she acknowledges that large parts of these areas housed and continue to house a select group of wealthy people whose property rights or property values are enhanced by nature conservation.

At the time that the estates were invading the Oak Ridges Moraine, cautions were levelled with regard to the ecological disruptions they might cause. A dispersed settlement pattern called for an extensive road network that invited invasive species and disturbed local wildlife, and the septic systems threatened to pollute the groundwater (Regional Municipality of York, 1972; Punter, 1974; Gates, 1978). In some instances, municipalities approved estate developments in areas designated as environmentally sensitive by the provincial Ministry of Natural Resources (Gates, 1978). In Richmond Hill, parts of the Jefferson Forest were turned into the Trailwood Estates, an exclusive estate subdivision with two-acre plots and mansion-style houses (Gates, 1978). Social and environmental critiques of such estate developments have subsided over time. One rare instance occurred in early 2001 with the publication of the interim report stalling development on the Moraine. At the time, Gregor Beck of the Federation of Ontario Naturalists pointed out that the report's provision for the building of residences "opens the potentially dangerous door to estate housing developments that cater to the rich" (Mallan, 2001: A7). The point was reinforced by Liberal Member of Provincial Parliament Michael Colle on the same occasion: "It's a weak-kneed report that will please primarily people who want to build million-dollar estate lots, and multi-millionaire developers are very happy today ..." (ibid.) (figure 7.2).

With the passing of the *Oak Ridges Moraine Conservation Act* and *Plan* at the end of 2002, such concerns have largely disappeared, though new estates continue to be built on the Moraine. In April 2009 one residence on Forest Ridges Road in the Trailwood Estates was on sale for $4 million. At the same time, a building lot (0.8 hectare) on the estates was advertised for sale at $599,000 and advertised as "ready for submission of site plan and application for Building Permit." The advertisement illustrates the unknown areas of grandparented building permits that are available on Moraine lands. In 2011 the lot was still advertised for sale (Sandberg, Wekerle, and Gilbert, 2012). Ironically, the Trailwood Estates is designated a natural core area in the *Oak Ridges Moraine Conservation Plan*. Parts adjoining the Jefferson Forest have been turned into a subdivision that has appropriated the name of Jefferson Forest (figure 7.3).

Many other estate developments benefit from natural core area designation, effectively hiding their questionable environmental histories

Figure 7.2: Moraine for wildlife, *not* millionaires

The growth of rural estates on the Oak Ridges Moraine is seldom raised in the nature conservation discourse. In the rare instance above, precipitated by the interim report stalling developments on the Moraine in August 2001, a placard identifies the spread of rural estates on the Moraine as a threat to the natural integrity of the Moraine. Source: *Toronto Star*, 15 August 2001: A7; Paul Irish and Getstock.com

and sanctioning their current existence. In 2012 Ashton Ridge was building a gated golf community in the Palgrave Forest, named Legacy Pines, again in the natural core area of the *Oak Ridges Moraine Conservation Plan* (figure 7.4). Next to it, in the settlement zone, large rural estate homes are built as a routine feature of the landscape (figure 7.5). Other similar developments are now being built or planned in close proximity to the Moraine (Binstock, 2009).

The settlement pattern presents a paradox. In the late 1990s strong lobbying efforts by citizen groups of residents and environmentalists, and technical studies by bureaucrats and scientists, coalesced to paint the Oak Ridges Moraine as a sprawl-threatened landscape that sustains broader ecological values (such as the health of full watersheds and the habitats of a variety of species at risk) and as one of the last continuous corridors of green space left in south-central Ontario (Johnson, 1999).

Figure 7.3: Jefferson Forest

In 1976 Jefferson Forest in Richmond Hill represented one of the last substantial deer yards within an hour's drive of Toronto. It was also designated as a biologically sensitive area by the Ministry of Natural Resources. Yet approval was granted by the Town of Richmond Hill to proceed with development in the area in the mid-1970s. Trailwood Estates was one such community that now features multimillion-dollar homes. Subdivision developments still continue in and around the forest. In 2010 Jefferson Forest was known more as a real estate development than as a forest. Source: the authors, 2004

Yet the building of rural estates and subdivisions continues in a climate in which the Oak Ridges Moraine is increasingly aestheticized in conformity with a conservation and nature norm that supports an exclusive residential and recreational landscape.

In mainstream media and among environmentalists in the Greater Toronto Area the development industry is often accorded tremendous power over the fate of conservation policy. Newspaper columnist John Barber of the *Globe and Mail*, for example, frequently comments on the close connection between local politicians and developers in promoting

Figure 7.4: Legacy Pines, Caledon

Situated within a natural core area of the Oak Ridges Moraine, Legacy Pines is described as follows by the developer: "Situated in Palgrave, in the town of Caledon, Legacy Pines offers the allure of a private village enclave located in a convenient semi-rural setting. The finely detailed and aesthetically pleasing luxury condominium villas are designed for easy living and active adult life-styles. This gated community also boasts a newly opened 9-hole golf course, clubhouse, fitness centre and tennis courts. With its stunning views, scenic walking trails, natural ravines, tree lined properties and an abundance of wild-life, Legacy Pines is truly a leisure paradise" (www.ashtonridge.com). Source: the authors, 2012

unabated urban sprawl and on the often direct influence, even corruption, that exists in these relationships. There are also frequent allusions to the connections between the development industry and provincial politicians and to the backroom channels that developers may employ to reach the ears of the politicians (Ferguson 1991a, 1991b, 1991c; Brennan and Benzie, 2005). Robert MacDermid (2009) has documented the close ties between municipal campaign funding and the development

Figure 7.5: Home on the Moraine

This house was built recently in Caledon, in a settlement area of the *Oak Ridges Moraine Conservation Plan*. It combines an aesthetic that favours the building of rural estate homes on large lots and another that considers such estates to be an integral part of the Moraine, a "Moraine place." Source: the authors, 2011

industry in the Greater Toronto Area, especially in the municipalities that encompass parts of the Oak Ridges Moraine.

Developers have nevertheless adjusted to the conservation policy in the Greater Toronto Area. In 2000, prominent local developer Joe Lebovic claimed that he too had a "home" on the Moraine and that he was concerned about nature values. Lebovic, who was instrumental in building some of the housing developments in Richmond Hill, confirmed his bioregional commitment by stating: "Do you really think that we want to harm our environment? Of course not. We have to live here, too … I think I am as conscious of the environment as the people who are against us" (quoted in Lakey, 2000a: B2). Lebovic also stands the City of Toronto's environmental concerns on their head, accusing the City, which sponsored Save the Rouge Valley System's intervention at the OMB hearing on the Richmond Hill housing expansion, by stating: "Millions of litres per year of raw sewage is dumped by the City into Lake Ontario. It goes straight into the lake, which is why the beaches often have to be closed due to contamination ... So once again, taxpayers are victims to wasteful politics and weak- kneed politicians who cave in to any Tom, Dick or Harry from a special interest group. The Richmond Hill fiasco is another example as to how the so-called 'environmental' movement in this country is simply another excessive, unjustifiable set of expensive and questionable land claims" (quoted in Francis, 2000: D02).

Other developers played a key role in the formulation of the Oak Ridges Moraine legislation. Three of them were appointed to the Oak Ridges Moraine Panel: Fred DeGasperis, Peter Gilgan, and Mario Cortellucci, all of whom own land on the Oak Ridges Moraine. Fred De-Gasperis is president of Con-Drain Company Limited, a company started in the 1950s to install water services. His company has grown to be involved in all aspects of municipal construction, from buying land to building whole communities. DeGasperis has an interest in Metrus Development Inc., while his son and other relatives operate Aspen Ridge Homes. Peter Gilgan, owner of Mattamy Homes, is one of Canada's largest individual homebuilders. A chartered accountant, he started building large custom homes on the Burlington waterfront in 1978. In the three-year housing boom starting in 1986, Gilgan built hundreds of homes in the Glen Abbey area of Oakville. Gilgan and his firm won high praise from an environmental group for their plans for Morningside Heights, an 800-home subdivision on land in Scarborough (*Toronto Star*, 2001). In the summer of 2006, Mattamy's Halton division introduced various green features, such as programmable thermostats, bamboo floors, and power-generating windmills on roofs, in a subdivision, Hawthorne Village in Milton, to assess consumers' willingness to pay for these goods (Dubé, 2006).

These progressive developers have, in some instances, worked in unison with environmentalists. The Morningside Heights subdivision – not located on the Oak Ridges Moraine but part of the Rouge River Valley and the Ontario Greenbelt, the headwaters of which are on the Moraine – was backed by one of the two most prominent environmental organizations in the Oak Ridges Moraine struggle, Save the Rouge Valley System (then under the leadership of Glenn De Baeremaeker). According to De Baeremaeker, the housing development represented a good example of a win-win situation: "It is very rare that you see developers designing a subdivision in a way that protects the environment ... Usually it's a matter of pave it first and ask questions later. These developers went out of their way to identify the woodlot and build around it, and to protect the creek and the area around it. We got millions of dollars in concessions from them that they really didn't have to give us. I'm hoping that this can become a model of co-operation for developments all across the country" (quoted in Lakey, 2000b: B2).

In combination with its environmental consideration, this project has also bought into an exclusive environmentalism based on wealth and privacy. It is thus described as a "huge, upscale housing project on the last large piece of land available for residential development in Toronto" (ibid.). In another image, combining the visions of ecology and exclusivity, one proponent labels the project "very gutsy. It balances the interests of Mother Nature and those of capitalism" (Ashton quoted in Abbate, 1998: A10).

The development industry also sponsors studies on the hydrogeology of the Moraine that it feels are useful to accommodate rather than prevent development (Greater Toronto Home Builders' Association, 2001). Special consultants have worked on developing a clean-water collector system that will gather water from rooftops for recharge into the Moraine. The industry also has a proven record of building more densely populated subdivisions, a practice that has less of an impact on the environment. Both the Greater Toronto and the Ontario Home Builders' associations sponsor environmental research and promote such practices in their official trade journals. Indeed, the authors of this book were solicited to write a short piece for a special green issue of the Ontario Home Builders' journal published in the summer of 2007 (Wekerle, Gilbert, and Sandberg, 2007).

Folded into the conservation aesthetic promoted by the development interests is also a recreational landscape that is shaped by and that complements the natural landscape. Golf courses dominate and are often developed in conjunction with estate housing. Although not always welcomed, and sometimes resisted, they are by far the most extensive and growing recreational land use on the Moraine. They are also increasingly imagined and produced as ecological landscapes, spurring marketing and businesses that specialize in environmental golf ventures. We noted one particular golf venture in chapter 2. A recent study identifies forty-one golf courses in the Moraine area (Garfinkel et al., 2008). Although a project has not yet been realized, even the Ganaraska

Conservation Authority has courted Envirogolf Inc. (a company headed by former mayor of Toronto and environmental advocate David Crombie), which specializes in greening golf courses or "environmental restoration through golfing" (Paul, 2000), a growing trend. In Uxbridge the Estates of Wyndance, a 125-home golf community, with houses in the range of $569,000 to $874,990, claims to use a "least-disturbance" ethos, which "incorporates existing trees, streams, rocks, vegetation and the natural topography of the site to create a course that is eco-conscious and unique" (Noik-Bent, 2006) (figure 7.6). According to professional golfer and entrepreneur Greg Norman, who designed the course, "it is not only our desire to create a great golf course, but also find a perfect balance between maximizing the value of the residential component and creating a plan that is conducive to protecting its surroundings … I like to think that we leave the property in better environmental condition than we found it" (quoted in ibid.). The houses also include various energy-efficient devices, as well as a water filtration and sewage treatment plant that serves both the community and the golf course. When queried about the sometimes controversial issue of development on the Moraine, the developer replied: "This is not really a case of taking a pristine greenfield. This is a case of taking an operating gravel pit, which had come to the end of its commercial life, and we brought it back to a new use" (ibid.). The developer begins to articulate a nature aesthetic that dovetails with resource use, in this case aggregates, that we will address in more detail in the next section of this chapter.

There are other recreational ventures on the Moraine. These include horse farms and agritainment complexes, where the urban dwellers can go for a horseback ride on groomed trails or can picnic and pick their annual bushel of fresh apples. Bike paths and trails are built along the right of way of abandoned rail lines, and a central activity of the Oak Ridges Moraine and the Niagara Escarpment protection ventures is the maintenance of hiking trails along their spines. In one instance, the Moraine Train, an old narrow-gauge rail line with vintage trains, is maintained by volunteers for tourists and railway enthusiasts. As we noted before, the Oak Ridges Moraine also harbours extensive forest areas that were established as monocultural pine plantations in support of sawmilling in the 1920s and 1930s but have since been turned into recreational forests.

The Moraine is also dotted with spas and retreats that use their location as a major selling point. At one such establishment, the Moraine is described as providing "a tranquil setting among horse barns and

Figure 7.6: Club Link Wyndance Golf community

Golf courses and, as above, golf communities where estate developments are tied to golf courses and golf club membership proliferate on the Moraine. In the photo above, the view of the Wyndance Golf community is looking from the east to the west. At the bottom of the photo is Fourth Concession Road, to the left is Highway 47, and to the right Church Street. The housing estate is located to the right of the forested area in the middle of the picture. Source: Lou Wise, 2007. Additional materials are available at York University Libraries, Clara Thomas Archives and Special Collections, Lou Wise Fonds, F0539.

rolling fields" (HighFields Inn and Country Spa, 2004) where clients can indulge in alternative treatments. The latter include representations of the Moraine as a First Nations site where guests can enjoy a "new sweat lodge for traditional healing ceremonies and a tepee where individuals pursue shamanistic journeys" (ibid.). The presence of First Nations activities, as we suggested in chapter 2, here mirrors the concerns and worries of an elite segment of society, and the healing caters to the alienated urban residents who are looking for a reprieve and respite on

Figure 7.7: Signage along highways 400, 403, and 115

Roadside signs announce to car drivers their entry onto the Oak Ridges Moraine. The signage is supposed to educate and raise awareness about the Moraine. It no doubt also offers political benefits. However, it also obscures the fact that the very same highways disrupt the continuity of the Moraine as a landform. Source: the authors, 2004

the Oak Ridges Moraine. The relatively short distance of travel from the city to the Moraine makes such reprieve and respite possible.

Road infrastructure is an integral part of the growth prerogatives of the provincial economy and society. However, it is also part of the nature aesthetic. Although individual highways and highway extensions are routinely challenged (though rarely successfully), the highways per se remain firmly intact, indeed entrenched, as "economic corridors" –resembling the ecosystem language of *natural corridors* (see Ontario Ministry of Public Infrastructure and Renewal, 2006). There have been some recent concerns about the disruptions that roads cause to the landscape continuity and the ecological connectivity across the

Moraine (Kalinowski, 2008; Ontario Ministry of Transportation, 2006). However, in most instances, roads are discursively absent from or written out of the debates and maps on nature conservation on the Moraine. There is, thus, a general lack of concern over the already existing dense network of roads on the Oak Ridges Moraine both in the general discourse and in graphic illustrations of the Moraine. Fenech et al. (2006) report that the major paved roads on the Moraine increased from 126 kilometres in 1935 to 554 kilometres in 1965 and to 1,016 kilometres in 1995. Most of these roads, which by 1995 included four multi-lane highways, run south to north, creating barriers to wildlife movement, and continue to be widened and added to without systematic protests.

Visiting most of the natural and heritage features of the Moraine is premised on car travel, and information on access is typically addressed to automobile drivers. Following observations made by other students of modern conservation, it can be noted that the enjoyment of nature as scenery viewed from a car window is a prominent feature of nature planning; however, drivers have to be reminded by prominent highway signs that they are entering the Oak Ridges Moraine, Niagara Escarpment, and Greenbelt (figure 7.7).

The Development of a Private Conservation Aesthetic

One element of a public nature aesthetic celebrates specific conservation areas on the Moraine and public access to them. In the much celebrated 120-page book collection on the Moraine simply entitled *Oak Ridges Moraine*, published by Save the Oak Ridges Moraine Coalition in 1997, most of the twenty-eight chapters deal with specific public places or places open to the public. These places and trails encourage travellers to view and visit the Moraine. Aside from this volume, there are voices within various organizations that support the purchase of public lands for conservation. The City of Toronto, for example, has a land acquisition policy that has been invoked in buying land on the Moraine, the most recent purchase being Swan Lake in Richmond Hill (Kuitenbrouwer, 2008). Councillor and environmentalist Glenn De Baeremaeker has been particularly active in submitting proposals for the City of Toronto to purchase land in order to expand the Rouge Park so that it connects the Rouge River watershed with the Oak Ridges Moraine (Spears, 2009).

There is, however, a growing emphasis on a private conservation aesthetic with respect to the Oak Ridges Moraine. Within the nature conservation community, lands and ecosystem services are increasingly seen as commodities that can be bought and sold (Robertson, 2000). This view is reflected in the growing role and popularity of conserved private lands. Schemes include the use of policy instruments that allow for tax relief for private landowners who set aside their lands for nature conservation purposes. It is common for estate planners, business, and environmental groups to work collectively to promote private nature conservation schemes (Logan and Wekerle, 2008; Sandberg and Wekerle, 2010). This is consistent with the following current societal trends: a scepticism of state regulation and intervention; a general suspicion of politicians, government bureaucrats, and experts; and a heightened belief in the power of market forces to foster environmental well-being (ibid.). Examples of private conservation measures include the rise of private land trusts, stewardship programs, and various state measures providing tax incentives for private conservation.

Private conservation schemes involve federal and provincial parastatal institutions and environmental organizations engaging in partnerships for environmental governance, including Environment Canada (2010), the Ontario Heritage Trust (2012), the Oak Ridges Moraine Foundation (2011g), Friends of the Greenbelt Foundation (2012), the Federation of Ontario Naturalists, the Toronto and Region Conservation Authority (2004b), the Ontario Land Trust Alliance (2005), and the Ontario Ministry of Natural Resources (Canadian Urban Institute, 2006). Their programs enable individual and corporate landowners to protect their property in perpetuity, to retain title, and/or to be eligible for enhanced income tax benefits by donating ecologically sensitive land to a qualified registered charitable organization or government body.

The landowners who donate conservation easements tend to share several common characteristics; they are exurbanites, older, affluent, predominantly white and professional, and play a crucial role in informing their neighbours of donation options and opportunities and then introducing them to willing donation recipients (Environment Canada, 2010; Estrin and Swaigen, 1993). The programs note that private conservation schemes represent a significant opportunity to enhance the natural heritage by assisting landowners to increase the economic value of their properties through effective stewardship. The "socio-economics of natural heritage" is about focusing on the fact that "nature count$" (sic), and devising market strategies to promote nature conservation (Canadian Urban Institute, 2006). The private conservation discourse is permeated and driven by money and market incentives while less emphasis is placed on the public acquisition of conservation lands and the provision of public access to such lands.

Many government representatives and environmentalists strategically embrace and normalize private nature conservation schemes. Interviewees during the course of this study downplayed the classed dimensions of private conservation schemes. They felt that although such schemes may seem to primarily benefit the wealthy, they ultimately serve everyone and provide for a better economy and better place to live. A development lawyer commented that whereas "for people who live on a low income in a public housing project in Toronto, protection of the Oak Ridges Moraine does not mean a lot ... ultimately [private] environmental protection benefits everybody" (Melling, 2004). Two representatives, from a provincial ministry and the Toronto and Region Conservation Authority, commented on the private profit motive, tax incentives, and recreational development to promote conservation, feeling that they are good hooks and societal buy-ins for nature conservation (Burnett, 2004; Doyle, 2004). The proponents of private conservation feel strongly that the emergence of more highly valued and more exclusive conserved lands, though in some regards regrettable, cannot be avoided. Accordingly, they state that land that was developable and highly valuable on the Oak Ridges Moraine before the legislation remains valuable after the conservation legislation. The act of development or the act of urbanization would have significantly increased those land values anyway (Melling, 2004; Rowe, 2004). Thus, these interviewees argued, even though some people will get wealthy because land will go up in value as a result of the legislation that restricts the supply of developable land in the region, this is not a reason not to do it. Restricting the supply of land is considered a cost that has to be paid in support of conservation. Meanwhile, the recreational and amenity needs of the urban or suburban poor, which could be served by investment in local green space and parks, are marginalized and substituted by the idea to conserve a distant Oak Ridges Moraine.

Private Conservation Arrangements on the Moraine

There is an increasing promotion of nature conservation areas on the Moraine that remain in the hands of private individuals, are poorly signed or advertised, and have limited access. Often conservation areas are named after their donors, such as the Bullen (65 hectares), Walker (70 hectares), Wright, and Smith properties held by the Ontario Heritage

Trust; the Wells (11.15 hectares), Campbell (38 hectares), and Fayden (10.34 hectares) properties held by the Oak Ridges Moraine Land Trust; and the Langtry Nature Reserve (29 hectares) held by the Nature Conservancy (Ontario Heritage Trust, 2012; Pavilons, 2012). Conservation areas may also be named after a donor's horse, as in the case of the University of Toronto's Koffler Scientific Reserve at Jokers Hill. Donated by businessman Murray Koffler, the area was held in a natural state during his occupancy. The property, as the University of Toronto calls it, is the sixth-largest private holding on the Moraine. It is held as an exclusive preserve for scientific study, though some public access is permitted in the eastern parts. Much of the research is focused on the past and current human impact on the Moraine and on the types of remedial action that can be taken. Examples of studies include the role of trees in restoring fertility to the soils of degraded sites, particularly with regard to organic matter addition, element cycling, and nutrient pumping, using the eroded soils of the area (Timmer, 2006).

The Oak Ridges Moraine Foundation identifies its land securement program as its most successful and popular activity (Oak Ridges Moraine Foundation, 2011b, 2011g). The Oak Ridges Moraine Land Trust worked closely with the foundation to promote the private conservation aesthetic. It advertises the number of hectares of land protected to date and lists prominent donors such as the Trillium, Schad, EJLB, Metcalf, and McLean foundations and the Nature Conservancy, as well as the conservation authorities, municipalities, and Ontario Nature (Shaw, 2004). It also reminds visitors that donating land is to "give a gift that lasts forever," and it displays its mandate as "protecting our legacy ... beyond policy" (ibid.). Describing the donation of land to a land trust as protecting it more securely than relying on policy feeds into the popular distrust of politics and politicians and the changes over time in political regimes and policies. Donated land will be held in conservation hands in perpetuity.

In the efforts to protect Moraine lands from development, little attention has been directed to the ways in which private land securement schemes may be uncritically driven by land use patterns, thereby neglecting the entities that are benefiting from and paying for conservation. There are also few comments explaining the Moraine's need for double protection through both regulatory and market mechanisms (Sandberg and Wekerle, 2010). Moreover, when the accumulation of lands is driven by individual decisions, the building of ecological integrity (which calls for a broader vision) may be easily compromised (Ohm,

2000). In addition, the provisions of some land securement schemes, such as conservation easements, can be terminated (ibid.). In 1999, for example, the Ontario Heritage Foundation (the Ontario Heritage Trust since 2005) sought to sell a piece of conservation lands, which had been bequeathed to it by a wealthy donor, for housing development in order to fund its other heritage projects; the transaction was only stalled by a group of activists who successfully argued in the courts that the sale would contravene the wishes of the donor (Ferenc, 1999). In this situation, private conservation programs may only satisfy their members, as opposed to public conservation schemes that must answer to the general public (Kline and Wichelns, 1998; Anderson and King, 2004). Further, with emphasis being placed on the number of hectares protected, few ask questions about the continued private nature of these lands. Public access to land is also restricted as most landowners contribute land donations through conservation easements. Through this arrangement the donors continue to live on their lands, and access remains restricted to the public. The landowners-donors merely agree to put limits or constraints on the development of their lands.

Privatizing Enforcement

Another element of the private conservation aesthetic is the delegation of monitoring and enforcement activities to citizens' groups. They in turn use volunteers for the monitoring activities. There are many who have cautioned against such developments, arguing that they result in corporatist tendencies in which elite positions are underwritten by sectoral negotiations (Bevir, 2006). The administrative role of the state is here shifting from control to coordination of non-elected partners' positions into a consensus. Some scholars question whether such arrangements lead to a democratic deficit because of the exclusion of some actors (Larner and Craig, 2005; Low, 2004; Bevir, 2006).

In the aftermath of the residents' struggle to preserve the Moraine and the enactment of provincial legislation to do so, citizens generally and residents on the Moraine specifically, while seeing the Moraine as a precious or unique place in which to live or to visit, were expected to perform conservation and monitoring tasks that were formerly undertaken by the state and state bureaucrats and experts. While there was far from a wholesale move from government to citizen monitoring of the Moraine, there was movement in that direction (for an earlier endorsement, see Tomalty et al., 1994; EcoSpark, 2012). There was also a

Figure 7.8: Koffler Scientific Reserve at Jokers Hill

The University of Toronto's Koffler Scientific Reserve at Jokers Hill in King Township. Source: the authors, 2004

distinct shift in the roles played by the conservation organizations that spoke on behalf of the Moraine. The previous struggles to "protect" and "save" the Moraine were replaced by efforts to "monitor," "sustain," and "celebrate" the Moraine, where residents applied for grants to the Oak Ridges Moraine Foundation or to Friends of the Greenbelt Foundation to pursue restoration, monitoring, and various other activities aimed at maintaining the ecological integrity of the Moraine. Monitoring the Moraine, an umbrella organization of Save the Oak Ridges Moraine Coalition, the Centre for Community Mapping, and Citizens' Environmental Watch, all sponsored in part by the Oak Ridges Moraine Foundation, provided assistance in these pursuits. Instead of the provincial government and its ministries taking on the responsibility and cost of monitoring the implementation of its own legislation, there was a growing acceptance of the provincial government giving grassroots citizen groups short-term project funding to take on this task. Non-profit organizations reliant on volunteers were thus taking on part of a task that in the past had been seen to be a core function of provincial ministries. This transfer in duties not only relieved the government of its responsibilities and public accountability but also left monitoring activities to community-based groups with limited funds, little time, lack of expertise, and no accountability to the public.

At the same time, however, these organizations often valorized the shift from state to civil society by arguing that it took, as we have noted, environmental conservation "beyond policy," that is, outside of the political cycle of changing governments and associated changes in ministry priorities and staffing. In its promotional material the Oak Ridges Moraine Foundation declared its mandate to stay clear of state intervention and command and control measures; the foundation "operates primarily by funding the work of others and through offering leadership or coordination for Moraine-wide activities where appropriate" (Oak Ridges Moraine Foundation, 2007) (figure 7.9). Thus, the non-profit and quasi-government agency set up by the state to conduct conservation measures may have channelled citizen activities into service functions rather than political activism. The possibilities for critical examination of Moraine policies were curtailed by the foundation's very meagre expenditures on research funding.

Yet the Oak Ridges Moraine Foundation's position on the role of government in conservation was ambivalent. In its most recent assessment of the Oak Ridges Moraine legislation the foundation found that the provincial government's role was generally lacking in the support of the conservation efforts on the Moraine (Oak Ridges Moraine Foundation, 2011a).

Marketing and Branding the Moraine

The marketing and branding of the Moraine as a unique landscape feature is also an important part of the private conservation aesthetic. The Oak Ridges Moraine is marketed as a name for a variety of purposes, not only private conservation but also business and ecotourism ventures, where it is understood that the Moraine has to earn its keep and contribute to the Greater Toronto Area's competitive position in the world economy (Sandberg and Wekerle, 2010). The conservation legislation itself is a way to brand the Moraine. Thus the Oak Ridges Moraine conservation legislation and the successor *Greenbelt Plan* and

Figure 7.9: The Gate House at Seneca College

The gatehouse of the former Eaton estate, at Seneca College, 13990 Dufferin Street North, is the home of the Oak Ridges Moraine Land Trust, the Oak Ridges Moraine Trail Association, and the Oak Ridges Moraine Foundation. These three organizations receive occasional state and private funds that vary in amount. Volunteers and some paid staff operate the organizations. In 2012 the Oak Ridges Moraine Foundation announced that it would fold by the end of the year if its provincial government funding was not renewed. Source: the authors, 2011

Growth Plan (which now include the Moraine) have been marketed to international observers as best-case examples of nature conservation that should be emulated by other jurisdictions (Josey, 2003). In 2003, for example, the Moraine figured as an "export commodity," being included in a study by the New Zealand Parliamentary Commissioner for the Environment (2003) entitled "Superb or Suburb? International Case Studies in Management of Icon Landscapes." The study identified the

Oak Ridges Moraine as one of three landscapes from which New Zealand could learn lessons about sustainable development.

Branding has also figured prominently in the efforts by different provincial governments to advance their status as conservation agents. Initial billboards along highways 400 and 404 declared for drivers, "Oak Ridges Moraine next 10 km," celebrating the achievement of the Conservative government that implemented the *Oak Ridges Moraine Conservation Act*. Since the election of the Liberal government in 2003, the signs telling drivers that they are entering the Oak Ridges Moraine have been changed to include the term *part of Ontario's Greenbelt* as a celebration of the Liberal government's *Greenbelt Act*. The change in signs supports Eidelman's (2010) thesis that the Moraine and Greenbelt legislation were a response to a public concern over urban sprawl, which reflects political entrepreneurship and the pursuit of electoral support.

The development industry has similarly used the Oak Ridges Moraine brand to market housing developments. As in the past, the industry is targeting wealthy professionals and retirees as customers who are looking for a second home or a home in a rural setting where a nature aesthetic and nature appreciation are keys to the enjoyment of a property (for an extensive treatment see Binstock, 2009). This aesthetic is seen in the numerous subdivisions that are named after the very same ecosystems that they have replaced. The Moraine is a key advertising tool for the property industry in those settlement areas that are still subject to development, and where developments are already present on or adjacent to the Moraine. Ravine lots, creek lots, or lots next to woods are marketed at a premium. Housing developments are portrayed as green communities that constitute privileged opportunities to live in harmony with nature. Site plans in promotional brochures show green spaces prominently and display conservation lands, kettle lakes, and nature trails in large print. Houses and roads, meanwhile, are peripheral; only in the fine print can the prospective buyer read that paths, walkways, and landscaping are conceptual and subject to change.

While still in possession of government funding, the Oak Ridges Moraine Foundation presented a whole battery of awards to groups and individuals to honour conservation efforts on the Moraine, which were then well advertised in the local media and on various websites (Oak Ridges Moraine Foundation, 2007). It also sponsored research projects that sought to raise the profile of the Oak Ridges Moraine, including designating the Moraine as a UNESCO world biosphere reserve, sponsoring photo contests and sports events, and advertising various agritourism activities. The Moraine is also part of a process of "faming" a landscape; for example, the Toronto and Region Conservation Authority awarded to the Oak Ridges Moraine Land Trust the funds of its annual Charles Sauriol Environmental Dinner for the Living City to "protect environmentally significant lands." The dinner couples the fame of the Moraine with an internationally famous environmentalist or other significant person as a speaker. Past speakers have included environmental lawyer Robert Kennedy Jr; Canada's first female astronaut, Roberta Bondar; primatologist Jane Goodall; oceanographic explorer and environmentalist Jean-Michel Cousteau; writer Margaret Atwood; environmental activist and presidential candidate Ralph Nader; and celebrity chef Michael Smith. In 2012, Mark Anielski, economist, and author of *The Economics of Happiness*, was the speaker.

The widespread funding, branding, "faming," billboards and signs, the UNESCO site aspirations, and the advertising of the number of land hectares protected have contributed to the status of the Moraine as a significant, iconic, mega, or star landscape. From one perspective, increasing the Moraine's policy visibility in order to raise money or to up its proponents' legitimacy in the eyes of donors may be seen as a magnanimous act, which lends its credibility to a new and underfunded cause. This perspective uncritically accepts the premise that corporate engagement is essential and that the Moraine as an object of nature conservation must be sold to sponsoring donors and the general public. There is virtually no incentive to examine the possible downsides of this approach, which may include the favouring of the preservation of one landscape or ecosystem over others, lost revenues from charitable land donations (for example, Ecogift Program), loss of public accountability in the operation of land trusts, and the development of exclusive landscapes (Logan and Wekerle, 2008; Sandberg and Wekerle, 2010).

The faming exercise is also fickle as fame is often ephemeral. In 2012 the Oak Ridges Moraine Foundation, in spite of several lobbying efforts, failed to secure future public funding and faced the prospects of closing its operations by the end of the year (Oak Ridges Moraine Foundation, 2011a, 2011b, 2011c, 2011d, 2011e, 2011f, 2011g, 2011h, 2011i, 2011j; Poisson, 2011; Gorrie, 2011; Schultz, 2011). It is likely that the current Liberal provincial government is favouring its own Greenbelt Foundation and sees the funding of two foundations as indefensible in what are often labelled "fiscally austere" times.

Producing a Resource Extractive Nature Aesthetic: Win-Win Ecologies

The second nature aesthetic of the exclusive landscape lies in the social construction of productive ventures as compatible with natural processes. Such accounts do not directly question the social structure of capitalist society but maintain that nature conservation and profit-driven development can be combined. We refer to this phenomenon as win-win ecologies. This is more than a crass greenwash in the form of green marketing and advertising; it is a deep and shared belief and philosophy that ecology can be accommodated, planned for, and even "improved" under growth. It makes references to ecological modernization, reconciliation ecologies, and business ecologies that can accommodate flora and fauna in productive and extractive landscapes (Rosensweig, 2003; Bullock, 1998; Abe, Bassett, and Dempsey, 1998; Roe and Van Eeten, 2002; Wilson et al., 1998; Lundholm and Richardson, 2010). Examples include fish ladders that allow migrant fish to circumvent hydroelectric dams, road culverts that allow amphibians to cross busy highways, sunk oil tankers that become fish habitats, and, as we shall argue, abandoned aggregate pits that can serve as biodiversity reserves.

We present the aggregate industry as a powerful example that promulgates and actively constructs a nature aesthetic compatible with growth. The aggregate industry is a highly invasive industry. Yet, the Ontario aggregate industry sector, including its partners in government and business, clothes itself in a conservationist aesthetic in the efforts of producing and selling its products, securing access to the resource, rehabilitating individually exhausted pits, and building a natural landscape from a collection of exhausted and sometimes active pits and quarries. On many scores this position is a powerful message since it claims to meet the needs of all Ontarians while taking into account both resource and environmental concerns in an integrated manner. These assertions, we suggest, provide an arresting image of overcoming the tension between growth and conservation while, in fact, failing to accommodate both.

The aggregate industry portrays itself as a good steward of the environment. This is a function of its own efforts to both reform its practices on the ground and discursively use words and ideas. Such measures are developed by individual companies as well as their central organization, the Ontario Stone, Sand, and Gravel Association, along with large international consultancy firms that do extensive work for the industry globally. Industry representatives have constituted a powerful voice on all boards and commissions struck to deal with the conservation of the Oak Ridges Moraine. A past environmental manager of the Ontario Stone, Sand, and Gravel Association, Peter White, served as chairman of the Oak Ridges Moraine Technical Working Committee, which was commissioned in the early 1990s by the Ontario Ministry of Natural Resources to prepare exhaustive studies on various aspects of the Moraine. The industry and its supporters thus use a powerful rhetoric that parallels that of its opponents.

At the very beginning of the aggregate cycle the industry employs the notion of *protection* (a term that is also entrenched in conservation policy) to guard aggregates from being built over or conserved before they have been extracted. Access to aggregates, in other words, needs to be protected just like any other ecosystem service or environmental amenity in nature. Both environmental resources and aggregates are presented as essential for human survival and the public good. The industry and environmentalists share the word *sterile* when referring to urban, constructed, or conserved conversions, that is, aggregate lands that have been paved, built over, or put into parks or conservation areas. In the 2010 state-of-the-resources study, Parkin et al. wrote: "The Oak Ridges Moraine Conservation Plan prohibits aggregate extraction in the Natural Core Area. As a result, over 50% of the selected aggregate area within the Oak Ridges Plan Area is sterilized (precluded from extraction) ... [a] small environmental feature has the potential to sterilize access to a 60 ha resource area" (quoted in Ontario Ministry of Natural Resources, 2009a: 12, 32). The industry refers to aggregate resources as having been sterilized by being buried under roads and buildings and thereby made inaccessible for extraction. It often laments, for example, that the largest aggregate deposits in Ontario are located under the City of Toronto (Chambers and Sandberg, 2007). Environmentalists similarly refer to built or paved over areas as barren of nature, desolate and unproductive (as in "paving paradise"). Often, of course, aggregate materials are used to sterilize nature. However, the terminology used by the combatants is the same: a so-called resource is *sterilized* in both instances.

Both the industry and environmentalists share the view that all ecosystems inevitably undergo succession. Ecologists note, for example, that local ecosystems may evolve from grasses and shrubs to

hardwoods and then to a mature softwood forest. The industry recognizes the same process in pits and quarries. Aggregate extraction is,
in fact, only considered a temporary or interim use, which is followed
by other uses. Pits and quarries are sometimes portrayed or imagined
as living or undergoing a constant succession of change. The industry
thus speaks boldly about the conversion of sandpits into golf courses,
housing developments, official areas of natural and scientific interests,
or a landscape of biodiversity cores (Ontario Stone, Sand and Gravel
Association, 2012b).

In the conversion of aggregate pits to golf courses the industry
can fashion the previous use as an advantage to the new use. At Empire Communities' Estates of Wyndance on the Oak Ridges Moraine,
a gated exurban community of estate and golf development, its golf
course is described as follows: "Sculpted with the eye of an artist and
the precision of a surgeon, the golf course bears the signature of its cre-
ator, world-class golfer Greg Norman. The least-disturbance approach
preserves the original features of the environment, taking advantage of
existing trees, terrain, and faces of the sand and gravel pits. The result
will be a stroke of landscape artistry" (Empire Communities, 2008). The
references to a "least-disturbance approach" and the preservation of
the "faces of the sand and gravel pits" point to the conception of what
are considered "the original features of the environment." The mention of sand and gravel pits reflects the aggregate industry's general
portrayal of its activities as "interim" and eventually yielding another
productive use (Sandberg, 2001). There is currently very little in provincial policy to further define the term *interim* and prevent it from being
invoked for multiple decades.

No doubt in response to the environmental turn, the aggregate industry and state supporters have increasingly come to imagine and defend
the successional process of gravel pits in ecological terms. Studies commissioned by the Ontario Ministry of Natural Resources now portray
abandoned sand and gravel pits on the Moraine as having the potential
to regenerate into biodiverse places that constitute important wildlife
habitats. This is quite different from the old approach of landfilling.
In 1998, Dance Environmental Inc., for example, produced a report entitled *Natural Rehabilitation of Gravel Pits on the Oak Ridges Moraine*. The
overall objective of the study was to document the naturalization and
degree of biodiversity at a series of gravel pits on the Moraine. Exploring twenty inactive pits on the Moraine, half of which had been rehabilitated and the other half abandoned without remediation, some of the

study's key findings were that time was the best remediation factor in healing gravel pits, though rehabilitation can be hastened by improving soil texture and drainage, leaving seed sources around the pit, and providing exposed water or wetlands.

At other sites on the Moraine, aggregate companies claim excellent results in rehabilitation efforts. In Uxbridge, Lafarge (2008) claims that post-extractive efforts can restore "the original landscape of the moraine." The rehabilitation of the Uxbridge pit notably received the 2003 Award of Excellence from the Ontario Stone, Sand, and Gravel Association. When the Oak Ridges Moraine legislation was declared, the forests surrounding this particular pit were designated as protected natural heritage forests, restricting the area of the Moraine available for extraction. In addition, the company used "techniques that would ensure the restored areas would be compatible with the adjacent natural environment. Soil preparation and landform replication techniques were designed to reproduce the hummocky topography typical of the moraine" (ibid.). The Lafarge description continues, stating that seedlings from sections of the pit that are cleared for extractions are transplanted to newly created terrain. "Natural seeding is also encouraged by planting the trees in an 'L' layout to catch and retain the seed from neighboring trees and allow micro-habitats to regenerate" (ibid.). One remarkable aspect of this situation is that extraction is occurring within the most protective zone of the Moraine. The result, according to Lafarge, is a situation where "rehabilitation works are coordinated with mining operations, a solution for satisfying local demand for sand and gravel products without jeopardizing environmental preservation." The Uxbridge experience is by no means an exception. In its corporate literature on Lafarge and biodiversity the company propounds that quarrying is but one phase in the life of a site. Lafarge's motto is actually "Bringing materials to life" (ibid.). In its wake specific wildlife habitats are often created, and rehabilitation "affords opportunities to recreate certain types of rare or disappearing ecosystems, such as wetlands" (ibid.).

The aggregate industry's trade organization and consultants do their share in promoting a similar message. They routinely give assurances of the slight environmental impact of the industry on the environment and of the industry's place in the culture and heritage of the Moraine. The Ontario Stone, Sand and Gravel Association (2012b) argues that recent land use history on the Oak Ridges Moraine provides us with evidence that disturbed landscapes are readily integrated with the natural environments which surround them. Aggregate extraction and other human-induced disturbances are part of the history and heritage of this landform. The document praises the ability of humans to interact with nature in profitable and harmonious ways, an activity that allegedly has improved with time: "The history of land use on the Oak Ridges Moraine is testimony of our ability to work with nature to repair previous damage. Portions of the Oak Ridges Moraine were once veritable waste land as a result of uncontrolled forestry and agriculture in the 1800s. These same areas, reforested in the mid 1900s, are now part of the Ganaraska Forest, a reserved core area on the Moraine. The success of the 1950s reforestation program which turned a denuded landscape into a core area forest should leave no doubt that today's aggregate industry with more sophisticated knowledge and stringent regulations can accomplish equal or better results" (ibid.: 3–4).

Examples of rehabilitated areas on the Moraine given by the industry include the Glen Major Conservation Area, which now "contains old field areas, coniferous and deciduous trees, which provide important habitat for a variety of significant fauna in the area"; a gravel pit of Highland Creek Sand and Gravel in Pickering Township that is now "successfully reforested"; the Sabiston Horse Farm on Bloomington Sideroad in Whitchurch-Stouffville, a former sandpit that has been rehabilitated as a pasture for horse farming; and Dufferin's Aggregates' Mosport Pit in Clarington, where "soil bioengineering has been successful in stabilizing slopes to create a naturalized after use" (ibid.: 4) (figure 7.10). A prominent consultant to the industry, James Parkin (2003), emphasizes that the industry can actually improve on nature, an action that paves the way for the potential to access additional aggregate reserves in natural core areas when the Oak Ridges Moraine legislation is due for review in 2015 (see below). As we have noted in the previous chapter, such potential incursions are allowed for in the *Oak Ridges Moraine Conservation Act*, but Parkin provides additional assurances that it is possible for rehabilitation to achieve natural self-sustaining vegetation of equal or greater ecological value and that the connectivity of key natural heritage features can be maintained. However, the rehabilitation paper of the Province's *State of the Aggregate Resource of Ontario Study* largely concludes that many aggregate producers have trouble arriving at this level of rehabilitation (Ontario Ministry of Natural Resources, 2009b).

Environmentalists typically view nature as sacred and worth preserving for its own sake. The most important quality of nature is

Figure 7.10: Win-win ecology

An award of excellence was given by the Aggregate Producers Association of Ontario (now the Ontario Stone, Sand, and Gravel Association) to Lafarge for its Uxbridge property on the Oak Ridges Moraine. The aggregate industry is working hard to depict itself as a responsible resource manager. Its wider claims rest on a win-win ecology assumption that resource extraction and nature conservation can coexist. Source: the authors, 2011

routinely considered to be biodiversity – the maintenance of diverse species, gene pools, and populations, and the ecological processes that achieve this. The visionaries of the aggregate industry have an answer for such a concern. The extraction of aggregates is often seen as capable of contributing to a perfect nature. Simulators and modellers claim that they "can produce any landscape you want" and that a biodiverse ecosystem is part of that process. Present studies by the Ontario Ministry of Natural Resources are trying to replicate the rehabilitation work of Lafarge on a much larger scale. Taking the Moraine as a whole, researchers are attempting to model a network of active, abandoned, and restored pits that move across the landscape over time (Fraser, 2004). In these computer-generated simulations and models, today's gravel pits can become tomorrow's naturally significant places. By implication, the reverse can also apply, though this option is seldom emphasized. On the whole, the modellers envision an Oak Ridges Moraine with a constantly moving network of active and rehabilitated or restored sand and gravel pits that can accommodate both the demand for construction material and the ecological and environmental concerns.

Within the sphere of ecology there has been a general rethinking about the role of catastrophic events. The old position is that natural catastrophes, such as fires, insect attacks, and storms, occur externally to ecosystems, are detrimental to ecological processes, and need to be prevented or mitigated (Pickett and Ostfeld, 1995). The new and current position is that catastrophic events may in fact be integral and beneficial to the renewal of ecosystems. Perhaps the most cited example of the old and new conceptions of natural catastrophes relates to forest fires. In the past, forest fires were seen as damaging and necessitating the establishment of forest-fire prevention and suppression services. Now, however, forest fires are seen as beneficial to the rejuvenation and even the prevention (through the periodic burn-off of fire loads). The new vision of natural catastrophes has also resulted in new modes of extraction, such as forest harvesting that emulates fires. However, such harvesting systems have received mixed verdicts. Some scientists are positive, while others see such systems as yet another way of excusing exploitative forest harvesting practices.

In the context of the Oak Ridges Moraine, catastrophic events are rare but may occur, particularly in the form of weather storms. The old vision of natural catastrophes may see such storms as destroying vegetation and causing erosion and eventual blowouts in the landscape. However, in the new vision, storm blowouts may be seen as opportunities for the formation of new and rejuvenated landscapes. Aggregate extraction can be seen in the same light, as a redeeming event that mimics a natural devastation, but one that can thereafter be restored into something natural and ecologically significant. Aggregate extraction may thus be able to remove early succession plantation forests of little ecological value and replace them with more valuable species. The removal of an old succession feature can similarly provide for renewal in protected areas. This intervention would prevent everything from becoming "old" in so-called protected or conservation areas.

A large part of the agenda of the aggregate industry, just like that of the environmentalists, is to promote the formation of nature preserves or parks. The industry portrays recreational parks in former quarries and sandpits in the city of Toronto as green oases that "would not have been there had it not been for the aggregate industry" (Sandberg, 2001). The industry association has given its highest rehabilitation awards for places like Smythe Park and the Don Valley Brick Works in Toronto. Abandoned pits on the Oak Ridges Moraine that have regenerated naturally to become areas of natural significant interest are identified as the evidence of aggregate extraction being an interim phase in transitional and successional processes. The Glen Major Management Tract in Uxbridge is the most prominent example on the Oak Ridges Moraine that has received a Bronze Plaque Award from the Ontario Stone, Sand, and Gravel Association (2012b).

There are other ways in which the industry claims environmental sustainability. These include recycling measures, pollution-abatement technology developments, and the manufacture of more durable building materials. Before the federal government pulled out of the Kyoto Protocol in December 2011, the industry also claimed that extraction sites close to the market reduced trucking distance, contributing to Canada's meeting of its reduction targets under the protocol (Patano and Sandberg, 2005). The pollution that road construction itself contributes, and the automobile and truck traffic that it generates, is conveniently written out of such claims. So is the demand for repaving, which results from aggregate truck movement since they are among the heaviest vehicles on the road.

We suggest that the above aspects of exclusive landscapes of power are in many ways shared by, and in most cases frame disputes between, development and conservationist interests on the Oak Ridges Moraine and in the Greater Toronto Area. The hidden power that underpins them compromises growth and conservation and obscures the social divisions within the city and region.

Conclusion

Exurban areas are often portrayed as landscapes of privilege, housing wealthy professionals and retirees who live in attractive and scenic spaces. When threatened with development or extractive activities, residents typically react strongly to fight them in "not in my backyard" fashion. However, commercial and extractive activities do often take place in exurban areas. On the Oak Ridges Moraine, combined growth and nature conservation plans promote not only an exclusive landscape defined by environmental values that accommodate residents of financial means but also extractive and infrastructural elements considered essential for an unproblematized and unquestioned public demand. Amenity and extractive aesthetics claim compatibility between extractive and ecological processes. Planning for growth and nature conservation at the urban fringe of the Greater Toronto Area may protect landscapes with a unique physical relief and geography, but it pays little attention to social topography. The current dominant policies in Ontario to preserve nature and promote growth share a common nature aesthetic that is essentially used to protect both development and nature, but in the end the system serves to maintain exclusive residential and industrial property values while excluding other interests and compromising nature in inadvertent ways.

Chapter Eight

Conclusion: Wrestling with Development, Sprawl, and Nature Conservation

We titled this book *The Oak Ridges Moraine Battles*, thereby suggesting that it might focus on the dominant story covered by newspaper headlines of citizens opposing sprawl development and the destruction of nature and ultimately winning the battle when legislation was passed in 2001. While our book does tell this David and Goliath story, it tries to go further. Lessons can be learned from the struggles on the Moraine, as it constitutes a mirror of critical self-reflection for all the actors involved. The battles for the Moraine have been diverse and go back a long time. We employ multiple lenses and standpoints to tease out the intersecting and overlapping strands of discursive battles over naming and framing the Moraine; the contestations over the science that describes Moraine landforms, hydrological flows, flora, and fauna; and the changing political, institutional, and regulatory frameworks that shape policies and programs. We examine the role and shifting influence of powerful actors that include politicians at three levels of government, state officials and agencies, and representatives of the development and aggregate industries. We also consider the agency of non-human actors, such as technologies, techniques, landforms, and ecological processes. We start and end with the people who live on the Moraine, whose material interests and emotional attachments are tied to its resources and amenities.

In fast-growing urbanized areas the proposals for changing land use routinely generate opposition. What is noteworthy about the campaigns to preserve the Oak Ridges Moraine is that they were successful in gaining protective legislation, thereby institutionalizing citizens' demands – an outcome that is rare in this type of land-use conservation battle. Our research started with a focus on the citizen campaigns to preserve the Moraine and the popular story of citizen challenges to the growth narrative from competing values of nature conservation. We documented a sustained campaign that moved beyond place-based activism to form a networked coalition of rural and urban interests, homeowners, and environmentalists who organized on a regional scale and drew upon a wider anti-sprawl and environmentalist network. We found that the Moraine campaigns engaged in both social protest and institutionalized political actions. This type of networked movement is becoming more prevalent when land-use conflicts occur in rural and exurban areas close to cities. Lessons learned from the history and organization of the Moraine campaigns may be useful in understanding land-based conflicts elsewhere.

In tracing the genealogy of the Moraine protests, we identified other stories about institutional and policy change that suggested a more nuanced politics of the Moraine battles. The shifting power dynamics of key actors reveal a more complex, contingent, historically situated story of the way in which the Oak Ridges Moraine came to be preserved through legislation. This is a story of the pervasiveness and mutability of the prevailing growth paradigm and the way it is not superseded but embedded in new ways of thinking about – and even selling – nature on the Moraine.

Perhaps more significant is that decades of contestation over the future of the Moraine introduced a new way of talking about the impacts of growth and made possible policy responses that linked conservation and planning on the urban periphery in a discourse of ecosystems planning. Our research on the Moraine struggles highlights the importance of ideas. The emphasis on ecosystems constituted a major paradigm shift from a focus on preserving specific sites to policies that preserve wider ecosystems that provide connectivity for vegetation and wildlife. We document the role played by changes and differences in scientific thinking about the Moraine and the ways in which individual scientific spokespersons, government agencies, and non-governmental organizations kept these ideas alive over time (despite numerous changes in political regimes) and disseminated ecosystems thinking both within expert communities and to the general public. An under-examined issue, on which we begin to touch, is the formation of epistemic communities and the importance of communicating ecosystem thinking to political actors through personal contacts, joint committees, staff, and technical papers.

In this book we highlight the importance of the repetition and popularization of this new way of thinking through the media, which offered special double-spread, full-colour graphics of some of the science underlying ecosystem-based proposals for the Moraine. Newspaper coverage and environmental organizations were so successful in educating the public that ordinary people used a specialized scientific language about aquifers, ecosystem cores, and corridors in letters to the editor and in public presentations (Swainson, 2001b). This substantial accomplishment of shifting policy discourse will be studied for years to come.

Our book shows the way in which the acceptance of an ecosystem approach to conservation planning provided an opening for wider institutional change in the province. In protecting the regional landscape of the Moraine, the provincial government was able to implement regulatory changes that had previously failed over three decades. As the Moraine is a regionally scaled landscape feature, the Province intervened in land use planning and reintroduced regional planning to southern Ontario. The Province also curtailed the powers of municipalities and regional governments to approve site-specific development applications. These lower-tier governments were forced to conform to the *Oak Ridges Moraine Conservation Plan*. This Plan became a precedent for more extensive provincial growth management legislation – the *Greenbelt Plan* and the *Growth Plan*. Both plans incorporated the language of ecosystems planning found in the *Oak Ridges Moraine Conservation Plan*. There was continued provincial intervention in land use planning on a regional scale, this time focusing squarely on directing, supporting, and managing growth in the Greater Golden Horseshoe. This conjunction of nature conservation and growth management policies illustrates the way in which governments can gain public acceptance of what is generally perceived as political suicide – intervention in private property markets. It also suggests that governments are not averse to using popular mobilizations as "cover" to introduce controversial new policies.

Our book also highlights the central role of planning and policy change through the planning system for a range of actors from large landowners to homeowners to environmentalists to government agencies and political parties. As our stories of changes in the planning of land use and conservation on the Moraine show, the planning system provides opportunities for citizens to intervene and articulate alternative futures for a region. Planning is also a regulatory system that favours powerful interests and often makes it difficult to challenge land-use change with arguments relating to nature's agency or quality of life.

For the development forces that are caught up in the discourse of growth, the environmental and hydrological threats to the Moraine constitute a warning about development in general. Current demand cannot be sustained, and alternative options must be found. In the lengthy negotiations to establish legislation for the Moraine, we document the ways in which key industries – the development and aggregate industries – as major landowners on the Moraine, articulated their interests in land-use change and engaged in negotiating a resolution to the ongoing contestations. These industries are very different from one another. The development industry is regional in scale, with many family-owned firms. It is not monolithic; individuals and their histories matter. The aggregate industry is dominated by multinational corporations, and this locates them and their decisions about operations on the Moraine within a global economy. The ways in which major industries engage in land use conflicts and their resolutions need substantial in-depth research, which has not yet been conducted in Canadian urban areas. Our book provides a beginning to such analyses.

Finally, *The Oak Ridges Moraine Battles* makes the argument that ordinary people matter. The Moraine has attracted residents who are willing to act on its behalf. They articulate a strong attachment to place. At the same time, the preservation-of-nature narrative has long been associated with privilege, raising questions about those whose view of nature is privileged and who benefit from preservation of the Moraine. There has been limited research on the social impact of exurban development. In the early 1970s and the 1990s, Punter (1974) and Walker (1987, 1994, 1995, 2000) raised questions about the privileged access of elites and the lack of attention to the expanding access to recreational facilities for urbanites. Our discussion of privatized conservation and the commodification of nature raises new questions about the pervasiveness of the capitalist growth paradigm and its ability to incorporate oppositional discourses. The role of the state as regulator and funder of conservation measures and the way this role relates to the conception of nature as a commons accessible to all remain under-studied, and we point to avenues to rectify the situation.

In the Aftermath of the *Oak Ridges Moraine Conservation Plan*

Frequently, stories of policy change or conflict end when the legislation has been passed or the conflict has been resolved. On 16 September 2008 the *Globe and Mail's* reporter John Barber (2008: A14) declared that "the sprawl that seemed to characterize it [the Toronto region] for so long ... has stopped." The new provincial policies that restrict green-field development in exurbia in favour of urban redevelopment, Barber further asserted, had turned new residents away from the suburbs and exurbs and had caused an unprecedented construction boom in condominiums in the downtown and some of the suburbs. Conservation policies at the urban fringe, such as the *Oak Ridges Moraine Conservation Plan* and the *Greenbelt Plan*, complemented by the *Places to Grow Plan*, seemed to have worked. However, this sentiment appears to have been premature. As the 2011 Canadian census has shown, growth in the five-year period between 2006 and 2011 in the regions that include the Moraine and environs has continued unabated and has far outstripped the growth in Toronto or the wider, Greater Toronto Area.

Competition for international finance capital and human skills is what drives prevailing urban and regional planning paradigms (Boudreau, Keil, and Young, 2009). The state is seen as an agent for creating a positive investment and lifestyle climate, which includes regulating regional and conservation planning to ensure orderly development and the protection of the natural environment. It is in this context that the Province of Ontario has rolled out a conservationist agenda that includes not only the Oak Ridges Moraine legislation but the *Greenbelt Plan*, which extends some of the principles of the *Oak Ridges Moraine Conservation Plan* more widely to cover the Greater Golden Horseshoe. The provincial government has also implemented the *Places to Grow Plan*, which integrates the conservation legislation and defines the places for growth in the region. In combination, the three plans firmly position the Province as the central controlling actor in land use planning and conservation policy in the wider region, thereby circumventing the jurisdictional fragmentation that had precluded effective policies to curtail or manage sprawl (Wekerle et al., 2007; Macdonald and Keil, 2012).

In this book we suggest that the conservation efforts fall into the category of the neoliberalization of conservation (McCarthy and Prudham, 2004; Boudreau, Keil, and Young, 2009; Logan and Wekerle, 2008; Sandberg and Wekerle, 2010). Neoliberalization is a process that is transforming the ways in which the governance of city regions and their non-human natures are thought about and managed. There is an extensive literature on the topic, but the gist of the message is that governance has undergone a substantial transformation. Governments no longer consider themselves regulators but rather facilitators of market forces. This does not necessarily mean a retrenchment in government spending, as it is so often described, but a redirection of government funds and priorities to support the market, on the assumption that it will serve the public good. Neoliberal policies also put growing emphasis on the individual rather than the collective as responsible for promoting welfare. The social welfare net and the bureaucratic state are therefore retrenched in favour of individual responsibility, private enterprise, volunteerism, and charitable activities.

The neoliberalization of conservation on the Moraine and the Greenbelt takes different shapes. The Oak Ridges Moraine and Greenbelt legislation show that different and seemingly opposed aesthetics of conservation and growth may have a lot in common. The legislation has become an important actor in consolidating the Oak Ridges Moraine as a hydrological, geological, and ecological entity within identified boundaries, while facilitating the provision of urban growth within and beyond its boundaries. As such, the *Oak Ridge Moraine Conservation Plan* and the *Greenbelt Plan* serve as lubricants rather than deterrents of growth (Wekerle et al., 2007). The bragging rights surrounding the Oak Ridges Moraine brand – and more recently the Greenbelt – present and market the Toronto region, as a green and attractive global city and region open for investments and as a home, to an international business class looking for not only a good investment climate but a good quality of life. In the effort to remain competitive, cities and regions often resort to the creation of the spectacular, or of spectacle, such as the building of museums, sports stadiums, and waterfronts, to attract investments, cultural events, and tourists (Lehrer, 2012). Those who promote the Oak Ridges Moraine and the Greenbelt similarly strive to frame these land areas as recognizable spectacles that charm and brand the Toronto region.

The Oak Ridges Moraine, along with many other conservation areas across the globe, maintains a division between humans and the non-human world, as well as between humans themselves, obscuring the view that culture and nature are indelibly linked, that a respectful relationship between both needs to be nurtured, and that all people, whether private landowners or not, need to be included. As Wendell Berry (referred to in Cronon, 1996: 89) once proposed, we need to think about building homes in nature where the prospect of use and interaction are ever present. Nature and culture are not separate. Conservation areas may well have a place in this scheme but not necessarily as the central feature of nature conservation. To be meaningful, nature conservation necessitates a change in overall human practices and interactions with non-human nature, rather than just isolating nature in a sea of unsustainable development. We need to rethink conservation areas as places that accommodate nature, farming, recreation, and some settlement without compromising the very landscapes and ecological processes that attract this range of activities.

But where do we begin to reverse the current trends that seem to promote both environmental unsustainability and growing social inequalities, a pattern that we note is also visible on the Oak Ridges Moraine? Our findings in this book suggest that nothing is given or absolute. The exurbia found on the Oak Ridges Moraine, we have argued, need not look the way it does today. It has taken on many shapes in the past, which suggests that it will continue to change in the future. From First Nations' home to re-settler farm and resource frontier to restoration object to recreational haven to nature conservation object to suburban and exurban commutershed, the Oak Ridges Moraine can also be transformed into a home for human and non-human nature and can provide people with equal access to its many qualities. The same will then apply to those regions beyond the Moraine that are now the hosts of leapfrog development.

However socially constructed natural areas may be, people feel an affinity to them, and these feelings of place attachment can be felt and expressed by residents and non-residents, environmentalists and scientists, alike. These feelings may have the potential to become an affinity for the protection of and the sense of belonging to a bioregion, a bioregion with a series of watersheds that can retain and filter water, within a region with unique flora and fauna. Attachment to the Oak Ridges Moraine has extended beyond its physical boundaries. We are struck by the proactive and effective intervention of the City of Toronto in the Oak Ridges Moraine debate, for example, even though it has been shut out of formal participation in the legal deliberations of the fate of the Moraine.

The emotional geographies of the Moraine provide a strong argument that goes beyond "not in my backyard"-ism to a genuine feeling of affect for a bioregion, however delimited, that has been constructed as an entity to which people forge a particular attachment and a sense of belonging. This argument counters the "not in my backyard" argument and the sense that attachment is only to one's own place, property, and backyard. However, while bioregionalism has so far attempted to bridge the divide between humans and non-human nature, it has yet to confront the more profound challenges posed by the continuing perception of a nature-culture divide and the social and environmental inequities between and within human communities themselves.

We are also hopeful on another score. William Adams (2009: 64) identifies two models of conservation: "state-protected wilderness" (derived from the United States) and "mixed tenure semi-natural habitat" (derived from the United Kingdom). The Oak Ridges Moraine model fits somewhere in between, where the land is largely privately owned and it is recognized that people have a place within it, but where the principle of a delimited and bounded "wilderness" or natural core space is acknowledged. Adams's conceptualization of a mixed tenure semi-natural habitat model suggests something more for the Oak Ridges Moraine. It acknowledges not only the ever-presence of humans in the more-than-human nature on the Moraine but also the possibility and the necessity of imagining other tenure arrangements that are more accommodating towards human equity and public access. Moreover, in a recent review of the field of conservation biology, Libby Robin (2009) adds fuel to the suggestion that specific natures like the Oak Ridges Moraine need to be seen in a larger spatial and social context. Robin (2009: 204) argues that any nature reserve model rests on the unfounded assumption that human-influenced environments are "essentially different from 'natural' environments." The implication is that a nature-culture divide does not help conservation biologists and managers make sense of environments.

The continued insistence on seeing the Oak Ridges Moraine as a distinct management unit reinforces a call for a more integrated approach to exurban development where human development needs to be seen as part of nature and where nature is embraced and respected. Moreover, the Moraine as a distinct home reminds us to be mindful of its gentrification, to challenge its becoming the exclusive preserve of the wealthy. The social always has to be part of any nature conservation scheme, including that of the Oak Ridges Moraine. We arrive at the paradoxical conclusion that the Oak Ridges Moraine, just like other nature preserves, needs to be transcended as a conservation object. Nature conservation is, in fact, something that should involve all places at all times, as well as being something that respects and acknowledges human diversity.

Oak Ridges Moraine Chronology

12,000 years ago	Retreat of glaciers forms the Oak Ridges Moraine
10,000 years ago	First record of Paleo-Indian habitation in the Lake Wilcox area (now Richmond Hill)
1280–1320	Date of earliest Iroquoian settlement in Lake Wilcox area (now Richmond Hill)
1787–8	The *Toronto Purchase* takes place between British colonial power and the Mississaugas
1791	John Graves Simcoe selects York as capital of Upper Canada
late 1700s–early 1800s	Extraction of timber from the Moraine
1920s–1930s	Reforestation (pine plantations)
1924	Creation of York Regional Forest (Regional Municipality of York)
1931	Formation of Federation of Ontario Naturalists
1946	Creation of conservation authorities by the Province of Ontario
	Planning Act imposes development limits; there can be no subdivisions without sewers
1947	Ganaraska reforestation
1954	Hurricane Hazel hits Ontario
	Consolidation of regional conservation authorities
	Formation of Metropolitan Toronto Advisory Planning Board (authority over parts of Moraine)
1967	Completion of Bruce Trail
1969	*Toronto Centred Region Plan* uses parkway belt to limit sprawl

1972	*Toronto Centred Region Concept Plan* sees Moraine as greenbelt
1973	Federal government spends $140 million to expropriate land for Pickering airport; People Not Planes organization created to fight against airport development
	Niagara Escarpment Planning and Development Act passes
1974	*Central Ontario Lakeshore Urban Complex* (COLUC) plan is presented
1975	Airport plan shelved owing to local opposition and lower-than-expected air traffic
late 1970s	Province talks about creating a community (of 90,000) on the Pickering lands; federal government gives the Province 3,600 hectares (9,000 acres) for the town
1985	*Niagara Escarpment Plan* passes
1986	*Mineral Aggregate Resources Policy Statement* passes
1987	Provincial Liberals propose for a new community (Seaton) the lands no longer needed for Pickering airport
	North Pickering is proposed as the site for new landfill
1989	Ontario Environmental Assessment Advisory Committee's report identifies Moraine as "a provincial resource" and a matter of "provincial interest."
	First mention of urban sprawl as an issue in reference to Seaton lands by People Not Planes
October 1989	Save the Oak Ridges Moraine (STORM) Coalition founded
June 1989	Town of Richmond Hill votes against high-density housing applications between Bayview Avenue and Yonge Street, north of Elgin Mills Road for more than 450 homes and a number of condominium units, generating a population of 3,500, three times the density designated under the Town's official plan
	STORM opposes argument that current servicing is not able to handle intensified development
	Richmond Hill Council awaits review of official plan for long-term development before deciding whether to allow intensified development in an urban fringe area
August 1989	Interim report of the Royal Commission on the Future of the Toronto Waterfront (Crombie Commission) recommends a green strategy for the Greater Toronto Area bioregion linking the waterfront, river valley systems, headwaters, wetlands, and other significant natural features

October 1989	Premier David Peterson commissions MPP Ron Kanter to conduct a study and recommend options for a greenlands strategy for the Greater Toronto Area
1990	*Ontario Planning Act* passes
	Premier Peterson approves creation of North Pickering Corporation to oversee Seaton land development
	Save the Rouge Valley System opposes widening highway and destroying environmentally sensitive lands; proposes provincial park or recreation area instead
February 1990	Niagara Escarpment is designated a world biosphere reserve by UNESCO
July 1990	Liberal MPP Ron Kanter releases *Space for All: Options for a Greater Toronto Area Greenlands Strategy*; recommends long-term protection for Oak Ridges Moraine
	Liberal government issues "expression of provincial interest" in Oak Ridges Moraine within Greater Toronto Area and announces planning study
September 1990	New Democratic Party elected to provincial legislature
	Watersheds, report by Royal Commission on the Future of Toronto Waterfront, calls for tighter provincial protection for the Oak Ridge Moraine; highlights need for an ecosystem approach to land use planning
June 1991	Province issues *Interim Guidelines – Provincial Interest on the Oak Ridges Moraine Area of the Greater Toronto Area* to implement expression of provincial interest
August 1991	Ontario Minister of Natural Resources establishes Oak Ridges Moraine Technical Working Committee (will produce fifteen background studies over next three years, serving as background for the *Oak Ridges Moraine Conservation Plan*)
December 1991	Final report, *Regeneration*, of the Royal Commission on the Future of the Toronto Waterfront reinforces the need for protection based on connectivity of core features.
1992	Oak Ridges Trail Association formed
November 1993	Town of Richmond Hill Official Plan Amendment no. 129 contains "environment first" principles intended to protect the Moraine; appealed at the Ontario Municipal Board by developers
March 1993	Province establishes Oak Ridges Moraine Citizen's Advisory Committee, chaired by STORM's Debbe Crandall

April 1993	Geological Survey of Canada initiates a five-year Oak Ridges Moraine geology and hydrogeology study
1994	Ministry of Natural Resources and Oak Ridges Moraine Technical Working Committee confirm and consolidate the principles of natural heritage system
December 1994	Royal Commission on the Future of the Toronto Waterfront releases *Oak Ridges Moraine Strategy: An Ecosystem Approach for Long-Term Protection and Management; Draft for Public Discussion.* Seven public meetings held
	Toronto Waterfront Commission and STORM present *Oak Ridges Moraine Strategy for the Greater Toronto Area* to Ministry of Natural Resources
1995	Seaton lands development committee is advised by John Sewell and David Crombie to go ahead with the Seaton community with a population targeted at 90,000.
	Markham's farmland known as Cornell is sold for development
	Progressive Conservatives are elected in Ontario; they change the structure and membership of the Ontario Municipal Board and make drastic cuts to public services
April 1995	Natural Resource Minister Howard Hampton writes to Federation of Ontario Naturalists that he is setting up a working group to write the final document implementing the 1994 Moraine strategy as formal provincial policy
10 July 1995	Ontario Municipal Board approves Official Plan Amendment no. 129 to allow subdivisions on developable land in Town of Richmond Hill. Decision strongly supports protection and management of Oak Ridges Moraine based on linkage of natural areas through corridors
	Seaton lands are rezoned and readied for real estate market to pay down the provincial deficit
March 1996	Revised *Planning Act, 1996,* and *Provincial Policy Statement* are approved to guide land use decisions across Ontario
May 1996	Release of *Provincial Policy Statement*
1996–9	Province sells rented "agricultural preserve" lands to tenant farmers at $3,750–$10,000 per hectare ($1,500–$4,000 per acre). Pickering Council puts easements on the land to maintain it as agricultural preserve
1996	James Dick Construction Ltd. purchases 80 hectare farm known as the Rockfort farm property and applies for a licence to operate a quarry on the site

1997	York-Durham Trunk Sewer System Master Plan recommends Big Pipe extension to King City
June 1997	STORM releases coffee table book *Oak Ridges Moraine*
1999	Richmond Hill revises official plan; developers appeal directly to the Ontario Municipal Board for approval to build more than 11,000 housing units on almost 700 hectares of Moraine land along Yonge Street
	Agreement to preserve 320 hectares of farmland in north Pickering "in perpetuity" (Duffins-Rouge Agricultural Preserve)
January 1999	Mayor of Newmarket challenges regional councils of York, Durham, and Peel to initiate joint regional protection strategy for Moraine
September 1999	York, Peel, and Durham regions issue state-of-the-Moraine report urging provincial leadership
October 1999	Moraine campaign rekindled when Municipal Affairs Minister Steve Gilchrist resigns over wrongdoing allegations by Moraine developers
6 October 1999	Joint press conference of Save the Rouge Valley System, Richmond Hill Naturalists, STORM, and others calls for protection of two-kilometre strip pinch point in Richmond Hill
20 October 1999	Richmond Hill Council approves Official Plan Amendment no. 200 to urbanize 2,800 hectares of Moraine land in Richmond Hill. Save the Rouge Valley System and Richmond Hill Naturalists urge the council to reject
26 October 1999	Durham Region Planning Council rejects a 2,500 housing project in Uxbridge, Gan Eden
November 1999	Federation of Ontario Naturalists and other non-governmental organizations release action plan to protect Moraine
	Liberal MPP Mike Colle tables private member's bill to protect Moraine
15 November 1999	Approximately 40 protesters from Save the Rouge Valley System and Richmond Hill Naturalists hold a mock funeral for the Jefferson Forest impacted by the Bayview Avenue extension
19 November 1999	Ontario Municipal Board holds pre-hearing to consider proposals to build 8,000 homes on Bond and Philips Lakes. Save the Rouge Valley System and Richmond Hill Naturalists granted standing

29 November 1999	Road blockade by environmental groups (Save the Rouge Valley System, Richmond Hill Naturalists, and homeowners) to stop the bulldozing of Jefferson Forest for the Bayview Avenue extension; 12 people arrested
December 1999	Federation of Ontario Naturalists and STORM meet with Municipal Affairs Minister Tony Clement to press for Moraine protection
8 December 1999	The City of Toronto allocates $1.6 million to oppose large housing developments in Uxbridge and Richmond Hill
7 January 2000	Richmond Hill proposes to change agricultural zoning of 2,800 hectares to allow 17,000 new houses
	Save the Rouge Valley System volunteers distribute thousands of flyers door to door throughout the town to further publicize the 12 January meeting
12 January 2000	Special meeting of Richmond Hill Council for approval of proposed rezoning; Council favours the amendment. A thousand citizens and environmentalists attend. Meeting is known as "Oak Ridges Moraine landmark battle" by the media; MPP Mike Colle pushes for freeze on development in order to complete scientific assessment of the impacts
February 2000	Rockfort quarry dispute heats up in front of the Ontario Municipal Board
1 February 2000	465 scientists sign on to STORM and the Federation of Ontario Naturalists' demands to ban development on the Oak Ridges Moraine
11 February 2000	Ministry of Municipal Affairs and Housing sends letter asking the Town of Richmond Hill to provide a 600 metre corridor along the Oak Ridges Moraine but offers no legislation or financial assistance for the Town to acquire lands
10–12 February 2000	"Wilderness Not Wood Chips" campaign by Save the Rouge Valley System; three-day moraine workfest where 200 volunteers bag and tag remains of Jefferson Forest trees
13–18 February 2000	Save the Rouge Valley System volunteers deliver 20,000 wood-chip bags to residents across Richmond Hill, publicizing the need to attend the 23 February council meeting, and Richmond Hill's plan to urbanize 2,800 hectares of green space
	Save the Rouge Valley System also creates and distributes 65,000 flyers advertising the 23 February meeting

22 February 2000	Provincial government recommends that Richmond Hill maintain a 600 metre-wide green corridor through lands on the Moraine that are in the process of being rezoned for development
23 February 2000	Richmond Hill public meeting at the Sheraton Parkway Hotel; 1,600 residents attend, and environmentalists, residents, landowners, developers, provincial government, the Toronto and Region Conservation Authority, York Region, and the City of Toronto make more than 50 submissions Richmond Hill Council defers decision regarding Official Plan Amendment no. 200 to the Province, owing to local opposition
March 2000	Federation of Ontario Naturalists, STORM, and City of Toronto seek, under the *Environmental Bill of Rights*, provincial review of laws to protect Moraine
7 March 2000	Richmond Hill Council asks Queen's Park to freeze all development on the Moraine until environmental protection is established by the Province; Town rejects the building of 17,000 houses
24 March 2000	City of Toronto, Federation of Ontario Naturalists, and STORM, funded by Sierra Legal Defence Fund, use *Environmental Bill of Rights* to challenge existing provincial land use planning laws and policies to protect the Moraine
31 March 2000	Ontario Municipal Board delays start of Moraine hearing from 1 to 23 May
April 2000	New Democratic Party MPPs Shelley Martel and Marilyn Churley table private member's bill to protect Moraine
3 April 2000	Save the Rouge Valley System organizes parade of woodland creatures to promote awareness of the 6 April council meeting to consider proposal for 2,700 housing units on 240 hectares surrounding Bond Lake. Save the Rouge Valley System also distributes 20,000 flyers promoting the meeting
6 April 2000	Richmond Hill Council votes unanimously to deny application for 2,700 houses; 18 other cases on the Moraine are reviewed by the Ontario Municipal Board; 500–700 people attend meeting
12 April 2000	City of Toronto is denied standing at Richmond Hill hearing by the Ontario Municipal Board
May 2000	Province proposes Moraine protection at Ontario Municipal Board's hearing in Richmond Hill

Progressive Conservative MPP Steve Gilchrist tables private member's bill to protect Moraine

Three ministers turn down *Environmental Bill of Rights* request, stating that existing Moraine protection is adequate

Federation of Ontario Naturalists begins doorstep canvass in Moraine communities, spreading the word about Moraine protection

4 May 2000   Ontario government releases report that majority of proposed developments on Moraine are inappropriate

20 May 2000   City of Toronto and Save the Rouge Valley System urge Ontario Superior Court to overturn Ontario Municipal Board's decision to bar the City from Richmond Hill hearing on the Moraine

23 May 2000   City of Toronto loses its bid to participate in the Ontario Municipal Board hearing in Richmond Hill

29 May 2000   Ontario Municipal Board's hearing on Richmond Hill applications for two developments (8,000 homes) on Bond and Phillips Lakes begins; silent protests outside the hearing with signs reading "Silenced by OMB," "Scientists Stifled," and "Muzzled by Developers"

Save the Rouge Valley System is the only environmental group allowed at hearing

Originally slated for 12 weeks, the hearing lasted roughly a year before being put on hold temporarily by the provincial government in May 2001

June 2000   MPP Mike Colle's bill defeated at second reading vote

NDP Moraine Bill passes second reading, but government never sets legislative committee hearings on it

6 June 2000   Ontario Professional Planners Institute releases statement calling for protection of the Oak Ridges Moraine

August 2000   Divisional court grants King City citizen's group leave to appeal Ontario Municipal Board's decision on village expansion and Big Pipe sewer line

1 August 2000   Ontario Municipal Board's hearing extended for nine months

12 August 2000 Divisional court rules that King City Preserve the Village, Concerned Citizens of King Township Inc., Nobleton Alert Residents Association Inc., and STORM can appeal an Ontario Municipal Board decision approving the King City Official Plan Amendment, which would effectively allow the Big Pipe

September 2000	MPP Mike Colle tables new Moraine Bill
December 2000	Conservation Authorities Moraine Coalition formed by nine conservation authorities that incorporate parts of the Moraine
	MPP Mike Colle's Moraine Bill passes second reading, but government never sets legislative committee hearings on it.
15–18 January 2001	Save the Rouge Valley System brings in biologist Reed Noss to testify at Ontario Municipal Board hearing
18 January 2001	Save the Rouge Valley System holds a rally for the Moraine, featuring Reed Noss. Approximately 200 people attend
19 January 2001	Region of York, Town of Richmond Hill, and the Toronto and Region Conservation Authority announce plan to buy 5 per cent (20 hectares) of the roughly 400 hectares of the Jefferson Forest Wetland Complex threatened by extension of Bayview Avenue
31 January 2001	Premier Mike Harris tells the *Globe and Mail* that urban growth must leapfrog areas such as the Rouge Valley and the Oak Ridges Moraine
	Developers question the credentials of Province's witness on water quality issues and persuade the Ontario Municipal Board to reject the testimony of Garry Hunter
February 2001	Federation of Ontario Naturalists releases Oak Ridges Moraine Greenway policy paper showing how the Province can protect the Moraine
8 February 2001	At Ontario Superior Court hearing, the Province and Save the Rouge Valley System argue for the reinstatement of expert witness Garry Hunter at the Ontario Municipal Board hearing
12 February 2001	STORM mails out 35,000 copies of a map of the Moraine that presents it as a contiguous system to labour groups, environmental organizations, politicians, and conservation groups.
21 February 2001	Ontario Superior Court rules for reinstatement of Garry Hunter as expert witness at the Ontario Municipal Board hearing. Hunter testifies that development in the Richmond Hill section of the Moraine could contaminate groundwater and harm rivers
14 March 2001	"National Day of Protest": Farmers show frustration, and rally for more aid, with tractor convoys and by burning an effigy of the agriculture minister

23 March 2001	Federal government announces plans to donate 3,025 hectares on the Moraine (part of the proposed airport land north of Seaton) to protect green space and to link it up with the Rouge Valley Park system
April 2001	Earthroots organizes protest at Ontario legislature
April–May 2001	Federation of Ontario Naturalists and STORM blanket radio waves with advertisements urging Premier Mike Harris to protect Moraine
May 2001	Federation of Ontario Naturalists proposes an Oak Ridges Moraine Greenway Plan. The Greenway Plan would be developed under the Province's *Planning and Development Act* to identify protected areas and wildlife corridors
	Minister of Municipal Affairs and Housing, Chris Hodgson, appoints Oak Ridges Moraine Advisory Panel to recommend protection plan for Oak Ridges Moraine. Over the spring and summer of 2001 this panel developed a proposed approach for a draft Oak Ridges Moraine plan and conducted public hearings across the Moraine area. The panel included a large number of high-profile and influential stakeholders representing the environmental and business interests on the Moraine (for example, Urban Development Institute, Federation of Ontario Naturalists, STORM, and Aggregate Producers Association of Ontario)
11 May 2001	Tests showing bacterial contamination in King City High School bolster supporters of the Big Pipe
17 May 2001	Provincial government passes the *Oak Ridges Moraine Protection Act* (Bill 55), freezing all development on the Moraine for six months and halting the Ontario Municipal Board hearing in Richmond Hill
25 May–5 June 2001	Save the Rouge Valley System launches its "Do Not Destroy the Moraine" campaign, delivering thousands of Moraine flyers and inviting people to rally for the Moraine
5 June 2001	King City Council threatens to take the Region of York to court over Big Pipe
5–7 June 2001	"The People's Hearing for the Moraine," a three-evening event organized by Save the Rouge Valley System, gives people from across the GTA a chance to tell provincial representatives what they want to see happen to the Moraine after the six-month development freeze is lifted. About 800 people attended and urged MPPs Steve Gilchrist, Frank Klees, and Tina Molinari to permanently protect the Oak Ridges Moraine

28 June 2001	Government appoints an advisory panel made up of developers, environmentalists, politicians, and scientists to draw up recommendations for the Oak Ridges Moraine; David Crombie is appointed as mediator in Richmond Hill dispute
August 2001	Federation of Ontario Naturalists delivers 3,000 postcards demanding permanent Moraine protection to Premier Harris
19 July 2001	Out of 110 development proposals, 37 receive exemption from the Oak Ridges Moraine building freeze because they are so close to completion (4,250 houses to be built)
9 August 2001	Save the Rouge Valley System leaks contents of advisory panel's recommendations to the media and warns public that the plan, which would allow housing on half the Moraine and continued urban expansion, is a death sentence for the Moraine
15 August 2001	Provincial "Share Your Vision" document, with advisory panel draft recommendations, is presented; 30-day consultation with four public meetings. At the press conference in which Municipal Affairs Minister Chris Hodgson announces the "Share Your Vision" document, local residents, Save the Rouge Valley System, and other grassroots groups protest passionately, waving signs that say "Say no to mansions on the Moraine"
28 August 2001	Advisory panel recommends that Moraine be divided between protected and developed land, with no estate housing on protected land. This reverses their earlier position in "Share Your Vision"
28 August–13 September 2001	Government holds public meetings across the Moraine to receive citizen input on the impending Moraine legislation; more than 2,000 people attend, calling for strong protection and denouncing loopholes in the advisory panel's recommendations
7 September 2001	Environmentalists file an application for judicial review of the Bayview Avenue extension's environmental assessment, arguing that it endangers the habitat of the Jefferson salamander
26 September 2001	Oak Ridges Moraine Advisory Panel recommends protection for the Moraine, including boosting natural linkages with a two-kilometre corridor and protection of natural core areas, and a ten-year review

29 September 2001	Save the Rouge Valley System distributes thousands of flyers urging citizens across the Greater Toronto Area to contact Premier Mike Harris in favour of permanent Moraine protection and a $1 billion land acquisition fund
October 2001	King City citizen's groups lose Divisional Court appeal and apply to Ontario Court of Appeal
2 October 2001	Developers demand compensation for land owned on the Moraine
3 October 2001	City of Toronto sets aside $1.6 million for two Ontario Municipal Board hearings; $800,000 goes to Save the Rouge Valley Stystem and $480,000 goes to the Toronto and Region Conservation Authority
6 October 2001	Save the Rouge Valley System organizes "Thousand Child March for the Moraine" rally, which gives children and their families the chance to show their support for Oak Ridges Moraine protection
11 October 2001	York Regional Council votes to take away King Township's control over sewage planning and to build an extension of the Big Pipe into the area
23 October 2001	Canadian Environmental Defence Fund (Environmental Defence Canada since 2002) lawyer Linda McCaffrey and Save the Rouge Valley System face off with York Region in Superior Divisional Court to stop the extension of Bayview Avenue until a proper study of the road's environmental impact can be done. The group argues that the road will destroy the habitat of the nationally threatened Jefferson salamander
24 October 2001	Justice Nicholson McRae rules against allowing the Environmental Defence Canada case to proceed, arguing that while it is a vital issue, the road extension is essentially a political issue
November 2001	Based on input of the advisory panel, Minister Hodgson tables draft bill to protect Moraine – *Draft Oak Ridges Moraine Conservation Plan* – and announces negotiated settlement with developers to end Richmond Hill Ontario Municipal Board hearing Federation of Ontario Naturalists hosts public meeting to explain draft bill and Moraine Plan

With the help of the Canadian Environmental Defence Fund, Save the Rouge Valley System appeals to a higher court to try to save the Jefferson salamander and stop York Region from extending Bayview Avenue through the newly created Moraine park. In January 2002 the Ontario Court of Appeal rules against Save the Rouge Valley System and orders the environmental group to pay York Region $1,500 in court costs

1 November 2001   Municipal Affairs Minister Chris Hodgson announces Bill 122, a draft *Oak Ridges Moraine Conservation Act,* and *Oak Ridges Moraine Conservation Plan* to permanently protect 100 per cent of the Moraine's natural features and water resources, create at 440 hectare park in Richmond Hill, and preserve a minimum 2 kilometre–wide wildlife corridor across the Moraine except where existing development makes this impossible. Also announced is a swap of land in Richmond Hill for provincially owned land in Seaton. Save the Rouge Valley System congratulates the government

2 November 2001   Bill 122 and the draft land use plan are posted on the *Environmental Registry* for thirty days

4 November 2001   Pickering Ajax Citizens Together for the Environment (PACT) argues that Seaton lands are as environmentally sensitive as the Oak Ridges Moraine

20 November 2001   The Province announces $15 million start-up fund for Oak Ridges Moraine Foundation to oversee the Moraine's future

23–25 November 2001   Bayview Avenue extension protest: MPP Mike Colle, Earthroots, and local residents sit down in front of bulldozers to save the Jefferson Forest

13 December 2001   *Oak Ridges Moraine Conservation Act* passes unanimously

27 June 2002   Minister of Municipal Affairs and Housing exercises his authority under section 18 of the *Oak Ridges Moraine Protection Act* and orders eight official plan amendments and eight zoning by-law amendments to be enacted on behalf of the Region of York and the Town of Richmond Hill that will allow development on the remaining lands before the Ontario Municipal Board

11 September 2002   Minister Hodgson issues a ministerial order to halt an application for 583 homes on the Moraine

20 September 2002	North Pickering Land Exchange Review Panel releases a draft document for public advice, posts the "Draft Principles" document on the *Environmental Registry*, holds public meetings in Pickering, and receives and considers a number of written submissions
15 October 2002	King Township takes York Region to court over the take-over of sewage collection
	Ontario Municipal Board cannot overturn the deal that allowed 6,600 homes to be built on the Moraine
17 October 2002	Niagara Escarpment Commission approves gravel pit extension in Milton
24 October 2002	Poll of Greater Toronto Area residents on development on the Moraine reveals that 14% support it, 46% oppose it
November 2002	North Pickering Land Exchange Review Panel announces its planning principles. Pickering has six months to change secondary plans; the lands are environmentally sensitive and are to be protected when creating the community of Seaton
5 November 2002	Save the Rouge Valley System pulls out of an Ontario Municipal Board hearing on housing on the Oak Ridges Moraine, calling it a sham
8 November 2002	Environment Minister Stockwell turns down requests for a full environmental assessment of the Big Pipe sewer system in King
18 November 2002	Bayview Avenue extension is opened
26 November 2002	North Pickering Land Exchange Review Panel presents its final principles to the Minister of Municipal Affairs and Housing and appoints Justice Lloyd Houlden as "Fairness Commissioner" to oversee land swap
December 2002	Provincial government announces the creation of the Oak Ridges Moraine Foundation, which is mandated to purchase land on the Moraine, to research and monitor features on the Moraine, and provide public education programs. The Province allocates $15 million in cash and land donations to support the program
10 December 2002	Trillium Foundation withdraws $195,500 in its funding of Save the Rouge Valley System

2003	Ernie Eves' Conservative government announces protection of Duffins-Rouge Agricultural Preserve with a Minister's Zoning Order under the *Planning Act*, directed by the North Pickering Land Exchange Review Panel, and consistent with the principles of Smart Growth and the *Provincial Policy Statement*. The land is 1,960 hectares and is designated in Durham's official plan as "permanent agricultural reserve"
30 March 2003	Four protesters are ticketed for trespassing in their demonstration to stop illegal tree-cutting on the Duffins-Rouge Agricultural Preserve
21 April 2003	Ministry of Municipal Affairs and Housing moves to protect approximately 2,000 hectares of Pickering farmland
1 July 2003	Ontario Superior Court rejects King Township's case to overturn York Region's by-law controlling sewage collection
29 July 2003	King Township Council votes to appeal Ontario Superior Court ruling
27 August 2003	Anti–Big Pipe candidate Leah Werry announces intention to run for mayor in King City. She loses to encumbent Mayor Black in November 2003
18 September 2003	Ontario Superior Court awards York Region $182,000 in court costs for defending the Big Pipe
22 September 2003	David Crombie, chair of the North Pickering Land Review Panel, urges Province to protect the Duffins- Rouge Agricultural Preserve
2 October 2003	Dalton McGuinty elected as Ontario premier
17 October 2003	Environmental Defence, Earthroots, and the Jefferson Forest Residents Association keep vigil on the MacLeod's Landing development site to protect it until Dalton McGuinty can take over the provincial government and fulfil his promise to halt the 6,600 new houses on the Moraine; environmentalists picket and hand out brochures; developers continue to bulldoze large tracts of the Moraine for subdivisions
23 October 2003	Builders of MacLeod's Landing declare a two-week moratorium on sales while they negotiate with McGuinty Liberals
21 November 2003	Liberals announce that they are unable to fulfil their promise to halt the building of 6,600 houses on the Moraine. Instead, 5,700 houses are to be built
12 December 2003	King Township Council votes to abandon court appeal against the Region and allows the Big Pipe to proceed, after King residents elect a pro-Pipe council in November 2003

16 December 2003	Dalton McGuinty introduces Bill 26, *Strong Communities Act*, to change the *Planning Act* to weaken developers' hold on the Ontario Municipal Board, and Bill 27, a one-year ban on development around the Golden Horseshoe, to come up with a long-term Greenbelt Plan
3 January 2004	The Duffins-Rouge Green Space Coalition comes out against the King City Big Pipe, arguing for a full environmental assessment; Mayor Black of King City counters with the argument that septic tanks are polluting the Moraine
17 February 2004	Greenbelt Protection Task Force announced
3 April 2004	Ontario Greenbelt Alliance formed
22 April 2004	Provincial government donates 1,432 hectares, worth approximately $35 million, doubling the length of the Rouge Park
17 May 2004	Huron Nation wins case against the Ontario Realty Corporation, which wanted to build a cemetery on an ancient burial site
8–15 June 2004	Provincial government begins public consultations in an effort to curb powers of the Ontario Municipal Board
1 July 2004	Great Lakes United asks Province to deny certificates of approval for the extension of the Big Pipe into King City until a complete environmental assessment has been conducted
9–13 July 2004	Environmental Defence Canada and Friends of the Rouge Watershed launch a private prosecution against York Region, claiming that construction of the Big Pipe violates the federal *Fisheries Act*
12 July 2004	Release of *Places to Grow: A Growth Plan for the Greater Golden Horseshoe*
30 July 2004	Ministry of the Environment issues a certificate of approval to York Region for the York Region Sewer System link to King City (Big Pipe); completion of link set for 2008; anticipated that it will increase King City's population from 4,800 to 12,000 in 25 years
August 2004	McGuinty government approves plans for construction of the Big Pipe
20 August 2004	Greenbelt Protection Task Force delivers its final report
10 September 2004	York Region Council moves ahead with plan to connect King City to the Big Pipe
24 September 2004	Provinces finalizes land swap deal

28 October 2004	Municipal Affairs and Housing Minister Gerretsen introduces Greenbelt legislation
3 December 2004	Municipal Leaders for the Greenbelt issue letter asking Dalton McGuinty to expand the planned Greenbelt area by 324,000 hectares
12 December 2004	Provincial government delays Greenbelt legislation for three months
24 January 2005	Public meeting is held in King City over the construction of the Big Pipe
February 2005	Agricultural easements on 28 properties on the Duffins-Rouge Preserve are removed
24 February 2005	Provincial government passes the *Greenbelt Protection Plan*
1 March 2005	*Provincial Policy Statement* is passed
2 March 2005	Several thousand farmers bring their tractors to Queen's Park to seek $300 million in emergency aid for the spring planting
8 March 2005	Developer Silvio De Gasperis takes Province to court re Greenbelt lands
9 March 2005	Six hundred farmers drive their tractors on highways 401, 404, and 427 to meet five hundred protesters at Queen's Park to highlight the crisis in farm income
May 2005	City of Toronto allocates $2 million to Toronto and Region Conservation Authority to protect source waters
11 May 2005	Durham Region decides not to block Pickering Town Council's decision to permit development on the Duffins-Rouge Agricultural Preserve
14 May 2005	*Greenbelt Act* passes
19 May 2005	Silvio De Gasperis loses first attempt to turn 600 hectares of Duffins- Rouge land into a subdivision
30 May 2005	Durham Region votes to support Pickering to remove 1,900 hectares of the Duffins-Rouge Agricultural Preserve from the Greenbelt to build subdivisions
11 July 2005	King City Preserve the Village Inc. applies for judicial review at the Ontario Supreme Court, arguing that the Region has failed to live up to the *Oak Ridges Moraine Conservation Plan*
13 July 2005	*Places to Grow Act* passes
16 June 2006	*Growth Plan for the Greater Golden Horseshoe* passes
2006	*Planning and Conservation Land Statute Law Amendment Act* (Bill 51) passes

Notes

1 Development, Sprawl, and Conservation

1 While this rate has been significant in the Toronto region, some U.S. census metropolitan areas have grown faster. For example, Portland grew by 26.3 per cent between 1990 and 2000, Dallas and Houston grew by 29.3 per cent and 25.2 per cent respectively, Denver by 30 per cent, Atlanta by 38.9 per cent, and Las Vegas by 83 per cent (GHK Canada, 2002: 13).
2 Toronto Census Metropolitan Area is the largest in Canada, stretching from Ajax and Pickering in the east to Milton in the west, and to New Tecumseth and Georgina in the north (Statistics Canada, 2009).
3 The *Employment Equity Act* defines *visible minorities* as persons other than Aboriginal peoples, who are non-Caucasian in race and non-white in colour (Statistics Canada, 2006).
4 The *Greenbelt Act* of 2005 added 400,000 hectares of designated protected countryside to the 360,000 hectares already contained within the existing *Niagara Escarpment Plan* and the *Oak Ridges Moraine Conservation Plan,* for a total of 760,000 hectares (1.8 million acres) (Pond, 2009).

3 The Surfacing of a Landform

1 Referring to the belt in which the telephone area code is 905.

6 Conservation Planning in the Service of Growth

1 In a different section of the same document Hunter, Beck, and Smart (1997) state that the "approximate 275 m asl contour has been accepted as the 'toe and slope' definition of the Oak Ridges Moraine, and corresponds, for the

most part, to a natural boundary between the high density urban forms encroaching from the south and the sparse rural development historically characteristic of the Moraine." Hunter, Beck, and Smart appear to be the hydrogeologists of the exurban estate developments that at the time were dominant in many parts of the Moraine, including the Palgrave Estates in Caledon whose hydrogeological studies had been conducted by Hunter and Associates.

Bibliography

Abbate, Gay. 1998. Peace comes to the Rouge Valley developers. *The Globe and Mail*, 4 June: A10.

Abbate, Gay. 2003. Had no choice but to allow development, Minister says. *The Globe and Mail*, 22 November: A13.

Abbruzzese, Teresa V., and Gerda R. Wekerle. 2011. Gendered spaces of activism in exurbia: Politicizing an ethics of care from the household to the region. *Frontiers: A Women's Studies Journal* 32 (2): 186–231.

Abe, Joseph M., David A. Bassett, and Patricia E. Dempsey. 1998. *Business Ecology: Giving Your Organization the Natural Edge*. Woburn, MA: Butterworth-Heinemann.

Aberley, Doug. 1993. *Boundaries of Home: Mapping for Local Empowerment*. Gabriola Island: New Society Publishers.

Aberley, Doug. 1999. Interpreting bioregionalism: A story from many voices. In *Bioregionalism*, ed. Michael Vincent McGinnis, 13–42. New York: Routledge.

Adams, William M. 1997. Rationalization and conservation: Ecology and the management of nature in the United Kingdom. *Transactions of the Institute of British Geographers* 22 (3): 277–91. http://dx.doi.org/10.1111/j.0020-2754.1997.00277.x.

Adams, William M. 2009. Separation, proprietorship, and community in the history of conservation. In *Nature's End: History and the Environment*, ed. Sverker Sörlin and Paul Warde, 50–69. New York: Palgrave Macmillan.

Aggregates and Roadbuilding Magazine. 2001. Canada's top 20 sand and gravel operations. Retrieved 19 August 2001 from http://www.rocktoroad.com.

Aggregates Manager. 2005. *Canada & Province News*. June.

Alderville Black Oak Savanna. 2006. History/Partners. Retrieved 15 September from http://www.aldervillesavanna.ca/partners.html.

Alderville Black Oak Savanna. 2009. To know this place. Retrieved 15 September from http://www.aldervillesavanna.ca/index.html.

Alderville First Nation. 2006. A general history. Retrieved 15 September from http://www.aldervillefirstnation.ca/history.

Alexander, Donald. 1994. Planning as learning: The education of citizen activists. Unpublished PhD dissertation, University of Waterloo, Ontario.

Ali, S. Harris. 2004. A socio-ecological autopsy of the *e.coli* 0157:H7 outbreak in Walkerton, Ontario, Canada. *Social Science & Medicine* 58 (12): 2601–12. http://dx.doi.org/10.1016/j.socscimed.2003.09.013.

Allemang, John. 1985. Castles in the hills. *The Globe and Mail*, 26 January: CLL1.

Altman, Irwin, and Setha M. Low, eds. 1992. *Place Attachment, Human Behaviour and Environment: Advance in Theory and Research*. New York: Plenum Press.

Amenta, Edwin, and Neal Caren. 2004. The legislative, organizational, and beneficiary consequences of state-oriented challengers. In *The Blackwell Companion to Social Movements*, ed. David A. Snow, Sarah A. Soule, and Hanspeter Kriesi, 461–88. Malden, MA: Blackwell.

Anderson, Christopher M., and Jonathan R. King. 2004. Equilibrium behavior in the conservation easement game. *Land Economics* 80 (3): 355–74. http://dx.doi.org/10.2307/3654726.

Athanasiu, Andrew. 2005. Plug up the pipe: Why Province should ditch Moraine sewer plan. *Now Magazine*, 11–17 August: 24, 50.

Attfield, Peter. 2000. It's not just the water that counts on Moraine. *Toronto Star*, 10 April: 1.

Bachelard, Gaston. 1958. *La poétique de l'espace*. Paris: Presses Universitaires Françaises.

Bäckstrand, Karin. 2003. Civic science for sustainability: Reframing the role of experts, policy makers, and citizens in environmental governance. *Global Environmental Politics* 3 (4): 24–41. http://dx.doi.org/10.1162/152638003322757916.

Bäckstrand, Karin. 2004. Scientisation vs. civic expertise in environmental governance: Eco-feminist, eco-modern, and post-modern responses. *Environmental Politics* 13 (4): 695–714. http://dx.doi.org/10.1080/0964401042000274322.

Baker, Douglas, Christine Slam, and Tracey Summerville. 2001. An evolving policy network in action: The case of construction aggregate policy in Ontario. *Canadian Public Administration* 44 (4): 463–83. http://dx.doi.org/10.1111/j.1754-7121.2001.tb00901.x.

Barber, John. 2008. Condo boom helps drop curtain on the age of sprawl. *The Globe and Mail*, 16 September: A14.

Barnett, P.J., D.R. Sharpe, H.A.J. Russell, T.A. Brennand, G. Gorrell, F.M. Kenny, and A. Pugin. 1998. On the origin of the Oak Ridges Moraine. *Canadian Journal of Earth Sciences* 35 (10): 1152–67. http://dx.doi.org/10.1139/e98-062.

Berg, Peter, and Richard Dasmann. 1977. Reinhabiting California. *Ecologist* 7 (10): 399–401.

Berube, Alan, Audrey Singer, Jill H. Wilson, and William H. Frey. 2006. Finding exurbia: America's fast-growing communities at the metropolitan fringe. New York: Brookings Institution. Retrieved 28 November 2008 from http://www.brookings.edu/reports/2006/10metropolitanpolicy_berube.aspx.

Bevir, Mark. 2006. Democratic governance: Systems and radical perspectives. *Public Administration Review* 66 (3): 426–36. http://dx.doi.org/10.1111/j.1540-6210.2006.00599.x.

Bevir, Mark, and R. Rhodes. 2003. *Interpreting British Governance*. London: Routledge.

Bevir, Mark, and R.A.W. Rhodes. 2006. *Governance Stories*. London: Routledge.

Binstock, Matthew. 2009. Backyard for whom? Rural gentrification versus nature conservation on the Oak Ridges Moraine. Unpublished major paper, Faculty of Environmental Studies, York University, Toronto.

Binstock, Matthew. 2011. Personal communication with L.A. Sandberg. Toronto.

Binstock, Matthew, and Maureen Carter-Whitney. 2011. *Aggregate Extraction in Ontario: A Strategy for the Future*. Toronto: Canadian Institute for Environmental Law and Policy.

Birnbaum, Leah, Lorenzo Nicolet, and Zack Taylor. 2004. Simcoe County: The new growth frontier. Toronto: Neptis Foundation. Retrieved 10 November from www.neptis.org.

Blais, Pamela. 2003. The growth opportunity: Leveraging new growth to maximize benefits in the Central Ontario zone. Issue paper no.5. Toronto: Neptis Foundation.

Bocking, Stephen. 1997. *Ecologists and Environmental Politics: A History of Contemporary Ecology*. New Haven: Yale University Press.

Bocking, Stephen. 2002. The Moraine is about politics, not science. *Alternatives* 28 (2): 11–12.

Bocking, Stephen. 2004. *Nature's Experts: Science, Politics, and the Environment*. Piscataway, NJ: Rutgers University Press.

Bocking, Stephen. 2005. Protecting the rain barrel: Discourses and the roles of science in a suburban environmental controversy. *Environmental Politics* 14 (5): 611–28. http://dx.doi.org/10.1080/09644010500257896.

Bocking, Stephen. 2006. Constructing urban expertise: Professional and political authority in Toronto. *Journal of Urban History* 33 (1): 51–76. http://dx.doi.org/10.1177/0096144206290265.

Boudreau, Julie-Anne, Roger Keil, and Douglas Young. 2009. *Changing Toronto: Governing Urban Neoliberalism*. Toronto: University of Toronto Press.

Bourne, Larry S. 2000. Urban Canada in transition to the twenty-first century: Trends, issues and visions. In *Canadian Cities in Transition*, ed. Trudi Bunting and Pierre Filion, 26–51. New York: Oxford University Press.

Bourne, Larry S., Michael Bunce, Laura Taylor, and Nik Luka. 2003. Contested ground: The dynamics of peri-urban growth in the Toronto region. *Canadian Journal of Regional Science* XXVI (2–3): 251–70.

Braun, Bruce. 2002. *The Intemperate Rainforest: Nature, Culture and Power on Canada's West Coast*. Minneapolis: University of Minnesota Press.

Braun, Bruce, and Noel Castree. 1998. *Remaking Reality: Nature at the Millennium*. London: Routledge.

Brennan, Richard, and Robert Benzie. 2005. McGuinty claims developers are angry at him. *Toronto Star*, 8 March: A01.

Brenner, Neil. 2004. *New State Spaces: Urban Governance and the Rescaling of Statehood*. New York: Oxford University Press.

Bruce Trail Conservancy. 2008. About Us. Retrieved 14 November from http://brucetrail.org/pages/about-us.

Bruegmann, Robert. 2005. *Sprawl: A Compact History*. Chicago: University of Chicago Press.

Buller, Henry. 2004. Where the wild things are: The evolving iconography of rural fauna. *Journal of Rural Studies* 20 (2): 131–41. http://dx.doi.org/10.1016/j.jrurstud.2003.08.009.

Bullock, James. 1998. Community translocation in Britain: Setting objectives and measuring consequences. *Biological Conservation* 84 (3): 199–214. http://dx.doi.org/10.1016/S0006-3207(97)00140-7.

Bunce, Michael. 1994. *The Countryside Ideal: Anglo-American Images of Landscape*. New York: Routledge.

Burnett, David (Toronto and Region Conservation Authority). 2004. Interviewed by L. Iandoli, 2 June, Toronto.

Burnett, David. 2005. OMB hearings and the Oak Ridges Moraine Conservation Plan: Review shows OMB is quick study. *Ontario Planning* 20 (July/August): 19–23.

Buttle, James. 1995. Channel changes following headwater reforestation: The Ganaraska River, Ontario, Canada. *Geografiska Annaler* 77 (3): 107–18. http://dx.doi.org/10.2307/521224.

Cadieux, Valentine. 2011. Competing discourses of nature in exurbia. *GeoJournal* 76 (4): 341–63.

Caledon Citizen. 2006. Plenty to celebrate on the Oak Ridges Moraine. 21 June.

Calnan, Denis. 2000. Let's fight for natural surroundings. *Toronto Star*, 2 August: A 19.

Canadian Urban Institute. 2006. Nature Count$: Valuing southern Ontario's natural heritage. Prepared for the Natural Spaces Leadership Alliance. Retrieved on 1 August 2012 from http://canadianurbaninstitute.org/media/pdf/Nature_Counts_rschpaper_FINAL.pdf.

Cardwell, Jennifer. 1996. The origin and changing role of recreation in Ontario's conservation authorities. Unpublished master's thesis, Department of Geography, York University, Toronto.

Carr, Mike. 2004. *Bioregionalism and Civil Society: Democratic Challenges to Corporate Globalism*. Vancouver: University of British Columbia Press.

Carter-Whitney, Maureen. 2008. The Ontario's greenbelt in an international context: Comparing Ontario's greenbelt to its counterparts in Europe and North America. Toronto: Friends of the Greenbelt Foundation.

Casey, Edward. 1997. How to get from space to place in a fairly short stretch of time. In *Senses of Place*, ed. Steven Feld and Keith H. Basso, 14–51. Santa Fe, NM: School of American Research.

Castells, Manuel. 1997. *The Power of Identity*. Oxford: Blackwell Publishing.

Castree, Noel. 1995. The nature of produced nature: Materiality and knowledge construction in Marxism. *Antipode* 27 (1): 12–48. http://dx.doi.org/10.1111/j.1467-8330.1995.tb00260.x.

Castree, Noel. 2001. Socializing nature: Theory, practice, and politics. In *Social Nature: Theory, Practice, and Politics*, ed. Noel Castree and Bruce Braun, 1–21. Malden, MA: Blackwell.

Castree, Noel, and Bruce Braun, eds. 2001. *Social Nature: Theory, Practice and Politics*. Oxford: Blackwell.

Cement Association of Canada. 2004. Homepage. Retrieved 11 December from http://www.cement.ca

Cement Sustainability Initiative. 2002. Homepage. Retrieved 11 December from http://www.wbcsdcement.org.

Central Ontario Lakeshore Urban Complex Task Force (COLUC). 1974. Report to the Advisory Committee on urban and regional planning of the Central

Ontario Lakeshore Urban Complex Taskforce. Toronto: Ontario Ministry of Treasury, Economics, and Intergovernmental Affairs.

Chambers, Colin, and L. Anders Sandberg. 2007. Pits, peripheralization, and the politics of scale: Struggles over locating extractive industries in the Town of Caledon, Ontario, Canada. *Regional Studies* 41 (3): 327–38. http://dx.doi.org/10.1080/00343400600928319.

Chapin, Timothy S., Charles E. Connerly, and Harrison T. Higgins. 2007. *Growth Management in Florida: Planning for Paradise*. Aldershot, UK: Ashgate Publishing Limited.

Chapman, Lyman John, and Donald F. Putnam. 1951. *The Physiography of Southern Ontario*. 1st ed. Toronto: Ontario Ministry of Natural Resources.

Cherniak, Jason. 2005. Massive parks cause urban sprawl. 30 September. Retrieved 10 January 2006 from http://jasoncherniak.blogspot.com/2005/09/massive-parks-cause-urban-sprawl.html.

City of Toronto. 1998. Oak Ridges Moraine / Oak Ridges Moraine Steering Committee. Retrieved 24 June 2000 from http://www.toronto.ca/moraine/index.htm.

City of Toronto. 2001. Federal government commended for protecting the Oak Ridges Moraine. 23 March. Retrieved 22 June from http://www.city.toronto.on.ca/moraine/news_032301.htm.

City of Toronto. 2012. Backgrounder: 2011 Census; population and dwelling counts. Toronto: City of Toronto. 8 February. Retrieved from http://www.toronto.ca/demographics/pdf/2011-census-backgrounder.pdf

Cloke, Paul. 1996. Rural life-styles: Material opportunity, cultural experience, and how theory can undermine policy. *Economic Geography* 72 (4): 433–49. http://dx.doi.org/10.2307/144523.

Cloke, Paul, and Jo Little. 1997. *Contested Countryside Cultures: Otherness, Marginalisation and Rurality*. London: Routledge.

Conservation Authorities Moraine Coalition. 2012. Conservation Authorities Moraine Coalition. Retrieved 30 July from http://www.trca.on.ca/the-living-city/conservation-authorities-moraine-coalition.dot

Cooper, Matthew. 1999. Spatial discourses and social boundaries: Re-imagining the Toronto waterfront. In *Theorizing the City: The New Urban Anthropology Reader*, ed. Setha Low, 377–99. New Brunswick, NJ: Rutgers University Press.

Cowell, Richard, and Jonathan Murdoch. 1999. Land use and limits to (regional) governance: Some lessons from planning for housing and minerals in England. *International Journal of Urban and Regional Research* 23 (4): 654–69. http://dx.doi.org/10.1111/1468-2427.00221.

Cowell, Richard, and Susan Owens. 1998. Suitable locations: Equity and sustainability in the minerals planning process. *Regional Studies* 32 (9): 797–811. http://dx.doi.org/10.1080/00343409850117960.

Cowles, Fiona. 1995. Planning trail and greenway networks: The Oak Ridges Moraine Trail. Unpublished major paper, Faculty of Environmental Studies, York University, Toronto.

Crandall, Debbe (Save the Oak Ridges Moraine Coalition). 2003. Interviewed by L. Iandoli, Caledon, Ontario, 25 May.

Crandall, Debbe (Save the Oak Ridges Moraine Coalition). 2004. Interviewed by G. Wekerle and L.A. Sandberg, Caledon, Ontario, 5 April.

Cronon, William. 1992. A place for stories: Nature, history, and narrative. *Journal of American History* 78 (4): 1347–76. http://dx.doi.org/10.2307/2079346.

Cronon, William, ed. 1996. *Uncommon Ground: Rethinking the Human Place in Nature*. New York: W.W. Norton.

Cruikshank, Julie. 2005. *Do Glaciers Listen?: Local Knowledge, Colonial Encounters and Social Imagination*. Vancouver: University of British Columbia Press.

Crump, Jeff R. 2003. Finding a place in the country: Exurban and suburban development in Sonoma County, California. *Environment and Behavior* 35 (2): 187–202. http://dx.doi.org/10.1177/0013916502250207.

Dance Environmental Inc. 1998. Natural rehabilitation of gravel pits on the Oak Ridges Moraine. Mississauga, ON: Management of Abandoned Aggregate Properties Program.

Davidson, Joyce, and Christine Milligan. 2004. Embodying emotion, sensing space: Introducing emotional geographies. *Social & Cultural Geography* 5 (4): 523–32. http://dx.doi.org/10.1080/1464936042000317677.

Demeritt, David. 2001. Being constructive about nature. In *Social Nature: Theory, Practice, and Politics*, ed. Noel Castree and Bruce Braun, 22–40. Oxford: Blackwell.

Deverell, John. 1994. Naturalists rally to save marsh. *Toronto Star*, 28 April: SD03.

DeVries, Laura. 2011. *Conflict in Caledonia: Aboriginal Land Rights and the Rule of Law*. Vancouver: University of British Columbia Press.

Dewar, Elaine. 1997. Behind this door. *Toronto Life*, May: 85–92.

Dexter, Brian. 1989. Uxbridge's industrial park makes York official angry. *Toronto Star*, 14 December: E8.

Dierwechter, Yonn. 2008. *Urban Growth Management and Its Discontents: Promises, Practices and Geopolitics in US City-Regions*. New York: Palgrave Macmillan.

Dobson, Andrew P. 2003. *Citizenship and the Environment*. Oxford: Oxford University Press. http://dx.doi.org/10.1093/0199258449.001.0001

Dobson, Andrew P. 2005. Citizenship. In *Political Theory and the Ecological Challenge*, ed. Andrew Dobson and Robyn Eckersley, 481–561. Cambridge: Cambridge University Press.

Doyle, Victor (Ministry of Municipal Affairs and Housing). 2004. Interviewed by G. Wekerle, L.A. Sandberg, and L. Gilbert, Toronto, 20 May.

Drake, Bob. 2002. Large regional quarries provide a growing proportion of the crushed stone in the United States, but is bigger better? *Aggregates Manager*, June.

Dubé, Rebecca Cook. 2006. How much are "green" features worth? *The Globe and Mail*, 28 July: G1.

Duckworth, Peter. 1975. Paleocurrent trends in the latest outwash at the western end of the Oak Ridges Moraine, Ontario. Unpublished PhD dissertation, University of Toronto, Ontario.

Duncan, James S., and Nancy G. Duncan. 2004. *Landscapes of Privilege: The Politics of the Aesthetic in an American Suburb*. New York: Routledge.

Durham Regional Police. 2012. ATVs: Rules of the road; where to ride. Retrieved 30 July from http://www.drps.ca/internet_explorer/whatsnew/whatsnew_view.asp?ID=16918.

Eagles, Paul F. J. 1981. Environmentally sensitive area planning in Ontario, Canada. *Journal of the American Planning Association* 47 (3): 313–23. http://dx.doi.org/10.1080/01944368108976513.

Eaton Hall. 2012. A rich and varied past: A historic country estate. Retrieved 15 July from http://www.senecac.on.ca/eatonhall/main.html.

EcoSpark, 2012. An overview of EcoSpark: 1996–2011. Retrieved 20 March from http://www.ecospark.ca/history.

Edey, R. Christopher, Mark Seasons, and Graham Whitelaw. 2006. The media, planning and the Oak Ridges Moraine. *Planning Practice and Research* 21 (2): 147–61. http://dx.doi.org/10.1080/02697450600944632.

Eidelman, Gabriel. 2010. Managing urban sprawl in Ontario: Good policy or good politics? *Politics and Policy* 38 (6): 1211–36. http://dx.doi.org/10.1111/j.1747-1346.2010.00275.x.

Empire Communities. 2008. The Estates of Wyndance. Retrieved 15 September from http://itracphp.com/empirelatest/corp/newsdetail.php?n=43.

Environment Canada. 2010. Ecological gifts: Donor profiles. Retrieved 15 March 2012 from http://www.ec.gc.ca/pde-egp/default.asp?lang=En&n=12345678-1&xsl=mainhomeitem&xml=494F00EC-D643-4B9B-993B-D15C4BB6626E.

Escobar, Arturo, Dianne Rocheleau, and Smitu Kothari. 2002. Environmental social movements and the politics of place. *Development*. 45 (1): 28–36. http://dx.doi.org/10.1057/palgrave.development.1110314.

Estrin, David, and John Swaigen. 1993. *Environment on Trial*. Toronto: Emond Montgomery.

Evans, James. 2007. Wildlife corridors: An urban political ecology. *Local Environment* 12 (2): 129–52. http://dx.doi.org/10.1080/13549830601133169.

Eyles, N., J. Boyce, and J. Hibbert. 1992. The geology of garbage. *Geoscience Canada.* 19 (2): 50–62.

Feldman, T., and Andrew E.G. Jonas. 2000. Sage scrub rebellion? Property rights, political fragmentation, and conservation planning in Southern California under the federal Endangered Species Act. *Annals of the Association of American Geographers* 90 (2): 256–92. http://dx.doi.org/10.1111/0004-5608.00195.

Fenech, Adam, Brent Taylor, Roger Hansell, and Graham Whitelaw. 2006. Major road changes in Southern Ontario, 1935–1995: Implications for protected areas. Retrieved 12 March 2006 from http://www.utoronto.ca/imap/papers/road_changes.htm.

Ferenc, Leslie. 1999. Estate land becomes battleground. *Toronto Star*, 20 August: B1.

Ferenc, Leslie, and Tony Bock. 2000. Groups look to Ottawa to curb 407 extension. *Toronto Star*, 7 March: 01.

Ferguson, Jock. 1991a. Civic corruption target of Toronto police probe: Full-scale look at links between developers, politicians. *The Globe and Mail*, 17 May: A9.

Ferguson, Jock. 1991b. York Region plan could strike sparks: High development, low density at odds with Queen's Park objectives. *The Globe and Mail*, 26 September: A12.

Ferguson, Jock. 1991c. Unique cash problem highlights the givers. *The Globe and Mail*, 9 November: A8.

Ferguson, Jock. 1992. The sultans of cement. *The Nation* 255 (3–10 August): 130-2.

Filion, Pierre. 2003. Towards smart growth? The difficult implementation of alternatives to urban dispersion. *Plan Canada* 12 (1): 48–70.

Filion, Pierre. 2007. *The Urban Growth Centre Strategy in the Greater Golden Horseshoe*. Toronto: Neptis Foundation.

Finkler, Lilith. 2001. Faith-full planning: The case of the Wat Lao Buddhist Temple. Unpublished paper, Faculty of Environmental Studies, York University, Toronto.

Fischer, John, Frederick Helleiner, and Klaus Wehrenberg, eds. 1991. *Greenways and Green Space on the Oak Ridges Moraine: Towards Co-operative Planning*. Department of Geography and Frost Centre for Canadian Heritage and Development Studies. Peterborough, ON: Trent University.

Flint, Anthony. 2006. *This Land: The Battle Over Sprawl and the Future of America*. Baltimore, MD: Johns Hopkins Press.

Flyvbjerg, Bent. 1998. *Rationality and Power: Democracy in Practice.* Chicago: Chicago University Press.

Forester, John. 1989. *Planning in the Face of Power.* Berkeley: University of California Press.

Forsyth, Tim. 2003. *Critical Political Ecology: The Politics of Environmental Science.* London: Routledge.

Foster, Jennifer. 2006. The social construction of landscape continuity on the Niagara Escarpment and Oak Ridges Moraine: Whose continuity? Whose landscape? Unpublished PhD dissertation, Faculty of Environmental Studies, York University, Toronto.

Foster, Jennifer, and L. Anders Sandberg. 2004. Friends or foe? Invasive species and public space in Toronto, Canada. *Geographical Review* 94 (2): 178–98. http://dx.doi.org/10.1111/j.1931-0846.2004.tb00166.x.

Foucault, Michel. 1980. *Power/Knowledge: Selected Interviews and Other Writings, 1972–1977.* New York: Pantheon.

Francis, Diane. 2000. Green hypocrites should stay off Ontario moraine. *National Post.* 22 April: D02.

Fraser, Jackie. 2001. Public submission to the Corporation of the Town of Milton concerning the Dufferin Milton quarry expansion. Town of Milton: Planning Department. 13 February.

Fraser, John. 2004. Land succession, transition and conversion on the Oak Ridges Moraine: An approach for integrating succession modules in VDDT/TELSA. Peterborough: Southern Spatial Analysis Unit, Science and Information Branch. Unpublished manuscript.

Friedmann, John. 1998. Planning theory revisited. *European Planning Studies* 6 (3): 245–53. http://dx.doi.org/10.1080/09654319808720459.

Friends of the Greenbelt Foundation. 2006. Friends of the Greenbelt Foundation announces $1.4 million environmental farm practices grant. 3 October. Retrieved 3 August 2012 from http://greenbelt.ca/news/economy/friends-greenbelt-foundation-announces-14-million-environmental-farm-practices-grant.

Friends of the Greenbelt Foundation. 2012. Home page. Retrieved 24 July 2012 from http://greenbelt.ca/.

Frouws, Jaap. 1998. The contested redefinition of the countryside: An analysis of rural discourses in the Netherlands. *Sociologia Ruralis* 38 (1): 54–68. http://dx.doi.org/10.1111/1467-9523.00063.

Fung, Felix, and Tenley Conway. 2007. Greenbelts as an environmental planning tool: A case study of Southern Ontario, Canada. *Journal of Environmental Policy and Planning* 9 (2): 101–17. http://dx.doi.org/10.1080/15239080701381355.

Funston, Mike. 1996. Caledon residents try to keep tranquil life. *Toronto Star*, 20 June: BR01.

Furuseth, Owen J., and Mark B. Lapping, eds. 1999. *Contested Countryside: The Rural Urban Fringe in North America*. Aldershot, UK: Avebury, Ashgate Publishing.

Gabe, Gonda. 2006. Beneath our feet there's an old new world to discover. *Toronto Star*, 11 March: B1.

Galloway, Gloria. 2004. Farmers out in the cold as development frozen. *The Globe and Mail*. 30 October: A11.

Ganaraska Region Conservation Authority. 2012. History of Ganaraska forest. Retrieved 1 August from http://www.grca.on.ca/about-history.html.

Garfinkel, Josh, and Josh Kohler (Earthroots), Anastasia Lindner and Hugh Wilkins (EcoJustice). 2008. Ontario's water hazard: The cumulative impact of golf courses on our water resources. Toronto: Earthroots and EcoJustice. July. Retrieved from http://www.ecojustice.ca/publications/reports/ontarios-water-hazard/attachment.

Garrett, James. 1999. Moraine is valuable. *Toronto Star*, 1 December: 01.

Gartshore, R. Geoffrey, Michelle Purchase, Robert I. Rook, and Leslie Scott. 2005. Bayview extension, Richmond Hill, Ontario, Canada habitat and wildlife crossing in a contentious setting: A case study. Road Ecology Center, University of California Davis. September. Retrieved 30 July 2012 from http://repositories.cdlib.org/uc/redir-bepress/jmie/roadeco/Gartshore2005a.

Gates, Christopher. 1978. Land resource planning on the Oak Ridges Moraine: Issues and prospects. Unpublished major paper, Faculty of Environmental Studies, York University. Toronto.

Gates, Christopher. 2009. Interviewed by G. Wekerle and L. Anders Sandberg, Toronto, March.

GHK Canada. 2002. Growing together: Prospects for renewal in the Toronto Region. Report prepared for the City of Toronto. Toronto: City of Toronto Planning Department.

Gibbs, David, and Rob Krueger. 2012. Fractures in meta-narratives of development: An interpretive institutionalist account of land use development in the Boston city-region. *International Journal of Urban and Regional Research* 36 (2): 363–80. http://dx.doi.org/10.1111/j.1468-2427.2011.01061.x.

Giddens, Anthony. 1991. *Modernity and Self-Identity: Self and Society in the Late Modern Age*. Stanford, CA: Stanford University Press.

Gilbert, Liette, L. Anders Sandberg, and Gerda Wekerle. 2009. Building bioregional citizenship: The case of the Oak Ridges Moraine, Ontario. *Local Environment* 14 (5): 387–401. http://dx.doi.org/10.1080/13549830902903674.

Gilbert, Liette, Gerda R. Wekerle, and L. Anders Sandberg. 2005. Local re-
    sponses to development pressures: Conflictual politics of sprawl and envi-
    ronmental conservation. *Cahiers de Géographie du Québec* 49: 377–92.

Gillespie, Kerry. 2003a. Sprawl costs billions, Sierra says. *Toronto Star*, 29 July:
    B03.

Gillespie, Kerry. 2003b. Smart Growth strategies released. *Toronto Star*, 19 Feb-
    ruary: B01.

Gold, John, and George Revill. 2000. Landscape, defence, and the study of
    conflict. In *Landscapes of Defence*, ed. John Gold and George Revill, 1–20.
    London: Prentice Hall.

Goldstone, Jack. A. 2003. Bridging institutionalized and non-institutionalized
    politics. In *States, Parties, and Social Movements*, ed. Jack A. Goldstone, 1–24.
    Cambridge: Cambridge University Press.

Gorrie, Peter. 2011. Showdown on the Oak Ridges Moraine. *Nature* 51 (2): 25–
    9, 38.

Government of Ontario. 1973. *Niagara Escarpment Planning and Development
    Act*. Toronto: Queen's Printer.

Government of Ontario. 1985. *Niagara Escarpment Plan*. Toronto: Queen's
    Printer.

Grand River Conservation Authority. 2008. Report no. GM-04–08–16. 25
    April. Retrieved 15 September from http://www.grandriver.ca/governance/
    GM040816.pdf.

Gravel Watch Ontario. 2006. Homepage. Retrieved September 15 from www.
    gravelwatch.org.

Greater Toronto Home Builders' Association. 2001. Oak Ridges Moraine prin-
    ciples. Retrieved 3 August 2012 from http://www.bildgta.ca/government_
    reports_detail.asp?id=88&fragment=0&SearchType=ExactPhrase&terms=
    oak%20ridges%20moraine.

Great Ontario Outdoor Adventure. 2006. Portage through the past. Retrieved
    15 September 2006 from http://www.ontariooutdoor.com/en/getaways/
    spring/history/details.php?id=22.

Guselle, Katherine. 1991. Realities of Planning on the Oak Ridges Moraine: A
    Citizen's Perspective. In *Greenways and Green Space on the Oak Ridges Mo-
    raine: Towards Co-operative Planning*, ed. John Fischer, Frederick Helleiner,
    and Klaus Wehrenberg, 7–13. Department of Geography and Frost Centre
    for Canadian Heritage and Development Studies, Trent University, Peter-
    borough, Ontario.

Guselle, Katherine. 1996. Presentation to the Ontario Legislative Assembly.
    Retrieved 5 March 2012 from http://www.ontla.on.ca/committee-proceed-
    ings/transcripts/files_html/1996-02-22_r013.htm#P901_288153.

Haan, Henk de, and Norman Long. 1997. *Images and Realities of Rural Life: Wageningen Perspectives on Rural Tranformations*. Uitgeverij, Netherlands: Van Gorcum.

Haas, Peter M. 1992. Epistemic communities and international policy coordination: Introduction. *International Organization* 46 (1): 1–35. http://dx.doi.org/10.1017/S0020818300001442.

Halfacree, Keith H. 1995. Talking about rurality: Social representations of the rural as expressed by residents of six English parishes. *Journal of Rural Studies* 11 (1): 1–20. http://dx.doi.org/10.1016/0743-0167(94)00039-C.

Halfacree, Keith H., and Paul J. Boyle. 1998. *Migration into Rural Areas: Theories and Issues*. London: Wiley.

Hanna, Kevin, and Steven Webber. 2010. Incremental planning and land-use conflict in the Toronto region's Oak Ridges Moraine. *Local Environment* 15 (2): 169–83. http://dx.doi.org/10.1080/13549830903530625.

Hanna, Kevin S., Steven M. Webber, and D. Scott Slocombe. 2007. Integrated ecological and regional planning in a rapid-growth setting. *Environmental Management* 40 (3): 339–48. http://dx.doi.org/10.1007/s00267-006-0225-7. Medline:17562099

Hare, Melanie. 2001. Exploring growth management roles in Ontario: Learning from "who does what" elsewhere. A report prepared for the Ontario Professional Planners Institute. Toronto. September.

Harner, John. 2001. Place identity and copper mining in Sonora, Mexico. *Annals of the Association of American Geographers* 91 (4): 660–80. http://dx.doi.org/10.1111/0004-5608.00264.

Harpur, Tom. 1991. Why do we dirty and spoil the wonders of nature. *Toronto Star*, 5 May: B7.

Harpur, Tom. 1992. Choosing between two evils produces mixed results. *Toronto Star*, 19 January: B7.

Harris, Cole. 1997. *The Resettlement of British Columbia: Essays on Colonialism and Geographical Change*. Vancouver: University of British Columbia Press.

Harris, Richard. 2004. *Creeping Conformity: How Canada Became Suburban, 1900–1960*. Toronto: University of Toronto Press.

Hays, Samuel P. 1987. *Beauty, Health and Permanence: Environmental Politics in the United States, 1955–1985*. Cambridge: Cambridge University Press. http://dx.doi.org/10.1017/CBO9780511664106

Heather Green Golf Course. 2006. Homepage. Retrieved 1 February from http://www.heatherglen.ca/

Heidenreich, Conrad E., and Robert Burgar. 1999. Native settlement to 1947. In *Special Places: The Changing Ecosystems of the Toronto Region*, ed. Betty I.

Roots, Donald A. Chant, and Conrad E. Heidenreich, 63–75. Vancouver: UBC Press.

Helferty, Natalie. 2001. Urgent appeal to save the salamander!!! Stop the Bayview extension!!! 30 October . Retrieved 17 May 2006 from http://home.eol. ca/~donbar/persons/Natalie.htm.

Helferty, Natalie (Richmond Hill Naturalists). 2004a. Interviewed by L. Iandoli. Caledon, Ontario, 15 April.

Helferty, Natalie (Richmond Hill Naturalists). 2004b. Interviewed by L. Orsi, 4 May.

Heynen, Nik, Maria Kaika, and Erik Swyngedouw. 2006. *In the Nature of Cities: Urban Political Ecology and the Politics of Urban Metabolism.* New York: Routledge.

Higgs, Eric. 2003. *Nature by Design: People, Natural Process, and Ecological Restoration.* Cambridge, MA: MIT Press.

HighFields Inn and Country Spa. 2004. *Toronto Life.* 1 March.

Hill, Alan. 1976. The effects of man-induced erosion and sedimentation on the soils of a portion of the Oak Ridges Moraine. *Canadian Geographer. Geographe Canadien* 20 (4): 384–404. http://dx.doi.org/10.1111/j.1541-0064.1976. tb00250.x.

Hintz, John. 2007. Some political problems for rewilding nature. *Ethics Place and Environment* 10 (2): 177–216. http://dx.doi.org/10.1080/1366879 0701344774.

Howard, Bryan. 1991. A Greenways Network for Ontario. In *Greenways and Green Space on the Oak Ridges Moraine: Towards Co-operative Planning,* ed. John Fischer, Frederick Helleiner, and Klaus Wehrenberg, 14–21. Department of Geography and Frost Centre for Canadian Heritage and Development Studies, Trent University, Peterborough, Ontario.

Howard, Kenneth W.F. 2008. Homepage. Retrieved 8 March from http://www. scar.utoronto.ca/~gwater/index.html.

Howard, K.W.F., N. Eyles, P.J. Smart, J.I. Boyce, R.E. Gerber, S. Salvatori, and M. Doughty. 1995. The Oak Ridges Moraine of southern Ontario: A groundwater resource at risk. *Geoscience Canada* 22:101–20.

Howitt, Richard. 2002. Scale and the Other: Levinas and geography. *Geoforum* 33 (3): 299–313. http://dx.doi.org/10.1016/S0016-7185(02)00006-4.

Hudson, Kellie. 1999. Defenders of Moraine take action: Group fights to protect sensitive Oak Ridges area. *Toronto Star,* 16 October: 01.

Hunter, G., P. Beck, and P. Smart. 1997. Oak Ridges Moraine hydrogeological study: Overview. 27 October 1999. Retrieved from http://www.hunter-gis. com/WS_Services/HAndH/ORMPAPER/ormovr.htm.

Hunter and Associates. 2001. Oak Ridges Moraine experience. 30 November 2001. Retrieved 17 December from http://www.hunter-gis.com/ws_services/HAndH/ORM1.htm.

Hunter Geographic Information Systems. 2008. Hydrogeology and hydrogeochemistry: Oak Ridges Moraine hydrogeology study; Overview. Retrieved 8 March 2008 from http://www.huntergis.com/ws_services/HAndH/ORM-PAPER/exfig2z.htm.

Huntington, Ellsworth. [1951] 1971. *Civilization and Climate*. Hampden, CT: Archer Books.

Hurley, Patrick T., and Peter A. Walker. 2004. Whose vision? Conspiracy theory and land-use planning in Nevada County, California. *Environment & Planning A* 36 (9): 1529–47. http://dx.doi.org/10.1068/a36186.

Immen, Wallace. 1999a. Showdown brewing with developers over Oak Ridges Southern Ontario's water system at risk as proposed housing projects threaten to destroy region's unique kettle lakes, activists charge. *The Globe and Mail*. 8 November: A11.

Immen, Wallace. 1999b. Chain saws in the forest. *The Globe and Mail*. 8 November: A11.

Immen, Wallace. 2000a. Fragile moraine poorly managed: Scientists. *The Globe and Mail*. 2 February: A17.

Immen, Wallace. 2000b. Environmentalists propose massive moraine greenway. *The Globe and Mail*. 10 May: A21.

International Association for Great Lakes Research. 2002. Linking science and policy for urban nonpoint source pollution in the Great Lakes region. Retrieved 11 December from http://www.iaglr.org/scipolicy/nps/index.php.

Izzard, Dorothy, and Ene Leivo. 1990. It's environmentally crucial to save the Oak Ridges Moraine. *Toronto Star*, 23 August: E4.

Jacob, Katherine. 2003. *Oak Ridges Moraine Trails*. Ontario: Conservation Ontario.

Jasanoff, Sheila. 1997. NGOs and the environment: From knowledge to action. *Third World Quarterly* 18 (3): 579–94. http://dx.doi.org/10.1080/01436599714885.

Jefferson Commemorative Committee. 1980. *Jefferson Public School Commemorative Book*. Goodwood, ON: The Committee.

Jefferys, C.W. 1953. *The Picture Gallery of Canadian History*. Toronto: Ryerson.

Johnson, Jon. In press. The great Indian bus tour. In *The Nature of Empires and the Empires of Nature: Indigenous Peoples and the Great Lakes Environment*, ed. Karl S. Hele. Waterloo, ON: Wilfred Laurier University Press.

Johnson, Lorraine. 1999. Hiking the Oak Ridges Moraine. *Seasons*. 39 (3): 24.

Johnston, Teresa. 2002. Commentary from the trenches. *Seasonal Storms*, newsletter of Save the Oak Ridges Moraine (STORM) Coalition, spring: 4. Retrieved 2 August 2012 from http://www.stormcoalition.org/resources/Seasonal%20Storms-Spring%2002.pdf.

Jonas, Andrew E.G. and Stephanie Pincetl. 2006. Rescaling Regions in the State: The New Regionalism in California. *Political Geography* 25: 482–505.

Josey, Stan. 2003. Province to curb development on Pickering land. *Toronto Star*, 21 April: A4.

Kalinowski, Tess. 2008. Putting the brakes on wildlife deaths. *Toronto Star*, 24 May: A7.

Kanter, Ron. 1990. *Space for All: Options for a Greater Toronto Area Greenland Strategy.* Toronto: Queen's Printer.

Kawartha Regional Conservation Authority. 2006. East Cross Forest Conservation Area. Retrieved 15 September from http://www.kawarthaconservation.com/conservation_areas/east_cross_forest.html

Keung, Nicholas. 2000. Buddhists battling for Caledon site. *Toronto Star*, 30 October: 1.

Keung, Nicholas. 2001. Laotian group wins struggle to build temple. *Toronto Star*, 7 May: B3.

Kline, Jeffrey D., and Dennis Wichelns. 1998. Measuring heterogeneous preferences for preserving farmland and open space. *Ecological Economics* 26 (2): 211–24. http://dx.doi.org/10.1016/S0921-8009(97)00115-8.

Kuitenbrouwer, Peter. 2008. Toronto chips in $1.1 million to buy lake in Richmond Hill. *National Post*, 9 October: A1.

Lafarge. 2008. Canada coordinated rehabilitation of a quarry in a protected area. Retrieved 11 December from http://www.lafarge.com/wps/portal/2_4_4_1-EnDet?WCM_GLOBAL_CONTEXT=/wps/wcm/connect/Lafarge.com/AllCS/Env/QR/CP1610625190/CSEN

Laidley, Jennefer. 2011. Creating an environment for change: The "ecosystem approach" and the Olympics on Toronto's waterfront. In *Reshaping Toronto's Waterfront*, ed. Gene Desfor and Jennefer Laidley, 203–23. Toronto: University of Toronto Press.

Lakey, Jack. 2000a. Developer vows Moraine won't suffer. *Toronto Star*, 25 July: B2.

Lakey, Jack. 2000b. Authorities give Rouge River housing plan final approval. *Toronto Star*, 17 November: 1.

Landsberg, Michele. 1991. Another paradise could be lost in rush to build homes. *Toronto Star*, 27 April: K1.

Larner, Wendy, and David Craig. 2005. After neoliberalism? Community activism and local partnerships in Aotearoa, New Zealand. *Antipode* 37 (3): 402–24. http://dx.doi.org/10.1111/j.0066-4812.2005.00504.x.

Latour, Bruno. 1987. *Science in Action: How to Follow Scientists and Engineers through Society*. Cambridge, MA: Harvard University Press.

Latour, Bruno. 2004. *The Politics of Nature*. Cambridge, MA: Harvard University Press.

Latour, Bruno, Steve Woolgar, and Jonas Salk. 1986. *Laboratory Life: The Construction of Scientific Facts*. Princeton: Princeton University Press.

Law, John, and John Hassard. 1999. *Actor Network Theory and After*. London: Blackwell.

Leahy, Stephen. 1995. Group working to preserve Ganaraska rural area of Durham called a "green jewel." *Toronto Star*, 12 October: OS4.

Lee, Susan W. 2009. The myth of citizen participation: Waste management in the Fundy region of New Brunswick. In *Environmental Conflict and Democracy in Canada*, ed. Laurie E. Adkin, 209–28. Vancouver: UBC Press.

Lee-Macaraig, Clarine, and L. Anders Sandberg. 2007. Assessing municipal lawn care reform: The case of a lawn pesticide by-law in the Town of Caledon, Ontario, Canada. *Electronic Green Journal* 1(25). Retrieved from http://escholarship.org/uc/item/2js5m5b8.

Lehrer, Ute. 2012. Urban images and privatization in Toronto. In *Local Space/ Conflict: Grounding Neoliberalism*, ed. J. Kunkel and M. Mayer, 99–109. New York: Palgrave.

Leopold, Aldo. 1949. *A Sand County Almanac*. New York: Oxford University Press.

Levy, Harold. 2000 Housing will affect Moraine: Expert – but changes would be "acceptable," witness tells OMB hearing. *Toronto Star*, 7 July: 1.

Light, Andrew. 2003. Urban ecological citizenship. *Journal of Social Philosophy* 34 (1): 44–63. http://dx.doi.org/10.1111/1467-9833.00164.

Light, Andrew. 2005. Ecological citizenship: The democratic promise of restoration. In *The Humane Metropolis: People and Nature in the 21st Century City*, ed. Rutherford H. Platt, 169–81. Amherst, MA: University of Massachusetts Press.

Lindgren, R.D. 1996. *Submissions by the Canadian Environmental Law Association to the Standing Committee on General Government Regarding Bill 52 (Aggregate and Petroleum Resources Statute Law Amendment Act, 1996)*. Toronto: Canadian Environmental Law Association.

Logan, Shannon, and Gerda R. Wekerle. 2008. Neoliberalizing environmental governance? Land trusts, private conservation, and nature on the Oak Ridges Moraine. *Geoforum* 39 (6): 2097–2108. http://dx.doi.org/10.1016/j.geoforum.2008.08.009.

Low, Murray. 2004. Cities as spaces of democracy. In *Spaces of Democracy: Geographical Perspectives on Citizenship, Participation and Representation*, ed. Clive Barnett and Murray Low, 129–46. London: Sage.

Luke, Timothy. 2002. The people, politics, and the planet: Who knows, protects, and serves nature best? In *Democracy and the Claims of Nature*, ed. Ben A. Minteer and Bob Pepperman Taylor, 301–20. Lanham, MA: Rowan and Littlefield.

Lundholm, Jeremy, and P. Richardson. 2010. Habitat analogues for reconciliation ecology in urban and industrial environments. *Journal of Applied Ecology* 47 (5): 966–75. http://dx.doi.org/10.1111/j.1365-2664.2010.01857.x.

Macaraig, J. Marvin R., and L. Anders Sandberg. 2009. The politics of sewerage: Contested narratives on growth, science, and nature. *Society & Natural Resources* 22 (5): 448–63. http://dx.doi.org/10.1080/08941920802046437.

MacDermid, Robert. 2009. *Funding City Politics: Municipal Campaign Funding and Property Development in the Greater Toronto Area*. Toronto: CSJ Foundation for Research and Education and Vote Ontario.

Macdonald, Sara, and Roger Keil. 2012. The Ontario Greenbelt: Shifting the scales of the sustainability fix? *Professional Geographer* 64 (1): 125–45. http://dx.doi.org/10.1080/00330124.2011.586874.

Mackintosh, E.E. 1982. *Agriculture and the Aggregate Industry: Rehabilitation of Extracted Sand and Gravel Lands to an Agricultural After-Use*. Toronto: Ministry of Natural Resources.

Mackintosh, E.E. 1985. *Rehabilitation of Sand and Gravel Pits for Fruit Production in Ontario*. Toronto: Ministry of Natural Resources.

Mallan, Caroline. 2001. Plan puts the brakes on new housing on Oak Ridges Moraine. *Toronto Star*, 15 August: A1, A7.

Mallan, Caroline. 2004. Moraine land deal a boost for green space. *Toronto Star*, 24 September: A1, A7.

Marsden, Terry, Jonathan Murdoch, Phillip Lowe, Richard Munton, and Andrew Flynn. 1993. *Constructing the Countryside*. London: Routledge.

Marsh, Gloria (York Region Environmental Alliance). 2003. Interviewed by L. Iandoli. Richmond Hill, Ontario, 28 August.

Martin, Jenn. 2004. Media frames and the fight for the Oak Ridges Moraine: Framing, tactics, and lessons to be learned. Unpublished paper, Department of Communications and Culture, York University, Toronto.

Masden, B., N. Carroll, and K. Moore Brands. 2010. State of biodiversity markets report: Offset and compensation programs worldwide. Ecosystem marketplace. Retrieved from http://www.ecosystemmarketplace.com/documents/acrobat/sbdmr.pdf.

Mason, R. 2004. The Pinelands. In *Big Places, Big Plans: Large-Scale Regional Planning in North America*, ed. Mark Lapping and O. Furuseth, 29–54. Aldershot, UK: Ashgate.

Matlow, Josh (Earthroots). 2005. Interviewed by G.Wekerle and S. Rutherford, Toronto, 8 June.

McAndrew, Brian. 1995. Rural retreat fears being swallowed up. *Toronto Star*, 13 February: A1.

McAndrew, Brian. 2000. Scenic green space or urban sprawl? *Toronto Star*, 13 February: 1.

McCarthy, James. 1998. Environmentalism, wise use, and the nature of accumulation in the rural west. In *Remaking Reality: Nature at the Millenium*, ed. Bruce Braun and Noel Castree, 126–49. New York: Routledge.

McCarthy, James, and Scott Prudham. 2004. Neoliberal nature and the nature of neoliberalism. *Geoforum* 35 (3): 275–83. http://dx.doi.org/10.1016/j.geoforum.2003.07.003.

McClean, Marc. 2001. Natural systems and alternative urban development. FES Outstanding Graduate Student Paper Series. Faculty of Environmental Studies, York University, Toronto. Retrieved 30 July 2012 from http://www.yorku.ca/fes/research/students/outstanding/docs/marc-mcclean.pdf.

McEachern, Alan. 2001. *Natural Selections: National Parks in Atlantic Canada, 1935–1970*. Montreal and Kingston: McGill Queen's University Press.

McElhinny, Bonnie. 2006. Written in sand: Language and landscape in an environmental dispute in Southern Ontario. *Critical Discourse Studies* 3 (2): 123–52. http://dx.doi.org/10.1080/17405900600908087.

McGinnis, Michael Vincent. 1999. *Bioregionalism*. New York: Routledge.

McGreevy, Patrick V. 1994. *Imagining Niagara: The Meaning and Making of Niagara Falls*. Amherst: University of Massachusetts Press.

McLellan, Janet, and Marybeth White. 2005. Social capital and identity politics among Asian Buddhists in Toronto. *Journal of International Migration and Integration* 6 (2): 235–53.

McMahon, Michael. 2000. Oak Ridges Moraine: Environmental challenge and opportunity. GTA Forum co-sponsored by the Centre for Urban and Community Studies, University of Toronto; Ryerson University; Urban Studies Program, York University.

McMahon, Michael. 2003. Moving beyond sprawl in the Toronto bioregion: The case of King City and the Big Pipe. Unpublished paper, Faculty of Environmental Studies, York University, Toronto.

McPherson, T. Scott, and Vic. R Timmer. 2002. Amelioration of degraded soils under red pine plantations on the Oak Ridges Moraine, Ontario. *Canadian Journal of Soil Science* 82 (3): 375–88. http://dx.doi.org/10.4141/S01-084.

Melling, Michael (Davis, Howe Partners). 2004. Interviewed by Sandra Patano, Toronto, 11 June.

Meriano, Mandana, and Nick Eyles. 2003. Groundwater flow through Pleistocene glacial deposits in the rapidly urbanizing Rouge River–Highland Creek watershed, City of Scarborough, southern Ontario, Canada. *Hydrogeology Journal* 11 (2): 288–303. http://dx.doi.org/10.1007/s10040-002-0226-4.

Mesch, Gustavo S., and Orit Manor. 1998. Social ties, environmental perception, and local attachment. *Environment and Behavior* 30 (4): 504–19. http://dx.doi.org/10.1177/001391659803000405.

Miller, Gord. 2005. Running out of gravel and rock, but what is the true state of our aggregates resources? *Toronto Star*, 6 January: A22.

Mitchell, Don. 2002. Cultural landscapes: The dialectical landscape – Recent landscape research in human geography. *Progress in Human Geography*. 26(3): 381–89.

Mitchell, William J.T., ed. 1994. *Landscape and Power*. Chicago: University of Chicago Press.

Monitoring the Moraine. 2006. Status report on the implementation of the Oak Ridges Moraine Conservation Plan: Implications for the Greenbelt Plan. Retrieved 1 August 2012 from http://www.ecospark.ca/sites/default/files/mtm/2006statusreport.pdf .

Mortimer-Sandilands, Cate, ed. 2009. Nature matters. *Topia: Canadian Journal of Cultural Studies* 21 (special issue): 5–8.

Mulkewich, Jane, and Richard Oddie. 2009. Contesting development, democracy, and justice in the Red Hill Valley. In *Environmental Conflict and Democracy in Canada*, ed. Laurie Adkin, 243–61. Vancouver: University of British Columbia Press.

Murdoch, Jonathan. 2001. Ecologising sociology: Actor-network theory, co-construction and the problem of human exceptionalism. *Sociology* 35 (1): 111–33. http://dx.doi.org/10.1017/S0038038501000074.

Murdoch, Jonathan, and Graham Day. 1998. Middle class mobility, rural communities, and the politics of exclusion. In *Migration into Rural Areas: Theories and Issues*, ed. Paul Boyle and Keith Halfacree, 186–99. New York: Wiley.

Murdoch, Jonathan, and Andy C. Pratt. 1997. From the power of topography to the topography of power: A discourse on strange ruralities. In *Contested Countryside Cultures: Otherness, Marginalisation and Rurality*, ed. Paul Cloke and Jo Little, 51–69. London: Routledge.

New Zealand Parliamentary Commissioner for the Environment. 2003. Superb or suburb? International case studies of iconic landscapes. Wellington, New Zealand: Parliamentary Commissioner for the Environment. Retrieved 1

August 2012 from http://www.pce.parliament.nz/assets/Uploads/Reports/
pdf/suburb_full.pdf.

Noik-Bent, Sherry. 2006. Low-rise builders reaching for Energy Star. *National
Post*, 1 June: PH3.

Norton, Bryan. 2003. *Searching for Sustainability: Interdisciplinary Essays in the
Philosophy of Conservation Biology*. New York: Cambridge University Press.

Noss, Reed F. 1992. The Wildlands Project land conservation strategy. *Wild
Earth*, special issue: 10–25.

Noss, Reed, and Allen Cooperrider. 1994. *Saving Nature's Legacy*. Washington,
DC: Island Press.

Nuissl, Henning, and Dirk Heinrichs. 2011. Fresh wind or hot air: Does the
governance discourse have something to offer spatial planning? *Journal of
Planning Education and Research* 31 (1): 47–59. http://dx.doi.org/10.1177/0739
456X10392354.

Oak Ridges Moraine Foundation. 2007. Moraine for Life Symposium: Stakeholders' report. In authors' possession.

Oak Ridges Moraine Foundation. 2011a. The Oak Ridges Moraine: One kind of
an ecological jewel. Retrieved 5 November 2011 from http://www.moraine-
forlife.org/resources/documents/FINALSummary-MeasuringSuccess.pdf

Oak Ridges Moraine Foundation. 2011b. The Oak Ridges Moraine: An assessment of stakeholder awareness, support, and concerns for the implementation of the Oak Ridges Conservation Plan. Retrieved 5 November 2011 from
http://www.moraineforlife.org/resources/documents/01_ORMFStakehold-
erReport-WEB.pdf

Oak Ridges Moraine Foundation. 2011c. Compliance assessment: Assessing
the health of the Oak Ridges Moraine in a watershed context. King City:
Oak Ridges Moraine Foundation. Retrieved 5 November 2011 from http://
www.moraineforlife.org/resources/documents/02_ORMFComplianceRe-
port-WEB.pdf

Oak Ridges Moraine Foundation. 2011d. Watershed health assessment: Assessing the health of the Oak Ridges Moraine in a watershed context. Retrieved 5 November 2011 from http://www.moraineforlife.org/resources/
documents/03_ORMFWatershedReport-WEB.pdf

Oak Ridges Moraine Foundation. 2011e. Landscape health assessment: Assessing the health of the Oak Ridges Moraine in a landscape context. Retrieved 5 November 2011 from http://www.moraineforlife.org/resources/
documents/04_ORMFLandscapeHealthReport-WEB.pdf

Oak Ridges Moraine Foundation. 2011f. Land stewardship: Achievements
in land stewardship since the establishment of the Oak Ridges Moraine

Foundation. Retrieved 5 November 2011 from http://www.moraineforlife.
org/resources/documents/05_ORMF-LandStewardshipReport-WEB.pdf

Oak Ridges Moraine Foundation. 2011g. Land securement: Achievements in
land securement since the establishment of the Oak Ridges Moraine Foundation. Retrieved 5 November 2011 from http://www.moraineforlife.org/re-
sources/documents/06_ORMF-Land_SecurementReport-WEB.pdf

Oak Ridges Moraine Foundation. 2011h. Research and education: Achievements in research and education since the establishment of the Oak Ridges
Moraine Foundation. Retrieved 5 November 2011 from http://www.mo-
raineforlife.org/resources/documents/07_ORMFResearchandEducationRe-
port-WEB.pdf

Oak Ridges Moraine Foundation. 2011i. Oak Ridges Moraine Trail: Improvements to the Oak Ridges Moraine Trail since the adoption of the Oak
Ridges Moraine Conservation Plan. Retrieved 5 November 2011 from http://
www.moraineforlife.org/resources/documents/08_ORMFTrailReport-WEB.
pdf

Oak Ridges Moraine Foundaton. 2011j. Oak Ridges Moraine red flags. Retrieved 5 November 2011 from http://www.moraineforlife.org/projects/doc-
uments/RedFlagsontheORM.pdf

Oak Ridges Moraine Research Group. 1995. *The Oak Ridges Moraine of Southern
Ontario: A National Groundwater Resource Threatened by Urbanization*. Scarborough, ON: Oak Ridges Moraine Research Group, University of Toronto.

Oak Ridges Moraine Technical Working Committee. 1994a. The Oak Ridges
Moraine strategy for the Greater Toronto Area: An ecosystem approach for
long-term protection and management. Ontario Minister of Natural Resources. November.

Oak Ridges Moraine Technical Working Committee. 1994b. Land use
patterns on the Oak Ridges Moraine area within the Greater Toronto Area. Background study no. 1. Ontario Ministry of Natural Resources. Retrieved 15 May 2006 from http://www.york.ca/Departments/
Planning+and+Development/Long+Range+Planning/ORM+Facts.htm

Oak Ridges Moraine Technical Working Committee. 1994c. A cultural heritage
study of the Oak Ridges Moraine area. Background study no. 7. Ontario
Ministry of Natural Resources.

Oak Ridges Trail Association. 2006. Homepage. Retrieved 15 September from
http://www.oakridgestrail.org.

Oak Ridges Trail Handbook. 2006. Aurora, ON: Oak Ridges Trail Association.

Oddie, Richard. 2009. Alternate routes, new pathways: Development, democracy, and the political ecology of transportation in Hamilton, Ontario,

Canada. Unpublished PhD dissertation, Faculty of Environmental Studies,York University, Toronto.

Ohm, Brian W. 2000. The purchase of scenic easements and Wisconsin's Great River Road: A progress report on perpetuity. *Journal of the American Planning Association* 66 (2): 177–88. http://dx.doi.org/10.1080/01944360008976097.

Ontario Divisional Superior Court of Justice. 2006. Court file no. 285/06. Retrieved 3 November 2009 from http://www.constitutional-law.net/Hiawatha.pdf

Ontario Heritage Trust. 2012. Natural heritage. Retrieved 1 August 2012 from http://www.heritagetrust.on.ca/Conservation/Natural-heritage.aspx.

Ontario Land Trust Alliance. 2005. About the Ontario Land Trust Alliance. Retrieved 11 December 2009 from http://www.ontariolandtrustalliance.org.

Ontario Ministry of Finance. 2011. *Ontario Population Projections Update: 2001–2036; Ontario and Its 49 Census Divisions (based on the 2006 Census).* Ottawa: Queen's Printer for Ontario. Retrieved from http://www.fin.gov.on.ca/en/economy/demographics/projections/

Ontario Ministry of Municipal Affairs and Housing 2001a. *Oak Ridges Moraine Conservation Act 2001.* 13 December. Toronto: Queen's Printer.

Ontario Ministry of Municipal Affairs and Housing. 2001b. *Share Your Vision.* Toronto: Queen's Printer.

Ontario Ministry of Municipal Affairs and Housing 2002a. *Oak Ridges Moraine Conservation Plan 2002.* Toronto: Queen's Printer. April.

Ontario Ministry of Municipal Affairs and Housing. 2005. *Provincial Policy Statement, 2005.* Toronto: Queen's Printer.

Ontario Ministry of Municipal Affairs and Housing. 2008a. More facts about the Oak Ridges Moraine. Retrieved 10 November 2009 from http://www.mah.gov.on.ca/Page1705.aspx

Ontario Ministry of Municipal Affairs and Housing. 2008b. Oak Ridges Moraine Conservation Plan technical paper series. Retrieved 22 April 2010 from http://www.mah.gov.on.ca/Page4807.aspx.

Ontario Ministry of Natural Resources. 2009a. *State of the Aggregate Resource in Ontario Study.* Paper 2, *Future Aggregate Availability and Alternative Analysis.* Toronto: Queen's Printer. Retrieved 6 November 2011 from http://www.mnr.gov.on.ca/stdprodconsume/groups/lr/@mnr/@aggregates/documents/document/stdprod_067830.pdf.

Ontario Ministry of Natural Resources. 2009b. *State of the Aggregate Resource in Ontario Study.* Paper 6, *Rehabilitation.* Toronto: Queen's Printer. Retrieved 6 November 2011 from http://www.mnr.gov.on.ca/stdprodconsume/groups/lr/@mnr/@aggregates/documents/document/stdprod_067739.pdf.

Ontario Ministry of Natural Resources. 2010a. *State of the Aggregate Resource in Ontario Study: Aggregate Resource Advisory Committee Consensus Recommendations to the Minister of Natural Resources.* Toronto: Queens Printer for Ontario. Retrieved 6 November 2011 from http://www.mnr.gov.on.ca/stdprodconsume/groups/lr/@mnr/@aggregates/documents/document/stdprod_067787.pdf.

Ontario Ministry of Natural Resources. 2010b. Natural Heritage Information Centre: Natural Areas list. Retrieved 15 February 2012 from http://nhic.mnr.gov.on.ca/.

Ontario Ministry of Public Infrastructure Renewal. 2005a. *Places to Grow Act, 2005.* Toronto: Queen's Printer.

Ontario Ministry of Public Infrastructure Renewal. 2005b. *The Greenbelt Plan, 2005.* Toronto: Queen's Printer.

Ontario Ministry of Public Infrastructure Renewal. 2006. *Places to Grow; Better Choices, Brighter Future; A Growth Plan for the Greater Golden Horseshoe.* Toronto: Queen's Printer.

Ontario Ministry of the Environment, Environmental Assessment Advisory Committee. 1989. The adequacy of the existing environmental planning and approvals process for the Ganaraska watershed. Report no. 38. Toronto: Queen's Printer.

Ontario Ministry of Transportation. 2006. Environmental standards and practices. Retrieved 15 September from http://www.mto.gov.on.ca/english/engineering/envirostandards/.

Ontario Municipal Board. 2006a. Decision/Order no. 1633. June 6. PL040712, PL040713. Retrieved 22 April 2010 from http://www.omb.gov.on.ca/e-decisions/pl040712_%231633.pdf.

Ontario Municipal Board. 2006b. Decision/Order no. 3289. November 23. PL 020446. Retrieved 22 April 2010 from http://www.richmondhill.ca/documents/planning_omb_3289.pdf.

Ontario Municipal Board. 2011. April 14. PL030997, PL090266, PL080014, PL090257. Retrieved 22 April 2011 from http://www.omb.gov.on.ca/e-decisions/pl030997-Apr-14-2011.pdf.

Ontario Stone, Sand and Gravel Association. 2012a. Home page. Retrieved 5 August 2012 from http://www.ossga.com/.

Ontario Stone, Sand and Gravel Association. 2012b. Rehabilitation of pits and quarries. Retrieved 6 August 2012 from http://www.ossga.com/Downloads/publicationsPFDs/rehabilitation2010.pdf.

O'Reilly, Dan. 1999. Moraine's hills a beautiful backdrop for Maple-area site. *Toronto Star,* 19 June: 01.

Osborne, Brian S. 1998a. Some thoughts on landscape: Is it a noun, a metaphor, or a verb? *Canadian Social Studies.* 32 (3): 93–7.

Osborne, Brian S. 1998b. Landscapes, waterscapes, inscapes: Putting the people back into Pukaskwa. In *Changing Parks: The History, Future and Cultural Context of Parks and Heritage Landscapes*, ed. John Marsh and Bruce Hodgins, 107–34. Toronto: Natural Heritage/Natural History.

O'Toole, Randal. 2009. Smart-growth plans are a failure in Portland. Cato Institute. Retrieved 2 August 2012 from http://www.cato.org/publications/commentary/smartgrowth-plans-are-failure-portland.

Oziewicz, Estanislao. 2000. Bacterial outbreak kills four in Ontario. *The Globe and Mail*, 25 May: A1, A8.

Parkin, James. 2003. Ontario aggregate resources management: Linkages between effective rehabilitation and long-term economic prosperity. Retrieved 2 August 2012 from http://www.techtransfer.osmre.gov/nttmainsite/Library/proceed/sudbury2003/sudbury03/120.pdf.

Parsons, James J. Jr. 1985. On "bioregionalism" and "watershed consciousness." *Professional Geographer* 37 (1): 1–6. http://dx.doi.org/10.1111/j.0033-0124.1985.00001.x.

Patano, Sandra, and L. Anders Sandberg. 2005. Winning back more than words? Power, discourse, and quarrying on the Niagara Escarpment. *Canadian Geographer* 49 (1): 25–41. http://dx.doi.org/10.1111/j.0008-3658.2005.00078.x.

Paul, Francis. 2000. Fairway trap. *Alternatives Journal*. Retrieved 11 December 2009 from http://findarticles.com/p/articles/mi_hb6685/is_/ai_n28784197.

Pavilons, Mark. 2012. Happy Valley is a real gem worth preserving. *King Weekly Sentinel*, 2 May. Retrieved 2 August 2012 from http://www.kingsentinel.com/news/2012-05-02/Community/Happy_Valley_Forest_is_a_real_gem_worth_preserving.html.

Pearce, Sean, 2011. OMB rules against Aurora on Westhill. *Aurora Banner*, 25 April.

Pembina Institute. 2007. The 2007 Ontario budget: Analysis from the Pembina Institute. Retrieved 11 December 2009 from http://pubs.pembina.org/reports/Pemb_An_2007ON_Budget.pdf.

Persico, Amanda. 2008a. Town, developer battle over housing proposal. York Region. com, 13 May. Retrieved 22 April 2010 from http://www.yorkregion.com/news/article/563617--town-developer-battle-over-housing-proposal.

Persico, Amanda. 2008b Residents prepared to defend Moraine. 5 September. Retrieved 22 April 2010 from http://www.yorkregion.com/YorkRegion/Article/559666.

Persico, Amanda. 2008c. Newmarket, developer begins OMB hearing. York
    Region. 14 December. Retrieved 5 April 2008 from www.theliberal.com.

Phillips, Martin. 1998. Investigations of the British rural middle classes: Frag-
    mentation, identity, morality and contestation. *Journal of Rural Studies* 14 (4):
    427–43. http://dx.doi.org/10.1016/S0743-0167(98)00031-X.

Pickett, S.T.A., and Richard Ostfeld, 1995. The shifting paradigm in ecology.
    In *A New Century for Natural Resources Management*, ed. Richard Knight and
    Sarah Bates, 261–78. Washington, DC: Island Press.

Pim, Linda, and Joel Ornoy. 2002. *How to Protect Nature and Curb Urban Sprawl
    in Your Community.* Ontario Federation of Ontario Naturalists.

Pincetl, Stephanie. 2006. Conservation planning in the west: Problems, new
    strategies, and entrenched obstacles. *Geoforum* 37 (2): 246–55. http://dx.doi.
    org/10.1016/j.geoforum.2005.05.001.

Planscape. 2003. Greater Toronto Area agricultural profile: An update of the
    GTA Agricultural Impact Study (1999). 7 November. Retrieved on 20 July
    2012 from http://www.york.ca/NR/rdonlyres/mtwocueieiiowcxqyi6ljz-
    vibl7kb32gjshdsgtyo4yccgler5pgjpv7pqvp6ajcdr4neucxmfk76gpqo57bu-
    supdf/rpt+1+cls+10.pdf.

Poisson, Jayme. 2011. The Oak Ridges Moraine: Not safe yet. *Toronto Star*,
    10 August. Retrieved 12 December from http://www.thestar.com/news/
    article/1037814--oak-ridges-moraine-not-safe-yet

Pond, David. 2009. Institutions, political economy, and land-use policy:
    Greenbelt politics in Ontario. *Environmental Politics* 18 (2): 238–56. http://
    dx.doi.org/10.1080/09644010802682619.

Pratt, Andy C. 1996. Discourses of rurality: Loose talk or social struggle?
    Journal of Rural Studies 12 (1): 69–78. http://dx.doi.org/10.1016/0743-0167
    (95)00046-1.

Priorities for Ontario. 2007. Greenbelt. Retrieved 11 December 2009 from
    http://www.prioritiesforontario.ca/greenbelt.

Prudham, Scott. 2004. Poisoning the well: Neo-liberalism and the contami-
    nation of municipal water in Walkerton, Ontario. *Geoforum* 5 (3): 343–59.
    http://dx.doi.org/10.1016/j.geoforum.2003.08.010.

Puck's Farm. 2006. Trees of the Oak Ridges Moraine. Retrieved 6 October 2008
    from http://www.pucksfarm.com/pdf/trees.PDF.

Pugin, A., S.E. Pullan, and D.R. Sharpe. 1999. Seismic facies and regional ar-
    chitecture of the Oak Ridges Moraine area, Southern Ontario. *Canadian Jour-
    nal of Earth Sciences* 36 (3): 409–32. http://dx.doi.org/10.1139/e98-104.

Pulido, Laura. 1996. *Environmentalism and Economic Justice: Two Chicano Strug-
    gles in the Southwest.* Tucson: University of Arizona Press.

Pulido, Laura. 2000. Rethinking environmental racism: White privi-
    lege and urban development in Southern California. *Annals of*

the Association of American Geographers 90 (1): 12–40. http://dx.doi. org/10.1111/0004-5608.00182.

Punter, John. 1974. Urbanites in the countryside: Case studies of the impact of exurban development on the landscape in the Toronto-Centred Region, 1954–1971. Unpublished PhD dissertation, Department of Geography, University of Toronto.

Purcell, Mark. 2001. Neighborhood activism among homeowners as a politics of space. *Professional Geographer* 53 (2): 178–94. http://dx.doi. org/10.1111/0033-0124.00278.

Puric-Mladenovic, Danijela, and Silvia Strobl. 2006. Delineating conservation areas on the Oak Ridges Moraine using a systematic conservation planning approach. *Forestry Chronicle* 82 (3): 395–402.

Regional Municipality of York. 1972. *An Interim Policy on Rural-Residential Development: York Region.* Regional Municipality of York Planning Department.

Regional Municipality of York. 1974a. *Interim Policy on the Urban Settlements in Rural York Region.* York Region: Regional Municipality of York.

Regional Municipality of York. 1974b. *Oak Ridges Moraine Study: An Interim Policy Approach to Development; York Region.* Regional Municipality of York Planning Department.

Regions of York, Durham, and Peel. 1999. The Oak Ridges Moraine: Towards a long-term strategy. Retrieved 22 April 2010 from http://www.york. ca/NR/rdonlyres/x3rfzwudlr4h7smnjezf63nhv2jbnrztrcsxfj4vjtbs2l4etb-smviqlld3fh72wcfiyqjgfaafyippgppcyppgpwg/ORM+1999+report.pdf

Reid, Ron. 1991. Perspectives on regional planning in Ontario. In *Greenways and Green Space on the Oak Ridges Moraine: Towards Co-operative Planning*, ed. John Fischer, Frederick Helleiner, and Klaus Wehrenberg, 1–6. Department of Geography and Frost Centre for Canadian Heritage and Development Studies, Trent University, Peterborough, Ontario.

Relph, Edward. 1976. *Place and Placelessness.* London: Pion.

Richardson, A.H. 1944. *A Report on the Ganaraska Watershed: A Study in Land Use with Plans for the Rehabilitation of the Sea in the Post-War Period.* Toronto: King's Printer.

Richardson, A.H. 1974. *Conservation by the People: The History of the Conservation Movement in Ontario to 1970.* Toronto: University of Toronto Press.

Richardson, Mary, Joan Sherman, and Michael Gismondi. 1993. *Winning Back the Words: Confronting Experts in an Environmental Public Hearing.* Toronto: Garamond Press.

Richmond Hill Council Public Hearing. 2000. Submissions: Input to draft official plan amendment 2000. 23 February. Richmond Hill Public Library, Reference Section.

Richmond Hill Naturalists. 2004. *The Bulletin*, no. 438 (August/September). Retrieved 11 December 2009 from http://www.rhnaturalists.ca/news/The_RHN_Bulletin_2004_08.pdf.

Richmond Hill Naturalists. 2006. *The Bulletin*, no. 451 (January), 1–8. Retrieved 11 December 2009 from http://www.rhnaturalists.ca/news/The_RHN_Bulletin_2006_01.pdf.

Riley, John, and Pat Mohr. 1994. *The Natural Heritage of Southern Ontario's Settled Landscapes: A Review of Conservation and Restoration Ecology for Land-Use Planning*. Aurora, ON: Ontario Ministry of Natural Resources.

Robbins, Paul. 2004. *Political Ecology: A Critical Introduction*. Malden, MA: Blackwell.

Robbins, Paul. 2007. *Lawn People: How Grasses, Weeds, and Chemicals Make Us Who We Are*. Philadelphia: Temple University Press.

Robin, Libby. 2009. New science for sustainability in an ancient land. In *Nature's End: History and the Environment*, ed. Sverker Sörlin and Paul Warde, 188–214. New York: Palgrave Macmillan.

Robertson, Morgan. 2000. No net loss: Wetland restoration and the incomplete capitalization of nature. *Antipode* 32 (4): 463–93. http://dx.doi.org/10.1111/1467-8330.00146.

Roe, Emery, and Michel J.G. van Eeten. 2002. *Ecology, Engineering, and Management: Reconciling Ecosystem Rehabilitation and Service Reliability*. Oxford: Oxford University Press.

Rome, Adam. 2001. *The Bulldozer in the Countryside: Suburban Sprawl and the Rise of American Environmentalism*. Cambridge: Cambridge University Press.

Rootes, Christopher. 2007. Acting locally: The character, contexts, and significance of local environmental mobilizations. *Environmental Politics* 16 (5): 722–41. http://dx.doi.org/10.1080/09644010701640460.

Rosensweig, Michael L. 2003. *Win-Win Ecology: How Earth's Species Can Survive in the Midst of Human Enterprise*. New York: Oxford University Press.

Rowe, Steven (Environmental Planner, Hardy Stevenson Associates). 2004. Interviewed by L. Iandoli, Toronto, 27 May.

Royal Commission on the Future of the Toronto Waterfront. 1992. *Regeneration: Toronto's Waterfront and the Sustainable City: Final Report*. Toronto: Queen's Printer of Ontario.

Rusk, James. 2000. City funds moraine preservation groups. *The Globe and Mail*. 10 June: A26.

Russell, H., C. Logan, T. Brennand, M. Hinton, and D. Sharpe. 1996. Regional geoscience database for the Oak Ridges Moraine project (Southern Ontario). In *Current Research 1996-E*, 191–200. Geological Survey of Canada.

Sandberg, L. Anders. 2001. The discourse of rehabilitated and constructed natures: Pit and quarry landscapes of the Greater Toronto Area. In *Leading Edge 2001: Proceedings.* Burlington, ON: Niagara Escarpment Commission. Retrieved from http://www.escarpment.org/_files/file.php?fileid=fileuaMEC dNteo&filename=file_Sandberg.pdf.

Sandberg, L. Anders, and Lisa Wallace. 2013. Leave the sand in the land, let the stone alone: Pits, quarries, and climate change. *ACME: An International E-Journal for Critical Geographies,* 12 (1): 65–87. http://www.acme-journal.org/ vol12/SandbergWallace2013.pdf

Sandberg, L. Anders, and Gerda R. Wekerle. 2010. Reaping nature's dividends: The neoliberalization and gentrification of nature on the Oak Ridges Moraine. *Journal of Environmental Policy and Planning* 12 (1): 41–57. http:// dx.doi.org/10.1080/15239080903371915.

Sandberg, L. Anders, Gerda Wekerle, and Liette Gilbert. 2012. Collection of real-estate advertisements and brochures in Greater Toronto Area from 2000 to 2012.

Sandlos, John. 2008. *Hunters at the margin: Native people and wildlife conservation in the Northwest Territories.* Vancouver: University of British Columbia.

Save the Oak Ridges Moraine (STORM) Coalition. 1997. *Oak Ridges Moraine.* Erin, ON: Boston Mills Press.

Save the Oak Ridges Moraine (STORM) Coalition. 2002a. Is our work over yet? *Seasonal Storms,* spring. Retrieved 2 August 2012 from http://www. stormcoalition.org/resources/Seasonal%20Storms-Spring%2002.pdf.

Save the Rouge Valley System. 2000. Stand up for clean water! Flyer. In authors' archives.

Schein, Richard H. 1997. The place of landscape: A conceptual framework for interpreting an American scene. *Annals of the Association of American Geographers* 87 (4): 660–80. http://dx.doi.org/10.1111/1467-8306.00072.

Schlosberg, David, and John S. Dryzek. 2002. Political strategies of American environmentalism: Inclusion and beyond. *Society & Natural Resources* 15 (9): 787–804. http://dx.doi.org/10.1080/08941920290069353.

Schmalz, Peter S. 1991. *The Ojibwa of Southern Ontario.* Toronto: University of Toronto Press.

Schmidt, Stephan, and Kurt Paulsen. 2009. Is open-space preservation a form of exclusionary zoning? The evolution of municipal open-space policies in New Jersey. *Urban Affairs Review* 45 (1): 92–118. http://dx.doi. org/10.1177/1078087408331122.

Schultz, Caroline. 2011. On guard for the Moraine. *Nature* 51 (2): 7.

Schuurman. Nadine. 2004. *GIS: A short introduction.* Malden MA: Blackwell.

Scott, Alan. 1990. *Ideology and the New Social Movements.* London: Unwin Hyman.

Sewell, John. 1993. *The Shape of the City: Toronto Struggles with Modern Planning.* Toronto: University of Toronto Press.

Sewell, John. 2009. *The Shape of the Suburbs: Understanding Toronto's Sprawl.* Toronto: University of Toronto Press.

Sgroi, Barbara 2005. Rebuilding the past. *Canadian House and Home* 27 (8), July: 74–81, 147.

Shamai, Samuel. 1991. Sense of place: An empirical measurement. *Geoforum* 22 (3): 347–58. http://dx.doi.org/10.1016/0016-7185(91)90017-K.

Sharpe, David R., P.J. Barnett, H.A.J. Russell, T.A. Brennand and G. Gorrell. 1999. Regional geological mapping of the Oak Ridges Moraine, Greater Toronto Area, Southern Ontario. In *Current Research 1999-E,* 123–36. Geological Survey of Canada.

Sharpe, David R., M.J. Hinton, H.A.J. Russell and A.J. Desbarats. 2002. The need for basin analysis in regional hydrogeological studies, Oak Ridges Moraine, Southern Ontario. *Geoscience Canada.* 29 (1): 3–20.

Shaw, Frank G. 2004. The Oak Ridges Moraine Land Trust: Partnership and co-operation in land securement for conservation and protection of the Oak Ridges Moraine. In *Leading Edge 2004: Proceedings.* Burlington, ON: Niagara Escarpment Commission.

Shuff, Tim. 2011a. Green gravel. *In the Hills,* 9 September. Retrieved 6 November from http://www.inthehills.ca/2011/09/back/green-gravel/.

Shuff, Tim. 2011b. Melanchthon megaquarry by the numbers. *In the Hills,* 16 June. Retrieved on 5 March 2012. http://www.inthehills.ca/2011/06/back/melancthon-mega-quarry-by-the-numbers/

Shutkin, William A. 2000. *The Land That Could Be: Environmentalism and Democracy in the Twenty-First Century.* Cambridge, MA: MIT Press.

Slack, Enid. 2002. *Municipal Finance and the Pattern of Urban Growth.* Toronto: C.D. Howe Institute.

Small, Peter. 2000. Planners urge province to act on Moraine. *Toronto Star,* 6 June: B4.

Smith, Cameron. 1999. Saving the birds of the Moraine. *Toronto Star,* 10 April: 01.

Smith, Donald. 1991. The dispossession of the Mississauga Indians: A missing chapter in the early history of Upper Canada. In *Historical Essays on Upper Canada: New Perspectives,* ed. Wilson Johnson, James Keith Johnson, and Bruce G. Wilson, 23–52. Ottawa: Carleton University Press.

Smith, Mark J. 1998. *Ecologism: Towards Ecological Citizenship.* Milton Keynes, UK: Open University Press.

Snow, David E., and Robert Benford. 1992. Master frames and cycles of protest. In *Frontiers in Social Movement Theory,* ed. Aldon Morris and Carol McClurg Mueller, 133–55. New Haven, CT: Yale University Press.

Song, Yan, and G.-J. Knapp. 2004. Measuring urban form: Is Portland winning the war on sprawl? *Journal of the American Planning Association* 70 (2): 210–25. http://dx.doi.org/10.1080/01944360408976371.

Soule, Michael, and Bruce Wilcox, eds. 1980. *Conservation Biology: An Evolutionary-Ecological Perspective*. Sunderland, MA: Sinauer Associates.

Spears, John. 2009. National park status sought for Rouge Valley. *Toronto Star*. 3 April: GT01.

Spectorsky, Auguste. 1955. *The Exurbanites*. Philadelphia: Lippincott.

Statistics Canada. 2006. Community profiles. Retrieved from http://www.statcan.gc.ca.

Statistics Canada. 2009. 2006 Census: Immigration in Canada; a portrait of the foreign-born population (2006 analysis series 97-557-XIE2006001). Retrieved on 4 August 2012 from http://www.statcan.ca.

Statistics Canada. 2012. *Focus on Geography Series*. Census Subdivision of Markham. 2 February. Ottawa: Statistics Canada. Retrieved from http://www.statcan.gc.ca.

Stein, David Lewis. 1999. Summit to test moraine plan. *Toronto Star*, 19 November: 01.

Stein, David Lewis. 2000. Saving moraine: It's all about water. *Toronto Star*, 30 March: 01.

Stein, David Lewis. 2001. No hopeless gesture will stop urban sprawl. *Toronto Star*, 8 March: OP01.

Stein, David Lewis. 2007. Closing plenary Moraine for Life symposium. Markham, Ontario. 13 February.

Stewart, Andrew. 2000. Science not issue in Moraine debate. *Toronto Star*, 5 June: A14.

Swainson, Gail. 1999. Protection sought for the Oak Ridges land. *Toronto Star*, 8 October: 01.

Swainson, Gail. 2000a. Step closer to development in sensitive ecological area. *Toronto Star*, 13 January: NE1.

Swainson, Gail. 2000b. Moraine ecological disaster fear. *Toronto Star*, 8 January: 1.

Swainson, Gail. 2000c. Expert explains new view on Moraine. *Toronto Star*, 13 July: D03.

Swainson, Gail. 2000d. Developers' theory "not tested." *Toronto Star*, 31 October: B2.

Swainson, Gail. 2001a. OMB rejects Province's Moraine witness. *Toronto Star*, 1 February: B01.

Swainson, Gail. 2001b. Rare species at risk, hearing warned. *Toronto Star*, 28 March: B02.

Swainson, Gail. 2001c. Road approved despite threat to salamander. *Toronto Star*, 11 September: B05.

Swainson, Gail. 2001d. Allow Moraine development, politicians say. *Toronto Star*, 14 September: NE25.

Swainson, Gail. 2001e. Salamander in middle of road extension battle. *Toronto Star*, 24 October: 1.

Swainson, Gail. 2002a. Secret vow to builders "betrays" Moraine deal. *Toronto Star*, 6 March: A01.

Swainson, Gail. 2002b. Crombie heading key Moraine group. *Toronto Star*, 8 March: B7.

Swainson, Gail. 2002c. Tories kill Moraine housing proposal. *Toronto Star*, 12 September: B1.

Swainson, Gail. 2002d. Tunnels under Bayview to protect rare salamander. *Toronto Star*, 17 September: A03.

Swainson, Gail. 2002e. Salamander tunnel scorned. *Toronto Star*, 18 September: B05.

Swainson, Gail, and Richard Brennan. 2002. Housing always part of plan: Hodgson. *Toronto Star*, 7 March: B1, B4.

Swainson, Gail, and John Mahler. 1999. Protest fails as Moraine trees fall. *Toronto Star*, 30 November: 1.

Swyngedouw, Erik. 1999. Modernity and hybridity: Nature, regeneracionismo, and the production of the Spanish waterscape, 1890–1930. *Annals of the Association of American Geographers* 89 (3): 443–65. http://dx.doi.org/10.1111/0004-5608.00157.

Symmes, Ric (Ontario Nature). 2007. Interviewed by G. Wekerle, Toronto, 13 February.

Tarrow, Sidney. 1996. States and opportunities: The political structuring of social movements. In *Comparative Perspectives on Social Movements: Political Opportunities, Mobilizing Structures, and Cultural Framings*, ed. Doug McAdam, John D. McCarthy, and Mayer N. Zald, 41–61. Cambridge: Cambridge University Press.

Tarrow, Sidney. 1998. *Power in Movement: Social Movements and Contentious Politics*. New York: Cambridge University Press.

Taylor, Laura. 2011. No boundaries: Exurbia and the study of contemporary urban dispersion. *GeoJournal* 76 (4): 323–39. http://dx.doi.org/10.1007/s10708-009-9300-y.

Taylor, Sterling. 1991. 407 threatens water, farmland, highway foes say. *Toronto Star*, 6 June: E1.

Theobald, D.M. 2004. Placing exurban land-use change in a human modification framework. *Frontiers in Ecology and the Environment* 2 (3): 139–44. http://dx.doi.org/10.1890/1540-9295(2004)002[0139:PELCIA]2.0.CO;2.

Thorpe, Jocelyn. 2012. *Temagami's tangled wild: Race, gender, and the making of Canadian nature*. Vancouver: University of British Columbia Press.

Timmer, Vic. 2006. Homepage. Retrieved 15 September from http://www.forestry.utoronto.ca/people/timmer/timmer.html

Tindal, C. Richard, and Susan Nobles Tindal. 2003. *Local Government in Canada*. Toronto: Nelson College Indigenous.

Tomalty, Ray, Robert Gibson, Donald Alexander, and John Fisher. 1994. *Ecosystem Planning for Canadian Urban Regions*. Toronto: Intergovernmental Committee on Urban and Regional Research.

Tomalty, Ray, and Andrejs Skaburskis. 2003. Development charges and city planning objectives: The Ontario disconnect. *Canadian Journal of Urban Research* 12 (1): 142–61.

Toronto and Region Conservation Authority. 2004a. Hurricane Hazel 50 years later. Retrieved 2 August 2012 from http://www.hurricanehazel.ca/index.html.

Toronto and Region Conservation Authority. 2004b. Conservation Foundation. Retrieved 16 April from http://www.trca.on.ca.

Toronto Environmental Alliance. 2009. *Dig Conservation, Not Holes: A Report on the GTA's Thirst for Gravel and How to Quench It*. Toronto: TEA.

Toronto Star. 1966. A greenbelt for Ontario. 26 November: 6.

Toronto Star. 1967. Robarts says escarpment to be saved for recreation. 11 March: 13.

Toronto Star. 2001. New in homes: These builders named to Oak Ridges Panel. 7 July: N02.

Town of Vaughan. 1972. Appendix B. In *Submission by the Regional Municipality of York on Toronto-Centred Region Concept*. Municipality Briefs.

Township of Uxbridge. 2005. Share your vision of the Oak Ridges Moraine: Submissions. Retrieved 23 July 2012 from http://www.town.uxbridge.on.ca/print/sustainability .

Tuan, Yi-Fu. 1980. Rootedness versus sense of place. *Landscape* 24: 3–8.

Underhill, Jane (King City). 2005. Presentation to ENVS 5161 Local Government, Faculty of Environmental Studies. York University, 11 March.

Urban Development Institute of Ontario. 2004. Growth plan for the Greater Golden Horseshoe. Toronto: Urban Development Institute of Ontario.

Valley Voices Residents Association. 2006. Homepage. Retrieved 15 September from http://www.valleyvoices.ca/index.htm

Valverde, Mariana. 2005. Taking "land use" seriously: Toward an ontology of municipal law. *Law, Text, Culture (Canadian Ethnology Society)* 9: 34–59.

Valverde, Mariana. 2008. The ethic of diversity: Local law and the negotiation of urban norms. *Law & Social Inquiry* 33 (4): 895–923. http://dx.doi.org/10.1111/j.1747-4469.2008.00127.x.

Walker, Gerald. 1987. *An Invaded Countryside: Structures of Life on the Toronto Fringe.* Geographical Monographs no. 17. Toronto: Department of Geography, York University.

Walker, Gerald. 1994. Planning the future of rural Toronto: Structure planning in the Greater Toronto Area. *Great Lakes Geographer* 1 (2): 54–65.

Walker, Gerald. 1995. Social mobilization in the city's countryside: Rural Toronto fights waste dumps. *Journal of Rural Studies* 11 (3): 243–54. http://dx.doi.org/10.1016/0743-0167(95)00019-J.

Walker, Gerald. 2000. Urbanites creating new ruralities: Reflections on social action and struggle in the Greater Toronto Area. *Great Lakes Geographer* 7 (2): 106–18.

Walker, Peter A. 2003. Reconsidering "regional" political ecologies: Toward a political ecology of the rural American west. *Progress in Human Geography* 27 (1): 7–24. http://dx.doi.org/10.1191/0309132503ph410oa.

Walker, Peter A. 2005. Political ecology: Where is the ecology? *Progress in Human Geography* 29 (1): 73–82. http://dx.doi.org/10.1191/0309132505ph530pr.

Walker, Peter A., and Louise Fortmann. 2003. Whose landscape? A political ecology of the "exurban" Sierra. *Cultural Geographies* 10 (4): 469–91. http://dx.doi.org/10.1191/1474474003eu285oa.

Walker, Peter A., and Patrick T. Hurley. 2011. *Planning Paradise: The Politics and Visioning of Landscape in Oregon.* Tucson: University of Arizona Press.

Walker, Richard. 2007. *The Country in the City: The Greening of the San Francisco Bay Area.* Seattle: University of Washington Press.

Walther, Melanie. 2011. Actors and ideas in local environmental campaigns: The case of Site 41. Unpublished major paper, Faculty of Environmental Studies, York University, Toronto.

Walton and Hunter Planning Associates, Betsy J. Donald, and J. Ross Raymond and Associates. 1999. Greater Toronto Area agricultural economic impact study. GTA Federations of Agriculture Project Management Committee. 19 November.

Wat Lao Veluwanaram of Ontario. 2008. About Wat Lao Veluwanh. Retrieved from http://www.watlao-veluwanh.com/

Watson, John W. 1947. Rural depopulation in southwestern Ontario. *Annals of the Association of American Geographers* 37: 145–54.

Webb, Margaret, 2002. Green goes green: Golf courses, those pesticide and water-gobbling environmental pariahs are turning natural. *Report on Business Magazine* 19(3): 38–9, 41.

Wekerle, Gerda R. 2001. Resisting sprawl: Environmental challenges and sustainable regional planning. In *Leading Edge 2001: Proceedings.* Burlington, ON: Niagara Escarpment Commission.

Wekerle, Gerda R., and Teresa V. Abbruzzese. 2009. Producing regionalism: Regional movements, ecosystems, and equity in a fast and slow growth region. *GeoJournal*. 75 (6): 581-94. Published online on 7 March. doi:10.1007/S10708-009-9271-2

Wekerle, Gerda R., Liette Gilbert, and L. Anders Sandberg. 2007. More to nature than marketing. *Ontario Home Builder Magazine*, summer: 69–70.

Wekerle, Gerda R., L. Anders Sandberg, and Liette Gilbert. 2009a. Regional resistances in an exurban region: Intersections of the politics of place and the politics of scale. In *Leviathan Undone? Towards a Political Economy of Scale*, ed. Rianne Mahon and Roger Keil, 247–64. Vancouver: University of British Columbia Press.

Wekerle, Gerda R., L. Anders Sandberg, and Liette Gilbert. 2009b. Challenging sprawl, preserving nature: Reframing environmentalism on the Oak Ridges Moraine. In *Environmental Conflicts and Democracy in Canada*, ed. Laurie Adkin, 279–97. Vancouver: University of British Columbia.

Wekerle, Gerda R., L. Anders Sandberg, Liette Gilbert, and Matthew Binstock. 2007. Nature as a cornerstone of growth: Regional and ecosystems planning in the Greater Golden Horseshoe. *Canadian Journal of Urban Research* 16 (1): 20–38.

Whatmore, Sarah. 1999. Rethinking the "human" in human geography. In *Human Geography Today*, ed. Doreen Massey, John Allen, and Philip Sarre, 22–41. Cambridge: Polity Press.

White, Richard. 2003. *Urban Infrastructure and Urban Growth in the Toronto Region, 1950s to the 1990s*. Toronto: Neptis Foundation.

White, Stephen. 1993. Naturalist's fight keeps frogs happy, drivers slower. *Toronto Star*, 5 August: NY01.

Whitelaw, Graham S. 2005. The role of environmental movement organizations in land use planning: Case studies of the Niagara Escarpment and Oak Ridges Moraine Processes. Unpublished PhD dissertation, University of Waterloo, Ontario.

Whitelaw, Graham, and Paul Eagles. 2007. Planning for long, wide conservation corridors on private lands in the Oak Ridges Moraine, Ontario, Canada. *Conservation Biology* 21 (3): 675–83. http://dx.doi.org/10.1111/j.1523-1739.2007.00708.x. Medline:17531046

Whitelaw, Graham, Paul Eagles, Robert Gibson, and Mark Seasons. 2008. Roles of environmental movement organisations in land-use planning: Case studies of the Niagara Escarpment and Oak Ridges Moraine, Ontario, Canada. *Journal of Environmental Planning and Management* 51 (6): 801–16. http://dx.doi.org/10.1080/09640560802423616.

Wiens, Mary. 2001. The Laotians vs the locals. *Harrowsmith Country Life*. February: 59–61.

Williams, Daniel R., and Joe W. Roggenbuck. 1990. Measuring place attachment: Some preliminary results. In *Proceedings of the Third Symposium on Social Science in Resource Management*, ed. James Gramann, 70–72. College Station: Texas A&M University.

Williams, Daniel R., and Susan I. Stewart. 1998. Sense of place: An elusive concept that is finding a home in ecosystem management. *Journal of Forestry* (May): 18–23.

Williams, Daniel R., and Jerry J. Vaske. 2003. The measurement of place attachment: Validity and generalizability of a psychometric approach. *Forest Science* 49 (6): 830–40.

Wilson, Alex, Jenifer L. Uncapher, Lisa McManigal. L. Hunter Lovins, Maureen Cureton, and William D. Browning. 1998. *Green Development: Integrating Ecology and Real Estate*. New York: Wiley.

Winfield, Mark S. 2003. *Building Sustainable Urban Communities in Ontario: Overcoming the Barriers*. Toronto: Pembina Institute.

Winfield, Mark S. 2004. *Towards Implementation? Building Sustainable Urban Communities in Ontario*. Toronto: Pembina Institute.

Winfield, Mark, and Greg Jenish. 1997. *Ontario's Environment and the "Common Sense Revolution": A Second Year Report*. Toronto: Canada Institute for Environmental Law and Policy.

Winfield, Mark, and Amy Taylor. 2005. *Rebalancing the Load: The Need for an Aggregates Conservation Strategy for Ontario*. Toronto: Pembina Institute.

Wonders, Karen. 2008. First Nations land rights and environmentalism in British Columbia / SPAET. 8 November. Retrieved from http://www.firstnations.de/development/coast_salish-spaet.htm.

Wood, J. David. 1991. Moraine and metropolis: The Oak Ridges and the Greater Toronto Area. *International Journal of Environmental Studies* 39 (1-2): 45–53. http://dx.doi.org/10.1080/00207239108710680.

Woods, Michael. 2003a. Conflicting environmental visions of the rural: Wind-farm development in Mid Wales. *Sociologia Ruralis* 43 (3): 271–88. http://dx.doi.org/10.1111/1467-9523.00245.

Woods, Michael. 2003b. Deconstructing rural protest: The emergence of a new social movement. *Journal of Rural Studies* 19 (3): 309–25. http://dx.doi.org/10.1016/S0743-0167(03)00008-1.

Woods, Michael. 2005. *Contesting Rurality: Politics in the British Countryside*. Aldershot, UK: Ashgate.

Woods, Michael. 2006. Redefining the "rural question": The new "politics of the rural" and social policy. *Social Policy and Administration* 40 (6): 579–95. http://dx.doi.org/10.1111/j.1467-9515.2006.00521.x.

Woods, Michael. 2007. Engaging the global countryside: Globalization, hybridity, and the reconstitution of rural place. *Progress in Human Geography* 31 (4): 485–507. http://dx.doi.org/10.1177/0309132507079503.

York Region. 1998. York Regional Forest management plan, 1998–2018. Retrieved 15 July 2012 from http://www.york.ca/NR/rdonlyres/s4tpa5ssqvwbcim7icv6xutsgaa5buyxzac6prabr42ldntlmszigdt5h-strf6iwcrz2jd47qtitwtvzofjv43c5fb/YR+Forest+MP+1998-2018_rev_section1-8%2c+Final+March+2010.pdf.

York Region. 2007. York Durham sanitary sewage system. Retrieved 1 August 2012 from http://www.york.ca/NR/rdonlyres/2ma6ikkk7joeisazlsd43tuw-gmzriyrogodjfv5f4v43a3oc7dikpetqxjihaxl2y7ewkh2lygito4bgnebbpcbklg/Need+and+Justification+Report+2007.pdf.

York Region School Board. 2006. Proposed West Gormley and Casa Development applications, Town of Richmond Hill. Retrieved 15 February 2009 from www.yrdsb.edu.on.ca/pdfs/a/agenda/mp/bd041125/yrdsb-bd041125-p54-59.pdf.

Young, Douglas, and Roger Keil. 2005. Urinetown to Morainetown? Debates on the reregulation of the urban water regime in Toronto. *Capitalism, Nature, Socialism* 16 (2): 61–84. http://dx.doi.org/10.1080/10455750500108328.

Zeller, Susanne. 1987. *Inventing Canada: Early Victorial Science and the Idea of a Transcontinental Nation*. Toronto: University of Toronto Press.

Zimmerman, Erich W. 1951. *World Resources and Industries: A Functional Appraisal of the Availability of Agricultural and Industrial Materials*. New York: Harper and Row.

Index

Throughout this index the abbreviation *ORM* is used to indicate references to the Oak Ridges Moraine.

320   Index